NARROW MINDS

Having saved her family from financial ruin by moving onto a houseboat in search of a less stressful, cheaper way of life, Marie Browne, her tea-fuelled husband Geoff and their children find themselves sucked back into normality. With a new job, a new rented house and a mountain of bills, they are pretty much back where they started, and the kids are planning mutiny. Facing perky postmen, ice-skating cows, psychotic villagers and outraged rodents, they're running out of time, their financial situation is getting desperate, and there's every chance life has conspired against them to make sure they never get back afloat. Until they find that the answer to their dreams lies with *Minerva*, a narrow boat even more run-down than their first . . .

NARROW MINDS

MARIE BROWNE

ISIS
LARGE
PRINT

First published in Great Britain 2011
by
Accent Press Ltd.

First Isis Edition
published 2016
by arrangement with
Accent Press Ltd.

A catalogue record for this book is available
from the British Library.

ISBN 978–1–78541–183–0 (hb)
ISBN 978–1–78541–189–2 (pb)

Published by
F. A. Thorpe (Publishing)
Anstey, Leicestershire

Set by Words & Graphics Ltd.
Anstey, Leicestershire
Printed and bound in Great Britain by
T. J. International Ltd., Padstow, Cornwall

This book is printed on acid-free paper

This book is dedicated to Geoff, Amelia
and Chris, Charlie and Sam:

To Geoff because he puts up with a huge amount
from all of us.

To Amelia and Chris because they are making us
Grandparents and that's just terrifying.

To Charlie because she keeps me on my toes and
makes me laugh.

To Sam because he never fails to surprise me.

I love you all.

Acknowledgements

This is a good place to say thank you to all those people who make our life what it is.

Those in houses: Helen and Dave, Ian, Vikki and Neil, Arwen and Carl and of course Mum and Dad.

Those in boats: Steve for always being a gentleman when I complain about his music, Lewis for not being as grumpy as I make him out to be, Dion and Charlie for being the best neighbours in the world and to Bill and Drew for mechanical insights and for instigating barbecues under adverse conditions.

Thank you.

CHAPTER
ONE

On Thin Ice

Shivering, stark naked and covered in semi-frozen cow poo, I realised that everybody, even members of the stoic, grumblesome English race, have their breaking point and I had just found mine. For the unlucky few, it may be something huge like the loss of a loved one or some other catastrophe that just can't be endured. However, for most of us it is the inevitable trickle of exasperating nonsense that finally forces stressed and hapless souls into out-of-character actions.

It could be that final demand hidden among the Christmas cards or another argument with the boss, bank charges, late buses, riotous rush hours, taxes, rising fuel costs and people cutting into queues (only the English see this as a mortal insult). Only a couple of months previously I had seen a woman scream at an assistant in a supermarket because the little treat that she allowed herself every week had been removed from their stock lists. All these little straws build up and build up and you never know which one will break the camel's back.

Earlier that bitterly cold November afternoon I had decided that winter is never a good time for positive thinking and had spent at least an hour staring glumly out of the lounge window. Enjoying my melancholy, I gazed out at the snow, hypnotised by the whirling eddies created by the wind racing around the buildings. Leaning on the sill, my forehead against the cold glass of the window and my thighs against the hot radiator, I watched our landlord, Kevin, chivvy his cows, slipping, sliding and pooing up the steep incline of the farmyard. He was trying to get them out of the snow and into the wonderful warm and cosy barn. The stupid animals fought him all the way, turning this way and that in an effort to find a way out of the yard.

Honestly, it was ridiculous, the wind howled around the farmyard. With nothing much to stand in its way (one or two irritable Swaledale sheep and some stunted and tenacious bushes at most); it had swept across the fells from the Pennines, carrying snow and sleet to batter the faces of the herd, and anyone else daft enough to be outside. Surely even an animal could see that the barn was better, why were they fighting it? It was good for them to be moved, in their best interests.

However, I just couldn't help myself, every time one broke free and headed back toward the field I cheered it on and booed when the poor thing was rounded up and forced to conform again. I was definitely on the side of the cows.

It seemed bizarre to identify with the antics of panicked bovines but, like them, I didn't want to be told what I could and couldn't do and certainly didn't want what was "best for me" or "acceptable". I stared over my shoulder at our new house. Like the barn it was comfortable and warm, the stone walls and thick carpet gave it a homely feel that the cows certainly wouldn't appreciate. Big pictures, way too big to fit on the walls of our last home, had been dragged out of storage in the hope that they would break up the vast expanses of magnolia-painted wall space. The huge leather sofa was just the right size for the whole family to warm its toes in front of the large open fire.

I shook my head and turned back to the window. This was the only area in the room I really liked, an odd little alcove, about seven foot wide, filled with overflowing, floor to ceiling, book shelves that loomed over a small dining room table. Cramped, confused and chaotic, it was definitely my favourite place to sit.

Compared to the narrow boat we had been living on for the last two years this house felt huge. I suffered slight agoraphobia as I shuffled around the mostly empty rooms trying not to notice that we only had enough possessions to fill a boat and not a house. It was too big, too empty and far too stable. I missed the continual rocking and odd bumps that had been almost unnoticed in the boat, however without them I had almost continual low level nausea. Being forced to sell our house after the downfall of the Rover company, we hadn't always enjoyed our somewhat odd lifestyle. The last three years we'd had to come to terms with some very odd situations, and we had laughed a lot. It had been our choice to buy a narrow boat and it had been our choice to attempt an alternative lifestyle and it had been our choice to embrace all the bizarre changes that went with living on a boat, even if most of our friends described us as "mad as a box of frogs".

There is something about living outside the social norm that really appeals to me. For one thing, it always lowers people's expectations. As soon as they find out that not only do you live on a semi-derelict boat, but you are also trying to raise children on that boat, they tend to scoff. However, as soon as they realise that all your dinner conversation leans towards moaning about nature, the price of diesel and you have a harrowing selection of stories that involve human poo, your average person will glaze over and almost perform circus tricks in the effort to be polite yet get away as quickly as possible.

If I'm entirely honest I think that may have been one of the main reasons I enjoyed it so much. I love to watch friends of friends stumble over their own brains as they try to come to terms with what, to most people, is a completely alien existence.

I sighed and tried to pinpoint that pivotal moment where we had taken our eye off the ball, had been swept away from the margins and stuck back into the herd. In short, I was trying to work out how the hell we had managed to end up in a similar situation to the one we had escaped only three short years ago: this had definitely NOT been the plan. I sighed again and, watching the cow circus vanish beneath the fog of my breath, whispered, "Oh Moo!"

I couldn't ignore the nagging feeling that, as we had been sucked back into "normality", escaping a second time was going to be much harder. Raising the fortifications after our previous escape, life had doubled the guard and installed CCTV. This time it was going to take a huge amount of planning to get away, I was worried that any possible plan would probably include tunnels and spoons.

With my husband Geoff desperate to retrain and get back into work, selling *Happy Go Lucky*, our old boat, had been our only option. Horrified at the ridiculous cost of courses, we'd sadly opted to sell the boat, put him through all his electrician exams, buy a new fixer upper and start all over again with the money that was left . . . Simples.

Geoff had indeed taken his exams and, as he usually does, passed with flying colours. Trying to save as much money as possible and with Lillian, Geoff's mother, out of the country we had taken over her house in Cumbria while he qualified and I searched for another boat. By the time he was a fully fledged electrician and had been offered a job across the Pennines in Durham, we still hadn't found anything suitable. So, in desperation, we had elected to take a six-month rent of a cottage over winter then, try again in the spring.

Unfortunately, the two children still at home, Charlotte and Sam, were ecstatic to be in a house again and were thoroughly enjoying all the little luxuries that came with being conventional. The fast computer, the large TV, washing machine that you didn't have to walk half a mile to use and the biggest enticement of all, the deep old bath. (I must admit even I was rather enamoured with that one).

Charlie at thirteen, was completely addicted to MSN, she spent hours on the computer either chatting to friends or enjoying eBay and other sales sites. Built like a small stick, she could still easily get into children's clothes but that was no longer acceptable so she spent days trolling through various sites looking for clothing. Ten-year-old Sam, luckily, couldn't care less what he looked like. He spent most of his life pushing his long mouse-coloured hair out of his strange amber eyes (a legacy from his father) and shouting mild obscenities at a computer game called "Space Chickens", and with Geoff enjoying his first proper job for about five years, life slipped relentlessly and inexorably toward "normal". Watching them, I could see that they thought I was mad to want to lose all this and go back to our previous mud-ridden, water-logged and insect-infested existence.

Amelia, the oldest, had left home the day we'd moved out of our last house. Unwilling to give up her lifestyle of college and friends, she had maintained from the outset that she wasn't going to deal well with life afloat, and had gone to live with her boyfriend, Huw.

Strangely enough she was the only one of my children who seemed to have any empathy with my desperate need to return to what I considered to be my normal life. At twenty-one, she was now living in Reading and was working as a letting agent for a well-known estate agency, she really hated the job. Like her mother, she loathed the set hours, the level of dress that was demanded of you and the ridiculous rules and management structure.

Two years in a flat of their own had opened the young couple's eyes to the bills and the struggle of trying to live on a starter income. The more irritated she became with the whole thing and the more her bank account failed to support her monthly expenses, the more she understood my point of view. It was quite refreshing, she would phone every two or three days, listen to me moan and gripe, moan and gripe back at me, then both of us, satisfied that neither of our lives were better than the other's, went on our way until the next support session: I missed having her around.

The small rented cottage that we currently inhabited was attached to a farm in the middle of rural County Durham. It was very pretty but cold, drafty and expensive to heat. The only good thing about the situation was that coffee with my long standing, and ever tolerant, best mate Helen was now much more frequent.

I had actually met up with her the day before. We had been developing a habit of meeting once a week in Barnard Castle. This pretty little market town was almost exactly halfway between my house on the outskirts of Durham and Helen's in Brough in Cumbria. Helen had been my best friend for more years than I cared to think about and her no nonsense attitude to life had given me a moral slapping on several occasions. This slapping, however, never managed to stop me griping and moaning whenever I saw her.

"Oh God, what's the matter now?" she had snapped as she had walked through the door of the Bowes museum cafe (I obviously had my "Oh poor me" face on). "You've got a face like a slapped bum." She wandered past me and over to the counter, polishing her glasses as she went, obviously walking into a warm room from the cold outside had seriously clouded her judgement.

I noticed, with some irritation, that she was only wearing jeans, boots, a shirt and a jumper. The woolly hat pulled over her hair more a nod to good taste than any need to keep warm. Even in the warmth of the cafe I was still snuggled into a huge puffy coat, my feet squashed into three pairs of socks, I had also picked the table directly beneath the big ceiling-mounted heater. I didn't feel the problem was with me but with the cafe. Set in a huge room with high ceilings, huge windows and stone floors, it was no wonder it felt cold.

Returning, she slapped down a cream-covered mocha for me, a plate of choccy thingies for both of us and a cup of Earl Grey for herself (yuck). Waiting until I was nose deep in my coffee she continued. "So, come on, what's the problem?"

After I had managed to get the cream out of my nostrils with a napkin, I sighed. There was no point lying, she'd see right through me in an instant. "I'm cold, there are too many hills up here and I can't understand a word anybody says. Every time someone speaks it sounds like that voice-over from Big Brother, I keep looking for hidden cameras. Everything smells of cow sh ... poo, and I know I'm just being narrow-minded and pathetic. Actually I'm beginning to irritate myself with my miseries I just want to go home."

Helen stared at me for a moment. "Look." She picked up one of the choccy things and took a big bite. "I could say, poor you, I could say that come summer you can go back to the river, go back to being a gypsy, go back to irritating those of us that pay council tax and go back to disappointing your mother. But quite frankly that isn't going to help you at the moment so really," she paused for another bite, studying me over the top of her glasses while irritably pushing the long strands of dark hair away from her mouth, "get over it."

Helen and I had originally met when working for an IT company when we both lived in Worcester many years ago. She had moved to Cumbria after giving up her IT management career to become a paramedic. She loved it up here and was always outraged when someone hated her adopted area. Raising an eyebrow at me, she continued, unstoppable in her righteous indignation. "You aren't going anywhere so you may as well make the best of it for the next six months, take some time to get to know the people in the village. I'm sure they're lovely." she paused again then spoke over me as I started to refute everything she said. "Just give it a try. You never know you may enjoy it so much you never want to leave." She pushed the plate of chocolate towards me. "Now have one of these and hurry up, I want to show you something that will make you feel more at home."

I stared out of the window, even washed and blurred by horizontal sleet, the sweeping lawns and elegant terraces of the museum were beautiful. However, I wasn't going to let something as pedestrian as outstanding splendour raise my mood so I resolutely turned my back on it all and stuck my nose, once again, into my coffee cup. It was a good job I hadn't seen it in the sunshine, it may have been hard to resist. "There's another small problem," I grouched.

Helen grinned. "What's that?"

"I don't think the kids are going to want another boat, especially not after the last one we went to see." I traced coffee rings on the table. "I think that pile of rubbish may have killed any enthusiasm they had for a life afloat."

"I didn't know you'd been to see a boat." Helen frowned. "Where was it?"

"Over at Hartlepool." I shook my head, remembering the terrible mess that had been described as a boat. "It was awful and actually reduced Charlie to tears, she was so worried that we were going to make her live on it."

Helen raised her eyebrows at me and I sighed, it looked as though the whole embarrassing story was going to have to be told.

"We'd just moved into Lillian's and I came up with one of my fantastic ideas that instead of another steel boat we buy a wooden one." I laughed, remembering the fantasy I had indulged in. "The ad said that it was an ex-fishing boat and that it was ready to sail away, and it was such a good price it would have left us with a huge amount of money to make any necessary repairs.

"So anyway, we made an appointment to see it and wandered over to Hartlepool for the day." I shook my head remembering the first impressions. "Helen, it was dreadful, it didn't help that the weather was appalling, but quite frankly bright sunshine and a Caribbean backdrop couldn't have made that boat look any better."

Helen frowned. "I remember how bad 'Happy' was when you bought her." She shuddered. "I can't imagine anything worse than that."

I laughed. "Happy was a palace compared to this thing."

Helen grimaced, obviously having trouble imagining anything so awful.

"She was about sixty foot long and was fairly cute from the outside. Well, apart from the gaping holes and obvious rot in a lot of her planks, but Geoff felt that these could all be replaced for a fairly reasonable price." I laughed, "What we didn't expect to find was an obvious telegraph pole for a mast, an engine that took up nearly a third of the boat and ceilings so low that we all had to walk about with our heads on one side."

"Wasn't it fixable at all?" Helen winced at my description.

I sighed. "If it had been just the two of us I suppose it might have been. Charlie, however, took one look at the beds, stinking, under two inches of water (the roof/deck was leaking due to all the holes in it), took one lungful of the stinking mould-laden air and just burst into tears. She stated that there was no way she was going to live on that and she'd actually rather go back to her father's than ever again set foot on the equivalent of the *Marie Celeste*."

Helen winced. "And since then I supposed she's not wanted to look at any others."

I shrugged. "My fault, I should have been far more careful, Charlie never saw Happy when we first got her so she doesn't remember the gruesome mess that we lived in." I sighed. "They seem happy here, they've got all their little gadgets, all the things they didn't have on the boat. School starts on Monday, so they're going to get friends, Geoff's got his job and feels that he shouldn't leave before he's done at least a year." I took another sip of coffee. "Everything we do just tightens the net and makes it harder and harder for us to escape."

Helen's grin had faded. "I didn't realise it was only you that wanted to get back home, I thought you were all working toward that."

I pushed the half-finished coffee away. "So did I, Geoff says he wants to but he hasn't bothered looking at boats, he's really intent on his new job." I shook my head. "God, I sound so self-pitying, it's really good that he's got this job and he's qualified." I paused. "I just wish we could've done it closer to home."

Helen sighed. "I don't have any answers for this one, if it's just you . . ." She tailed off and shrugged. "You can't just push off on your own and leave them all behind."

I smiled sourly. "It might be the best thing, they'd soon come running when the food and the clean washing ran out."

Nodding, Helen checked her watch then leapt up and grabbed my arm. "Talking of things running out, come on we're running out of time, you have to see this." She pulled me toward the door. "Honestly you're going to love it."

Out of the coffee shop we wandered back past the little shop and into the impressive entrance hall. Helen bounded away toward the stairs and spoke over her shoulder at me, "*Come on*, it's nearly two o'clock."

"Come on, come on." She shouted over the top of the banister before disappearing behind another big wooden door. I puffed along behind her thinking that cow print wellies probably weren't right for this place and hoped I wasn't dropping mud on the carpet. Distracted, I stopped to study some of the portraits on the walls, their huge antique gold frames perfectly in keeping with the decor. The eyes of the long dead followed me as I slowly followed the sound of Helen's voice.

Lost in thought, I was surprised when a slim hand shot out through the door and grabbed my cuff. "Oh, good grief, come on!" Helen snapped. "I know you want to spend your life just drifting along the river, swatting mozzies and watching Geoff fall into the water but there really are times when you need to get a bloody move on." She pointed to a glass case in the middle of the room, surrounded by silent onlookers. "Look at this."

I approached the glass case curiously, the other people standing around moved aside for me and we all stood staring at this most beautiful "thing".

13

Within the case a life-sized silver swan rested on a glistening streambed of twisted glass rods. Silver fish hovered above the "stream" and all was framed within a bed of large silver leaves, as old as it obviously was, the "thing" was breathtakingly beautiful.

I was right about it being an antique, a description from 1773 lists it as:

A swan, large as life, formed of silver, filled with mechanism, beating time with its beak to musical chimes terminating at the top with a rising sun upward of three feet diameter, the whole eighteen feet high.

I looked again at the swan. The aforementioned sun was no longer present and the case was now about six foot. It was obviously no more than a beautiful statue, which was a shame but it would be ridiculous to hope, after 236 years, that it still worked.

I was still marvelling at the workmanship when a hush fell on the small crowd and a smiling man approached the case, there was a definite sense of anticipation.

Helen appeared beside me and grinned. "Isn't it gorgeous?"

I nodded then jumped as the glass rods began to rotate. Pressing closer to the glass, I jumped again as the swan's gleaming silver head bent left toward me then away to the right, it then twisted around and appeared to preen its own back. Rotating back again, it sighted a fish in the water and bent down, a fish appeared in its mouth which it seemed to swallow.

When the fish had disappeared the swan's head returned to its upright position and the whole thing became a statue again, as the music stopped all was silent and still. I firmly stifled a childish impulse to grab the man and shout "again, AGAIN!" It had only lasted about forty seconds but it was forty seconds I would remember for a fair while: incredible.

As we wandered around the other exhibits Helen poked me. "Well?"

"Well what?"

She grinned. "Oh come on let's hear it."

"What?" I pretended to have no idea what she was talking about.

"Swans don't eat fish."

I laughed. "Swans don't eat fish, they may be beautiful but they are also aggressive, scary, and plain stupid most of the time. They wait in the dark for you to come out on the front of the boat then they hiss loudly, and laugh as you leap two or three foot into the air. But for something that old and beautiful I'm willing to be tolerant of its reality failings."

"Good." She looked at me sideways.

"What?"

"Well, if you extend that tolerance to your neighbours and give them a chance, they may surprise you as well." She gave me a beaming, self-satisfied, smile.

"If my neighbours were old and beautiful I would. And, if I stayed up here for two hundred and thirty-six years, those neighbours might, just might, stop thinking

15

of me as a southerner and actually talk to me." I paused for a moment.

"Helen?"

"Yes?"

I gave her a "look". "I don't know if anyone's ever told you this, but you can be intolerably smug when you're right."

"See you next week." She gave me a huge grin.

I turned round and stuck my tongue out at her. "Oh shut up." After a quick hug I was back in my car and away. Maybe she was right, maybe I shouldn't keep hankering after the past. I've always told the kids, especially Amelia, who has a tendency to revisit situations in the hope they'll turn out differently the second time, "Never go back, always go forward." There was a distinct possibility I should take my own advice.

A heavy knocking on the back door returned me to my fairly mindless perusal of Kevin's ice-skating cows and sighing heavily I dragged my face away from the window. I noticed that my face and hands were blue from the cold but my thighs were a fiery red from where they'd been in contact with the radiator: they were beginning to tingle alarmingly.

I limped through the kitchen toward the back door. This was the only other room I really liked. Tiny and poorly equipped, it boasted just a couple of cupboards, a sink unit, a small cooker and a washing machine. It reminded me of home, even the lino on the floor was the same pattern as the one we'd had on the boat. As I opened the door to the grinning postman. I noticed that the snow was getting heavier, each flake was now the size of a fifty pence piece and I was sure I could hear a slight thud as they hit the ground, each one adding to the rapidly thickening blanket.

"Afternoon!!" John stuck his head through the door and smiled alarmingly. "More bills, what a swine eh? Never mind we all have to live with it, better to smile and take it on the chin, than moan about it."

I stretched my face into what I hoped resembled a smile and quashed my temptation to quip about "morning" postal rounds. I just couldn't be bothered to listen to a long list of excuses about the weather and low staff levels.

He pointed to the grey and yellow sky. "Bet you don't see a lot of this down south." He carefully pronounced this as "darn sarth", presumably in an effort to make sure I could understand what he was saying. Sorry sweetheart, I originally come from Surrey and I've recently come from Cambridge. Lose any form of chin, stick a couple of plums in each cheek then stretch each vowel to snapping point and I might just stand a chance of understanding you.

"Oh, this one needs signing for." He held out a thick envelope. "It's for the farm, I couldn't get an answer at the door but it looks important, could you sign for it?"

"They're just up there." I pointed up at the barn at the top of the farmyard.

"Oh right." He grinned at me and pushed the letter into my hand.

It was definitely the day for heavy sighs and taking the post from him I nodded, then bared my teeth at

17

him again. He gave me a cheery wink and swivelled on his heel.

"No rest for the wicked eh?" He waved and headed down the passageway between the cottage and the horse barn, stamping his feet as he went, leaving clods of snow to melt and fill the passage with water. "See you tomorrow," he called over his shoulder, "no doubt there'll be more bills . . . there always is."

Shutting the door with a thud just to show him what I thought of him and his bills, I studied the post then sighed again. There really was no point in waiting, the weather was just going to get worse and it was rapidly getting dark. I might as well sling my wellies on now and go and give them the stupid letter.

Glancing out of the window I could see the diminutive Kevin and his two huge sons pushing through the milling cattle. The boys' names were Jack and Simon but I had come to think of them as Huge one and Huge two, both of them had a neck that was wider than his head, both were red-faced and blushed horribly whenever they were spoken to. If you asked either of them a question, he would give you a quietly spoken answer then rush off to do whatever people did with cows.

Kevin was appropriately proud of his huge sons and had recently regaled me with the tale that, while on a night out in their mother's small car, the boys had suffered a flat tyre. Evidently, unable to find the jack, Simon had merely lifted the little Ford Ka while his brother had changed the wheel. Looking at them, I didn't doubt the story for an instant.

Just for a moment, I considered getting dressed but decided that my dressing gown, while not really winter wear, would be good enough for a twenty-second trip up the farmyard especially if I threw my plastic mac on as well. The coat had been a slightly humorous present from Helen. It was an old-fashioned, strong, plastic mac, white with huge black cow print all over it: seriously retro. I think she had found it in a 1960s store and had laughed for ages when she first saw me in it, especially as it matched my wellies. As a special thank you I had worn it every time I had seen her since and her smile was beginning to look slightly strained. It probably wasn't acceptable to the farmers either but it kept out the rain and snow better than any other coat I owned so frankly, I didn't give a damn how I looked.

Once out of the back door I realised, with a shudder, that it was much windier than I had expected. I struggled up the steep farmyard, my eyes half-closed against the stinging snow, trying desperately to avoid the many piles of new cow plop that were rapidly freezing over. Unable to see, I kept stepping into half frozen puddles of dubious liquid that were lurking under the pristine layer of new snow. I slipped and slid on each frozen puddle, my arms pin-wheeling with each staggering step.

"KEVIN!!" I screamed into the wind, hoping that he would see me and meet me halfway, but the wind was too loud and he was concentrating on the cows that bumped and warbled at each other, still eager to get away from the seductively warm barn.

If I'd had any sense, I would have given up, turned around and carefully retraced my steps. I should have waited for the lads to go in for tea and then dropped the letter round by way of the nice clear path. For some reason this didn't even occur to me. So, slipping, sliding, swearing and staggering, I pressed on up the farmyard.

Right at the top Simon finally noticed me, and pushing his way through the cows, came over to meet me. "You all right Mrs Browne?" He looked me up and down obviously taking in my wellies and the mad mac, then raised his eyebrows slightly at the sight of my pale blue dressing gown peeking from beneath. His expression spoke volumes about the sanity of the woman in front of him.

"Yes ... (Huff) ... Hi ... Simon ... letter ... (Huff)." I stopped speaking for a moment desperately trying to get my breath back. "I thought I would give it you now ... (Huff) before the weather really got nasty and I'm not going to want to go out later ... (Huff)."

Simon took the letter and stared at it. "Well ... thanks for that ..." He frowned a little. "You be careful going back down." He scuffed his foot through the snow. "It's getting a bit slippery under there."

I nodded but, as I turned, my foot slid on one of the icy puddles. Waving my arms in an attempt to keep my balance I endeavoured to run on the spot, and like most people would I failed horribly.

Down I went in a fluffy flurry of pale blue dressing gown, cow-print mac and matching wellies. As I fell my only thought was, oh great, now I'm going to have to attempt to stand up again and that's just not going to be an elegant exercise on this surface. However, as it turned out, I needn't have worried at all. As my backside hit the ground I began to slide back toward the house, the strong plastic mac slipping easily over the icy slurry; I had flashbacks of being twelve and sledging on a coal bag.

As I slowly travelled down the farmyard, I became aware of a certain warm stickiness that was liberally covering the backs of my thighs and calves and panicked, thinking that I had cut myself on one of the cobbles. The fear was fleeting and soon pushed aside by nausea as I realised that the little cracks and pops preceding each wave of warmth meant that I was breaking the icy crust on each cow plop I encountered. It didn't make me feel any better to realise that the contents, scooped up by my coat were being carried along with me. I really think blood would have been preferable.

After about six feet I stopped and gingerly placed my hands on the ground, readying myself for an attempt to stand upright. With my hands wrist deep in snow and my feet slipping and slithering ahead of me I must have looked like an amateur Cossack dancer attempting the Casatchok for the first time. Finally giving up I rolled over on to my hands and knees, inelegantly stuck my poo-covered rear into the air and then slowly and carefully stood upright, my shaking legs feeling like wet spaghetti.

I turned to look at the short, steaming scar that was my route down the farmyard. Attempting to regain some poise I stepped, very carefully, down the steps and through the gate wincing as each step sent a fresh wave of warm and smelly stuff cascading down my legs to add to the squelching mess inside my wellingtons. (I do remember wishing I had taken time to put some socks on).

"You all right Mrs Browne?" a voice, filled with laughter, floated down from the top of the farmyard.

"Fine, fine," I called back. I knew that Huge one had been joined by his brother and his father, I could hear them trying not to laugh and failing. There was no way I was going to look back at them, that was an image that could scar a person's psyche for life.

Trying not to walk like a cat that had just had its paws buttered, I made my way carefully to the back door. After shutting it firmly behind me, I turned on the light against the rapidly approaching dark and stood, uncertain, on the mat.

"Oh my God." Charlie came into the small kitchen with her hands held firmly around her nose. "What on earth is that . . . SMELL?"

Sam, following closely on the heels of his older sister, crinkled up his nose and wailed, "Oh yurgh!" He coughed and clutched his throat theatrically. "WHAT is that?"

I gave them both the "look of doom" then began shedding clothes as quickly as I possibly could. I really needed to get everything off before the warmth in the room melted the rest of the frozen yuck and the smell became intolerable. My mad mac had a huge rip right down the backside, so I wouldn't be wearing that again.

My dressing gown was streaked in what *could* have been mud but the smell told me differently. My long T-shirt was mostly unscathed but just to be sure I dumped that as well. When I was standing, stark naked except for a pair of pants that were destined for the fire, I opened the door just enough to get my foot through and kicked every piece of clothing out into the snow. Yelping at the cold I heeled my wellies off, and then stared down at my slimy toes in disgust. I stank, even more horribly, I was beginning to crust over.

Stalking past the still wailing children, I suddenly realised that as I had turned the lights on and hadn't pulled the curtains. I had just given the farmers a complete eyeful of naked woman. Oh just great! A poo covered, naked, sliding southerner, this was a story that was going to get to the local farmers in about ten minutes flat. I was never going to be able to go out in public again.

After two showers, a long hot bath and a couple of medicinal doses of Jack Daniels, I began to feel better. Geoff had come home and after bringing me a cup of tea sat on the toilet to talk to me. He looked very professional in his bottle-green work gear. He was very good, I think that he actually managed to keep a straight face while I was whining on, but it's really difficult to tell when most of someone's face is hidden by beard, his shaking shoulders, however, told a very different story.

Later that evening, he helped out by rubbing Savlon into some of my more hard-to-reach scratches. I was worried that they might become infected from the cow poo, and that I would get mad cow disease. I had visions of standing in odd postures, showing nervous or aggressive behaviour and showing a lack of co-ordination. Geoff, safe behind my backside, just laughed and said that we had better get me tested because, from the list of symptoms I had just given him, nobody would be able to tell the difference.

"Look," he said and laughed, "you managed to last two years on the river and you never came down with Weil's disease, I think you're probably safe."

"I never bum-skated through six inches of frozen rat sh . . . plop." I said as I twisted myself around trying to see my own backside.

"Well," Geoff spoke over his shoulder as he headed to the kitchen to put the kettle on, "you threw me into a dilute eight foot of it on two separate occasions and I'm still here, I think you'll live."

He poked his head around the door and grinned at me, his teeth just showing through his rather exuberant salt and pepper beard. "How come you never fell in the river?" he asked. "Maybe this is just karmic retribution and I'm sorry I wasn't there to see it, I don't suppose you could do it again tomorrow could you?" He thought for a second or two. "If I rush out and buy a video camera in the morning we could make a quick two hundred and fifty quid from one of those funny clip shows." Then laughing at his own wit he disappeared off to deal with the kettle.

Giving his departing rear end a sarcastic sneer, I parked myself gingerly on the sofa, angling over to sit on one thigh in an effort to stop my poor, abused backside from making contact with the cold leather seat. "Don't you miss it?" I called toward the kitchen.

"Miss what?" Geoff appeared carrying two steaming cups. "The never-ending worry about getting disease?"

"No! The river, the boat, the life." I took the mug and took a deep breath, ah bless him, he'd doctored my coffee with a liberal splash of whisky. "Have you seen that lot on the table?" I gestured vaguely toward our so called dining room. "We've only been here two weeks and that whole pile of post is either bills or rubbish and every day more drops through the door. To make matters worse it's delivered by the cheery prat from hell who has made it his job to point out to me just how much rubbish we're getting and telling me I have to put up with it."

Geoff heaved himself back off the sofa and wandered into my weird little alcove by the window. We had managed to get every one of our thousand and some books out of storage and into the house. It took a little effort to wedge ourselves into the chairs at the table for food but we managed it . . . just.

"These are just mostly multiple letters from BT." He shuffled through the pile and began throwing some of them onto the table. "Just throw away anything marked "occupier" and see what the rest say. We can't have that many bills at the moment, we've only just moved in. These are mostly set-up correspondence about the telephone line and the broadband line. Most of these can just be dumped or filed for reference."

"So . . . do you miss it?" I pressed.

Geoff wandered back across the room and then stood warming his backside at the open fire, crinkling his toes into the rug and occasionally bouncing a little. With his hands stuck deep into the pockets of his new Snicker work trousers he jangled the odd collection of radiator bleed keys, fuses and other little bits of "stuff" that he carried around these days. He was the very picture of a man in deep thought. I waited, almost breathless in the fear that he would say no.

Eventually he sighed and turned around to give the fire a poke. "Yes and no." He put another log on top of those already there and then came over to flop onto the sofa. "I don't miss the lack of money or the never-ending walks to take the rubbish to the skip. I do miss a lot of things: the fish in the river, the morning mists, the chats with the neighbours." He paused and frowned, then ran his hand through his recently shorn hair. "Actually what I miss the most is that it didn't matter what problem you had, there was always someone willing to lend a hand." He nodded. "Yes I do miss it." He reached into the pocket of his huge green fleece, fumbling around in the monogrammed breast pocket for his tobacco. "How about you?"

I took a huge gulp of whisky sour hot coffee and coughed slightly, more to cover the moment of deep melancholy than too much alcohol. "More than I ever thought possible."

"Don't worry." Geoff leaned over and gave me a hug crinkling his nose at the smell of whisky (at least I hoped it was the whisky and not a lingering odour of ordure). "Wait until spring and there'll be loads of boats for sale and we can get back to where we're supposed to be."

Taking another gulp of coffee, I huffed. "Good, let's hope that we haven't run out of money by then. I was horrified when they filled the oil tank up and then charged me over six hundred quid." I drained my cup and getting to my feet reached out a hand to pull Geoff to his. "Come on, let's go to bed, I'm sure I'm going to dream of cows."

Geoff grabbed my hand and pulled me back down into his lap. "They're better than rats." He grinned and wriggled a finger between my ribs making me scream. "At least cows don't eat through your rope lockers, raid your bins and make nests in the woodpile, leaping out at you, screaming and gnashing their teeth when you go for some kindling."

Just for a moment I had a strange mental image of a cow nest in a woodpile, then, deciding I had had more than enough whisky I slapped his hand away and got to my feet. "Nah, I'll take the rats any day, much quieter, listen to that racket." We both fell silent, the cows could be heard still screaming their heads off at the top of the yard. (Probably laughing at the woman they'd caught in their poo.)

"Time for bed." Geoff heaved himself to his feet and wandered over to put the guard on the fire.

"I've always hated cows." I grabbed the mugs and headed out with them to turn the lights off in the kitchen. "I've never really trusted them, they look sweet with those big eyes and those wet pink huffing noses, but I've always felt that they are far too curious for 'our' own good."

As we climbed into bed I reached over to turn the light off. Geoff gave me a huge hug and a big slobbery kiss then almost immediately fell asleep. I lay awake for a long time, positive I could still smell cow poo and listening to the nonstop mooing that echoed around the farmyard, muted only slightly by the ever-increasing snow.

I really didn't care what people were like all over the country I just wanted my neighbours back, Charlie and Dion, Disco Steve, Grumpy Lewis, Steve, Jude and the kids. The house next door was occupied but they had been away since we moved in and I had yet to meet them. I yawned and snuggled down into the warm Geoff-filled space. Maybe I was being unfair, maybe they would be fine. As consciousness drifted away on my cow-filled dreams, I was ready to see what the next five months would bring.

CHAPTER
TWO

In Bed, No One Can Hear
You Scream

I awoke the next morning to that strange dead stillness that only thick snow can create, no birds and — wonder of wonders — no cows, no sound from the road, just that odd anticipation in the air. I lay there for about twenty minutes enjoying the warm bed before a blood curdling scream sent me up into the air like a cat that has just been confronted by a skunk.

"Mum . . . MUM! Arrrrgggghhhh!!"

Leaping out of bed, I winced as my feet hit the cold floor and my poor abused gluteus maximus reminded me that I had seriously overdone it the day before. So alternately wincing, limping and muttering I rushed into Charlie's bedroom. I found her dressed only in her pyjamas with her face pressed against the window.

"What?" I grabbed her arm. "What's the matter, are you all right?"

Charlie whipped round and screamed at me. "Look at the snow, look how thick it is, can we go sledging, can we?" She let go of my arm and rushed out of the door, I hurried after her.

"Sam, SAM!" She grabbed his covers and pulled them, and him, off the bed and onto the floor. Sam, unused to this behaviour and woken from an obviously deep sleep became wide awake and completely incoherent for a couple of minutes. He tried to stand up but both legs gave way simultaneously and he landed face down on his deposed duvet. It was at this point his subconscious noted that, as Charlie was screaming, obviously something was very wrong, so he'd better scream as well.

Charlie, wide-eyed and a bit overwhelmed by the sounds that her brother was making, shut up and backed away. Hiding behind me, she peered out at him from around my back.

Sam just lay face down and screamed and screamed. Geoff, worried that his young son was being murdered, arrived wild-haired, wild-eyed and resplendent in elderly underpants.

I laughed and picked Sam bodily up off the floor. "Sam!" He carried on screaming, completely stiff and unresponsive. I placed my face right in his line of vision. "SAM . . . SAMUEL!! Look at me!" The use of his full name usually meant that he was in big, big trouble and with a snap of teeth the screams cut off and I watched him focus on my face.

"Wha . . ." He looked around at the devastation of his bed, the shocked looks on the faces of his family, then at me, his little face crumpled slightly and I could see tears beginning to glimmer in those huge amber eyes of his.

"It's all right," I hurried to explain, "it's just Charlie woke you up a little too quickly and I don't think you were really with us for a while."

He looked at me, confused, then at Charlie as she bounced out from behind me and grabbed his arm. "Oh for goodness' sake you big twit, look."

She dragged him, resisting all the way, over to the window, then grabbing his long and sleep mad hair she turned him physically to look out at her personal nirvana. "Look at THAT."

Sam looked blearily out of the window and I could almost hear the "click" as he registered what he was seeing.

Fifteen minutes later Geoff and I were once again face down on our bed. We were pretending to get dressed but really were stealing five peaceful moments before facing the great outdoors. We tried not to listen as Chaos and Disorder planned their day (and ours) as they rushed backward and forward, each having ideas about what they should do first. I had to smile, first a big cooked breakfast, then they were going to make a big snowman. Then they were going to come in for hot chocolate, then sledging.

For a moment there was silence. Beside me Geoff muttered, "Here comes trouble. I give them to the count of 5 . . . 1,2,3,4,5."

"MUM!" Both of them came careering into the room. "We don't have any sledges, what are we going to do?"

Geoff clambered out of bed and rootled around in the pocket of his trousers, he then turned and threw his keys to Charlie. "Go and have a look in the van, I'm sure you can find something in there that will act like a sledge."

As the sound of feet faded into the distance I turned and raised my eyebrows at him, he laughed.

"I was in one of the DIY stores yesterday and they were selling sledges, as it was snowing outside I thought a couple might come in useful."

I laughed. "Oh that's not fair." I dragged myself off the bed and started searching in the cupboard for a pair of his thermal long johns to steal. "Aren't you going to be voted 'Best Dad in the World'? I can't compete with that."

By the time we were dressed and downstairs, the kids had finished their first snowball fight, Sam had been hit in the face twice and had had a big handful of snow forced down his back, Charlie hadn't even had to duck. Sam, irritated and frustrated at his own lack of aim had given up, leaving Charlie trying to use one of the new sledges on flat ground, much to her annoyance it wasn't going well.

Over a huge breakfast of hash browns, beans, bacon, sausages and Sam's favourite, fried bread, we decided that we were all going to trudge out to the big hill behind the house and test the sledges.

Charlie stared out of the window, the snow was still falling. "It's really deep." She looked a little hopeful. "We have to start school the day after tomorrow."

"It's not that deep," Geoff said, "it's only about seven or eight inches and the roads will be clear."

I laughed at her expression of woe. "This really isn't that bad love." I began to clear the plates away. "You've just never seen more than a couple of centimetres of snow before. I'm sure your dad has seen it much deeper, coming from Cumbria."

Geoff nodded. "I remember walking down a lane and after the plough had been through the snow at the side of the road was up to my waist."

Both kids looked at him and rolled their eyes. "Yeah right!" Charlie got up and went to put her wellies on. "Come on Sam, let's get out before they start on the *old days*." Both went out muttering about the parental lies that they had to put up with.

"Do you remember that day we were visiting my mum and the car got stuck halfway up that hill in the snow?" Geoff laughed.

"Yes I do." I poked him in the arm. "That was when I got out to push and you drove off and left me, I had to run to catch up."

"I didn't dare stop, I'd have got stuck again." He put on a wounded look. "I was only going slowly, I thought you'd be able to jump in."

I waved a knife at him. "I did jump in, but as soon as both feet were in the car, I found myself hanging on to the open door, couldn't hold on and fell out again."

"I had to stop the car and pull you out of that snow drift that you were bum-first in. We couldn't get the car going again and had to abandon it and walk to my mum's."

"Well if your mum didn't live halfway up bloody Stainmore we wouldn't have had any problem." I looked out at the snow. "It's amazing that this is the deepest snow the kids have ever seen."

Geoff took the plates out of my hand and dumped them on the table. "Come on, leave them, let's go sledging before it all melts."

Four hours later we arrived back home. The kids, soaked to the skin, were shivering uncontrollably. They had given up walking and were perched on their sledges forcing Geoff to drag Sam and me to drag Charlie. I couldn't feel my feet and the wild excitement about the snow had dulled to the usual moaning and griping.

"I can't feel my legs." Charlie staggered upright and kicking her boots off at the door fell into the lounge.

"Don't stand too near the fire," Geoff warned, "as you warm up it's going to really hurt."

Charlie looked at him dubiously. "Why?"

Geoff just winked at her. "Trust me, it's going to hurt."

I chivvied both children upstairs. "Come on out of those wet clothes, who wants the first bath?"

Charlie was quicker to shout for the bath than Sam and although I made it only lukewarm she still yelped as she got in. "It's really hot!" she moaned.

Sam stuck his head through the door all snug and warming up nicely in pyjamas, socks, slippers and big fluffy dressing gown.

"What's hot?" He ducked as a naked Charlie screamed at him and threw a bar of soap.

"Just get in," I coaxed, "in about ten minutes it will seem really cold and you'll have to put some hot in."

Hearing a car pull up, I checked out of the window. "I think our elusive neighbours have just arrived," I told Charlie, "come on get yourself warm, while I go and say hello." Leaving Charlie to her muttering and whinging I wandered downstairs and opened the front door, Geoff just behind me.

A tall dark woman, a robust-looking man and two children were just emerging into the snow. This looked fairly good, their kids were about the same age as ours and it would be really nice if they got on.

"Hello." I wandered toward them. "You must be the neighbours. Kevin and Val said you'd be arriving soon."

"Hello." Both of them smiled. The man came around the car to greet us. "I'm Mike and this is Gill." The woman nodded and huddled further into her coat, the two kids gave us a cursory once-over then shot into the house, hitting each other as they went, the boy wearing a Newcastle United football shirt and the girl a short pink skirt which clashed with her bright orange hair.

"I'm Marie and this is Geoff," I said. "Have you moved here from somewhere local?"

"Oh yes." Gill smiled and nodded emphatically. "We had a bit of a problem with the house we were living in so it was really nice of Kevin and Val to let us have this place at such short notice." She paused. "Especially as we have the baby."

"The baby?" I looked into the back of the car and sure enough there was a small carry seat containing a tiny, red-faced baby, I took a closer look. "He doesn't look very old."

35

"Three days." Mike gave Gill a hug, she smiled at him but I noticed that the smile was more of a wince.

"Good grief!" I poked Geoff with an elbow. "Don't stand around here in this cold, you get inside and we'll meet again when you've had some sleep, can we help with anything?"

Mike breathed a sigh of relief and shepherded his wife toward the door. "I don't suppose you could just bring the baby bag could you?" He turned and opened the back doors to the car, then handed a blue nappy bag to Geoff. I poked my head around my husband and was just about to coo over the baby when I noticed that, under the blanket, it was wearing a tiny little Newcastle United outfit. He'd already had one ear pierced, the gold stud looked huge and brassy jammed through the tiny, perfect pink ear. I recoiled in horror. Watching Geoff and Mike carry the bits and pieces indoors, I decided with the boys in football gear and one daughter in pink this probably wasn't going to be a friendship made in heaven.

I got exactly the response I expected from both Charlie and Sam later that evening.

"Football!" Sam turned his nose up. "Stupid game."

"Pink!" Charlie snorted. "Stupid colour."

The neighbours were never mentioned by the kids again, in fact over the next five months there seemed to be a certain intolerance that grew between the two sets of kids, if theirs went outside mine would come in, if mine went out theirs would go in, they never spoke to each other, just sneered and made snide comments. Between Charlie and the young lady it seemed to be a never ending round of "Barbie girl or Ginge" with a riposte of "Goth git or scruffy cow". Sam and the young man weren't so vocal but would follow their sister's lead and make menacing faces at each other.

On Monday morning I had two worried children to deal with. Starting a new school is always horrible and ours were expecting the worst.

Driving carefully through the snow I was determined that the school run was going to be excitement-free. We had left at least twenty minutes earlier than we needed to just in case I couldn't remember where the school was or the snow actually became a problem. I wanted the kids at school, on time and as calm as possible.

As we plodded along the country roads heading for Durham our Ford Maverick seemed to be making fairly light work of the snow-covered roads. Or at least it would have if we'd have been in hill-free Cambridgeshire. Feeling the wheels begin to skate on one fairly steep hill I put the car into 4X4 and began the climb, we so nearly made it. About ten meters from the top the car hit a rut and began to slide. I made the whole thing worse by jamming on the brakes and for about three minutes we followed our own tracks in the snow back down to the bottom of the hill.

I had a moment of déjà vu as we slid backward. There were, of course, some differences, this one wasn't covered in cow poo and my interesting slide yesterday hadn't been accompanied by Charlie and Sam screaming blue murder.

The screams finally cut off as our little trip finally terminated in a hedge. Making sure everybody was still in one piece, I pulled slowly out of the hedge and making sure I drove on virgin snow managed to make it to the top. It really wasn't that bad but the kids were now completely freaked out and neurotic, just the right frame of mind to start a new school. Ho hum.

Dropping Charlie at her secondary school in Durham, I took a couple of minutes to reassure her that everything would be fine, she had already visited the school so she knew what to expect. I watched her go with a slightly heavy heart, she didn't look at all happy.

It's always a little difficult to integrate into a new school, not just for the child but the mother can have a couple of problems as well. As we headed toward the gates of Sam's primary school both of us were nervous as children and mothers turned to watch us approach.

There were a few that, like me, were bundled up against the weather but most seemed to be dressed for a party. One group of women were dressed alike in tight tracksuits, high heels, and vast amounts of gold jewellery. Two of them were particularly brave and had on tight-fitting skinny jumpers designed to show off the pink jewels that pierced the blue and goose-bumped skin about their belly buttons. They winked occasionally in the winter sun as the overabundant folds of flesh parted at every movement. Huge gold hoops dangled from each ear, accented by the tight ponytails that sprung bi-coloured above stretched faces sporting pinched lips and hard eyes.

As we walked through the gate, the chattering group dropped into silence and turned to stare. Determined to be sociable I nodded to them and chirped a cheery, "Good Morning." There was no change of expression but as one they turned away, returning to the conversation they had been having before I arrived.

Each group of women I passed seemed to use their conversations as a barrier to keep the "off-comers" away, I chided myself that my paranoia was getting out of hand. Ignoring them all, I marched, with Sam, through the preschool crowd and went to find his teacher. I sincerely hoped the kids were friendlier than their parents.

Back at the house it seemed very quiet and even larger than I feared. I wandered about, vaguely tidying, determined not to think or worry about the kids. Finally I settled down at the computer desperate to find a new boat, the quicker I found one, the quicker they could go back to their old schools and all would be well. It didn't surprise me when, after two solid hours of searching, I came up with no options at all.

When I went to pick the kids up that evening I was relieved that both seemed to have had a good day, Charlie, as she always does, had immediately made friends with a mixed group of young teenagers. She thought it unbelievably funny that they had trouble understanding her accent and had spent most of the day trying to convince them that she wasn't actually Canadian.

Back at the Primary School, I once again ran the gauntlet of the staring, silent mothers ignoring them as they paused in their muttered conversations to throw quick glances and snide looks my way. It wasn't my imagination, I was definitely getting the silent treatment. I waited, alone, for Sam to come out. Finally he arrived with another small boy in tow.

"Hi, Mum," he shouted breathlessly, "this is Aaron, can he come and play?"

I groaned silently to myself, I really didn't want to have to approach any of the women with the pony-tail face-lifts and ask if her son could come and play, I desperately tried to think of an excuse but before I could cudgel my cold brain into action Aaron rushed off.

"Nan . . . NAN!" He shot over to an older woman, also standing alone, some distance away. "Can I go and play with Sam?"

I studied the small woman, she was well-dressed, not expensively, but sensibly for the sub-zero weather conditions. Strands of grey hair had escaped from under her warm blue hat and were blowing about her face; she had to flick them away as they crept behind her glasses. Aaron grabbed her heavily gloved hand and towed her over to us.

"Hello," she said and smiled at me, "I'm Mickey."

Oh, that London accent, I breathed a sigh of relief. "Hi, I'm Marie." I hesitated, aware that we were getting stares from the mothers around us. "Sam and Aaron would like to play." I paused and let the question hang.

"Oh, that would be lovely." Mickey laughed and taking off one of her sheepskin gloves she fumbled about in the pocket of her heavy blue and red ski jacket. "It's nice that Aaron's got a friend."

Finally finding a piece of paper and a pen in her pocket, Mickey wrote down her telephone number and we arranged that Aaron would come after school that Friday and left it at that. I found myself quite looking forward to it, here was a woman who could give me some much-needed answers.

The Friday visit went pretty much as expected, I picked both of them up from school and the two small boys ran about the house, irritated Charlie, traumatised her rats (she said), bickered, fought, played computer games, argued about who won and generally enjoyed themselves hugely. By the time Mickey arrived they had decided that they were firm friends. Mickey seemed massively relieved and accepted a coffee.

"Is it my imagination," I said, handing her a biscuit, "or am I being shunned by the locals?"

Mickey looked surprised. "Well, you've only just arrived."

I dunked a Hobnob into my coffee. "So?"

She laughed. "Marie, I've been up here five years and they still don't talk to me."

"Really?" She must be joking, please let her be joking.

"Yep. I have a couple of people I talk to at school but really it is only one or two." She smiled at me.

Oh great, I totted up in my head how many years Sam had left at primary school . . . three, three more years. I sighed, tomorrow I really needed to find a new boat, the women at Sam's old school were paragons of welcoming virtue compared to this lot.

Another four weeks meandered by and little by little Charlie and Sam settled into their new schools, making friends and generally enjoying life. Geoff was still having fun with his new job and as Christmas approached I began to worry that we were going to be stuck here for ever.

Every day I checked for new boats and fretted when each one I found was turned down for some reason or another by Geoff. When I mentioned that I had found one, the kids would groan and state emphatically that there was no way they were moving back onto a boat. They liked life here, they liked the huge television, the really fast internet connection, having a huge bedroom and a big bath was something they'd never been able to enjoy on our old boat. I began to realise with a sinking feeling that it was only me that was still yearning for the past.

Christmas was quite a rowdy affair. Our oldest, Amelia, and her boyfriend Huw arrived on Christmas Eve with presents and washing. I noticed that they no longer seemed to be "love's young dream". Although there were lots of comments and jokes about getting married, Amelia seemed to snap at Huw every time she spoke to him. He didn't bother to talk to her at all and just spent the time moaning about her to anyone that would listen. I mentioned to Geoff that I wouldn't really want to bet on another year for them.

Amelia has a knack for finding the present that causes Chaos and Disorder to state that she is the best sister in the world and me to threaten her with dismemberment. Last year, for Sam, it had been drumsticks that made drum sounds when you tapped them on anything, this year it was a computer game: World of Warcraft. For some time now, Charlie and Sam had been asking for this but it was an online game that had a monthly fee. We certainly hadn't had the bandwidth to play it on the boat but here it was possible and Amelia had purchased the disk, one month's subscription, and had presented it as a fait accompli before I could scream my objections.

Huw spent a couple of hours on the computer with Geoff, setting it up and explaining how it all worked. My heart sank as I saw Geoff's eyes light up, he really is still a student at heart. He had spent most of his university years playing Dragons and Dungeons and each Saturday had run about in the woods with a rubber sword doing something called LARP. This was the best game in the world to him, a complete land populated by real people from all over the world playing out their fantasies of being an elf or an evil wheelbarrow, or something similar.

However, when it was all working he handed the computer over to the kids and let them enter this massive fantasy world, become mad characters and go off on bizarre quests. It was sure to become an instant hit and I was determined that time limits should be set from the word go. My heart sank as once again I knew I was going to have to be the demon that said "no".

In an attempt to keep Sam in bed beyond four o'clock on Christmas morning, I had decreed that everybody was to have a stocking and that included me! So at three o'clock I was creeping around putting stockings at the end of everyone's bed, and I was looking forward to the next morning, hoping that Geoff would have purchased me a stocking full of "stuff". He had been dropping heavy hints for about a fortnight that I was going to love my "unusual" gifts and I had to admit to being a little excited.

After the stocking delivery I snuggled back into bed and thought about the previous Christmas, we had been so broke but we'd still had a good time and I dropped back to sleep with happy memories of *Happy Go Lucky* resplendently decked out in cheap Christmas lights that had turned the surrounding mist into an ever changing coloured haze.

Sam managed six o'clock this year and, on awaking to a loud set of giggles that emanated from his room, I rolled over with a hopeful smile at my husband. He gave me a quick kiss then, reaching under the bed, he pulled out a multi-coloured stocking bulging with exciting lumps and bumps, I really couldn't resist a juvenile squeal.

"Now, then," Geoff said, holding the stocking out of the reach of my grasping hands, "have you been a good little girl?"

I laughed and put on a terrible lisp, "Oh, yeth Thanta, I've been ever tho good, I haven't pulled any of my friendth pigtails, I haven't painted any petth pink and I haven't put gravy into your wellieth." I batted my eyelashes at him. "Ever tho, ever tho, good."

Geoff laughed and handed the stocking to me. Having finally got it in my hands I reached over and pulled his stocking from where I had hidden it in the bedside cabinet. I dumped it unceremoniously on his lap causing a slight wince. "Happy Christmas, you open yours first, I want to savour mine."

His first and best stocking present was a new watch, completely waterproof, it had all sorts of functions and was very swish. The previous year I had managed to throw him overboard while trying to get a new bath on to the boat. His old watch never actually stopped working but there was a huge blob of condensation across the glass that we never got rid of, I really felt I owed him a new one.

It took him about twenty minutes to open all his presents (I did feel that he was being deliberately slow) apart from the new watch there were CDs, books, a new computer game, socks, a tangerine and some nuts (just to keep it traditional). His big present, a mega tester, was downstairs under the tree. I had no idea what it did, something electrical but it had lights and made pinging noises and had had to be sort of tuned or something so it had come with a technical certificate of calibration, it looked ever so professional. I knew he had been coveting one of these things for months so I was definitely going to get brownie points.

Finally getting to open my first present I was a little disappointed to note that the box, once the wrapping was off, came from a well-known but not very exclusive jewellery shop. I didn't really wear jewellery and had a horrible vision of a huge pair of cheap gold earrings. I tentatively opened the box and winced when Geoff let out a roar of laughter. It was a lump of coal.

"I thought you said you'd been good?" Geoff guffawed.

I burst out laughing. "Oh, very funny, maybe I haven't been as good as I thought."

I picked up the next present, it was a small box of chocolates from Hotel Chocolat, very nice, just the thing to eat before breakfast and certainly the thing to eat before the kids saw them. I opened the box and frowned. Geoff had carefully taken out all the chocolates and replaced them with little pieces of coal. I smiled with a bit of an effort as I listened to my terribly happy husband snigger and giggle.

I reached for the next present. One was funny, two was amusing, surely he wouldn't push his luck that far and go for three would he? Oh surely not.

Oh yes he would, and a fourth and a fifth and a sixth. By the time I reached the last three lumps at the bottom of the stocking I had completely lost my sense of humour. Geoff wasn't laughing any more either; obviously the look on my face had told him that this had gone well beyond a joke.

I emptied the last of the "presents" out onto the bed and gave him a hard stare. "Should I even bother opening them?"

He gave me a sickly smile and shook his head. "I thought it would be funny." He ran a hand over his head and gave me a rueful look. "You know? Bad girl gets a stocking full of coal." He sighed. "The girls at the office said you would find one or two funny but any more than that and I was going to find myself spending Christmas in the car while wearing my turkey dinner."

"You should have taken their advice." I pursed my lips at him. "You have once chance and about thirty seconds to make it up to me."

Geoff looked horrified and scrabbled about under the bed coming up with a little plastic bag.

"What's that?" I weighed the bag cautiously in my hand.

"It's the chocolates out of that box, I saved them." He ripped open the little plastic bag and grabbing one popped it into my mouth, then grinned hopefully at me and said, "Your real present's downstairs."

I couldn't be angry at him, he looked so forlorn. "Exactly how long did it take you to wrap up all this coal?" I pointed to the pile of coal resting in my lap, carelessly dropping black dust all over our blue chequered duvet.

"About three hours." He shook his head. "It seemed like such a good idea at the time."

The thunder of feet interrupted us. Sam burst into the bedroom waving a DVD. "Look, look I got the new SpongeBob film, can we go and watch it?"

Charlie, following hot on the heels of her brother, sighed and rolled her eyes. "Thanks for the pressies." She grinned. "I especially liked the tiny bottle of Irish Cream."

"Hmmm," I sighed, "I take it that's already gone, has it?"

She nodded. "And the chocolates, and the orange," she paused, "in fact I feel a bit sick." She frowned as she caught sight of the bed covered in coal. "What's that?"

"Your mother hasn't been very good this year," Geoff muttered, obviously determined to keep the joke going.

Charlie gaped at the bed. "Oh, you didn't . . .?" she stepped around me and picked up one of the unopened presents. "Not every one . . . surely."

I scowled as Sam finally caught on to the joke and howled with laughter (obviously the same puerile jokes tickle both father and son).

Geoff, faced with frowns from both me and Charlie shook his head. "Yes, I know, it was a bad idea." He climbed out of bed and reached for his jeans. "Let's go and find Mum a real present shall we?" He scuttled out of the room with Sam following hot on his heels.

"I thought it was funny Dad," Sam said in a loud theatrical whisper as they exited stage left.

Charlie snorted and patted me on the arm. "Don't worry, I bought you something nice," she said, grinning.

The rest of the morning went fairly well, and after a huge dinner that included slightly burnt turkey and very undercooked roast potatoes, everyone settled down to their various tasks. Sam and Amelia spent most of the afternoon watching SpongeBob, the two of them laughing uproariously at the silly jokes (I do think that Amelia's extreme humour may have been slightly Southern Comfort-fuelled). Charlie and Huw played World of Warcraft and Geoff played with his new electrical testing gadget. With all of the others engaged, I finally got the chance to set up my new laptop. Well, I looked at it for a while and then called Geoff over to fix it for me; it seemed the right thing to do after all he had put me through.

That evening, out in the kitchen, Amelia was helping me with the washing up, she was still fairly tipsy but was now sporting a major headache as well.

"So how's the boat hunting going?" She paused to wash a couple of paracetamol down with a large glass of water. "Have you got anything yet?"

"Nope." I didn't really want to talk about this, I was feeling slightly guilty about the money I had spent over Christmas, I knew it had severely knocked our bank account around.

She picked up a saucepan and began an industrious if ineffectual drying movement. "So what are you going to do?"

Leaning on the edge of the sink I sighed. "I don't know, Mills, I really don't. Even if I find a boat, I don't think anyone else wants to move again." I tailed off, not knowing what to say.

Amelia frowned. "I didn't want to be the one to tell you." She nodded toward the lounge and its sleepy, overfed occupants. "But Charlie was saying earlier that there was no way she was going to move on to a boat again."

"I know." I stirred the murky water around in the sink, I could feel tears gathering and held my breath, this was NOT the time for a good cry.

Amelia grabbed one of the clean glasses and filled it with Southern Comfort. Holding it out toward me she gave me a big grin. "Don't give up yet." She stared out of the window at the sleet. "If it's like this in December, just imagine what it's going to be like in February." She pushed the glass towards me. "I shouldn't think spring even turns up here till about June, everybody will be completely fed up with it by then."

I stared at her over the rim of the glass. "When did you get so sneaky?"

Amelia blushed. "Sometimes you just have to wait for the right time to make your point."

"And your point would be?"

She flicked a nervous glance toward the living room. "Let's just say we're all hoping for some big changes in the New Year."

With that slightly enigmatic statement, she dropped the tea towel on top of the unfinished washing up and sailed out of the room.

Oh dear; Amelia in that sort of mood wasn't going to be good news for anyone.

As January and February slipped slowly away, I was still having no luck finding a new boat. Once again, everything was either too small or too expensive. I was also really concerned about our finances. Every week Geoff's wages just failed to cover our expenditure. Little by little we were eating away at the savings, a couple of hundred quid here, a set of new tyres there, we just needed the car serviced, the kids needed new shoes. As the savings went down, my boat search became more frenzied. Boats I wouldn't have considered three months ago were now out of our price range and I was becoming slightly panic-stricken about the whole thing.

I worked out that at our present rate of spending we had less than three months before we wouldn't be able to buy a boat at all. I firmly ignored the little voice in my head that suggested we may already be at that point. I wasn't going to listen to that rubbish, I *couldn't* let myself listen to that rubbish, if I did, I might well be inclined to just give up and there was no way I was going down without a fight.

I stared out of the window at the sleet-filled rain and deliberately screwed my pages of calculations up and threw them, with a certain amount of vindictiveness, into the already overflowing wastepaper basket. Typically, I missed and it bounced off across the carpet. I sighed and bent down to pick it up.

The only place to put the computer desk, printer and all the other IT paraphernalia we owned was a nice little niche under the stairs. As you walked in the front door you found yourself immediately in the living room with the stairs to your left. The space beneath them made a fairly good office. Unfortunately the stairs were wider than the computer table and as I stood up I smashed my head into the underside of the polished wooden treads. The sudden pain brought tears to my eyes and I staggered over to grab the back of the sofa, trying to stop my eyes watering. Honestly it was only the bump on the head that made me cry, nothing to do with the finances, and as long as I kept telling myself that I was fine. I gave the offending piece of paper a vicious kick telling myself that I just needed to talk to Geoff about the whole thing, between us there wasn't anything we couldn't accomplish.

Unfortunately it had become almost impossible to talk to Geoff about it. In fact it had become almost impossible to talk to Geoff about anything. Completely engrossed with the stupid online game, he had taken to coming home from work, eating dinner and getting straight on to the computer. I was seriously considering hitting either him or the equipment with a very large hammer. There was, of course every chance that I was being unreasonable so, as usual, I took my woes to Helen.

"He doesn't talk to me any more," I ranted at her one evening over gin and bitter lemon. "That stupid game is just taking over, every flaming night he just sits there till he can't stay awake any more then we go to bed and he passes out. He doesn't interact with the kids, we don't go out."

I sighed and looked at her. "We're running out of money, Hels, the savings are just going down and down, it's only me looking for a boat, the kids have made it clear they don't want to move and Geoff doesn't even live in this world any more, he's become some sort of Orc hairdresser or something." I took a deep breath, any more of this and I was just going to have a complete crying fit. "I can't bear it, when we had the boat we did everything together, there were things going on all the time, getting water, getting coal, running about, fixing things, we laughed." I frowned.

"We froze our bits off as well, got eaten alive by insects and fished Geoff out of the river a lot but," I hesitated as I tried to think of the right words, "it was fun."

Helen gave me a hug; obviously this was a real problem and not one for a good nagging. "Well, your life is pretty much the same as everybody else's." She laughed. "Lots of people spend too long on computer games, good grief I know I've nagged Dave about it often enough. There's never enough money and you rob Peter to pay Paul." She paused for a moment, "Look, what exactly is it that's so important to you about living on the boat, maybe if you went through it you'd see it wasn't all that good and you could concentrate on living here." She leaned forward with a curious look. "So come on convince me."

I gulped and could feel my face heating up. "You're going to laugh, it's such a corny thing but to me it was the best thing in the world."

Helen pushed her hair out of her eyes and frowned, trying desperately to give the impression that she wouldn't laugh.

"It's the sense of community." I gave her a slightly embarrassed smile. "Not something *I've* ever been worried about eh? I can't even remember a house where I haven't had some problem with the neighbours, even if it's something really paltry like their cat digging up my lawn." I took a sip of my drink. "You always knew where you were with the boaters, nobody ever bothered you, nobody judged. There were boats of every shape and size down that line, but there was no one-upmanship, none of the "I've got a better boat than you". People would always help out, if you ran out of coal or electricity or needed something; there were no worries about asking someone for help, you knew that in the same position they'd certainly ask you."

I paused as I tried to remember what had made it all so very special. "In the summer, there were early mornings where we'd all be drinking coffee and perched on steps, some in pyjamas, some in shorts, just chatting. People would join the group or wander off, everyone knew everyone else. If people had too much of something they just left the excess by the skip or offered it around." I grinned. "I remember someone had managed to pick up a load of paving slabs, far too many to pave the way to their boat. So that winter, there were about five of us that didn't need to skip through the mud, it was such a simple thing but it was so good."

I paused for breath and took a look at Helen to see if she understood, she frowned so I carried on. "And every year a set of boats get lifted out for blacking, the first two days just seem to be a bit of a party, someone brings a barbecue, there's far too much beer consumed, but eventually they start work but if your next door neighbour needs help then they would do that as well. Maybe I'm wrong, not having lived through it, but there seems to still be that sense of community that my gran used to talk about." I pondered the whole thing, then another thought occurred to me and I frowned. "There is one other thing, every morning that stupid postman comes to the door and delivers me a pile of letters."

Helen shook her head in confusion. "Yeah, so?"

"Well, it's just that if you're watching your budget and every day another bill comes in and another and another, and if it's not bills it's rubbish. Just bits of paper telling you that to live a fulfilled life you need to change your gas provider or your telephone provider." I huffed in exasperation. "On one hand they're telling you to pay up because you're in debt and on the other they're offering more debt, more money, more . . ." I paused trying to think of the word that would convey my utter disgust with the whole stupid process ". . . stuff." I shook my head, it wasn't a good word.

"It's obscene really and it's no wonder that everyone gets into debt." I looked up at her and took in the lifted lip and disbelieving look. "I told you it was pathetic, but it was the one thing I loved about being on the boat, no post. We had a box in the city and we went once a week and picked it all up, half of it went straight into the recycling and the rest we just ignored until they went away," I said giving her a big smile, "it was heaven."

Helen shook her head in complete disbelief. "Everybody deals with post Marie," she said still shaking her head, "you just learn to live with it."

"But I don't have to live with it, I know I don't and that's the thing. I've seen the other side and quite frankly it's really peaceful." I frowned and shook my head again remembering all the things about house living that I didn't have to put up with.

"Well, I can see the appeal although I'm not sure I agree with you about the post." Helen leant back in her chair and took a large sip of her drink, the ice cubes clinking as she lifted it. "But if you want your way and you're fairly sure that it's going to be good for everyone and not just you, you're going to have to do what we do best."

"And what exactly is that?" I sniffed at her.

"Pick your time and be really, really sneaky." She raised her eyebrows at me. "Fancy another?"

CHAPTER
THREE

Dignity Dissolves in Alcohol

As winter grudgingly gave way to a wet and windy spring, life, unfortunately, continued unchanged. Charlie happily added to her group of friends and often went out at the weekends. I had met most of the group she hung around with and they seemed a nice enough crowd, although it is always a bit difficult to tell in a large group of gabbling thirteen-year-olds.

Charlie decided she couldn't take the accent any more and had taken it upon herself to teach them "proper English" as she called it, consequently her closest friends now switched between barth and bath, Carstle and castle, glarss and glass with equal enthusiasm.

Sam on the other hand had taken to the local lingo like a pro. Asking him on one occasion if he would like ice cream after tea he responded with an enthusiastic "wae'aye mun". Geoff howled with laughter. I didn't find it funny at all and had to go and have a sit down.

Geoff, seeing I was upset, came and sat beside me. "What on earth's the matter with you?" He handed me a coffee. "You can't expect him to live somewhere and not pick up a couple of the local sayings." He frowned.

"I hadn't got you pegged for such a narrow-minded, dyed-in-the-wool southerner." He paused then shook his head. "But that's not it is it?" He stared at me. "You've never worried if someone's from Glasgow, France or flipping Timbuktu so what exactly is the big problem here?"

"It used to be like that." I sighed and took a sip of scalding coffee. "And it's really odd, I have no problems with the people from Durham, or Darlington or even Newcastle, they seem to be welcoming, chatty and just generally nice, pretty much like people all over the country." I paused for a moment. "But this village is like flaming anti-Stepford, the women at school are still not speaking to me." I shook my head. "That sounds really pathetic I know, it's not that I need them to like me but they won't even acknowledge that I'm standing there, and if one of them is talking to Mickey and I go and talk to her, the other women will walk away, it really is getting ridiculous."

Geoff snorted and looked dubious.

I took another sip of coffee and stared into the fire. "There was a woman standing about three feet from me yesterday and she was talking to her friend about how proud she was that she was umpteenth generation to live in the same house and that her grandfather had never gone further than ten miles out of the village his whole life. She said that she didn't understand why these people needed to move all over the country and take houses that locals could have.

They kept looking at me as they were talking then giggling, honestly it's really basic schoolyard bullying I couldn't care less about them or their stupid village; let's face it, what's here? A big fat nothing, but it does get really wearing."

Geoff shook his head. "Are you sure you're not just being paranoid?" He stretched his feet towards the fire. "Most people I come in contact with are lovely."

"You're never actually here," I moaned. "Let's face it, if a heavy fog came down I wouldn't dare enter the centre of the village because there is a huge and real possibility that if you tried to walk through the fog you'd end up in the Newcastle version of bloody Brigadoon or in Limbo where all the dead stand in silence and wait for judgement day." I pulled a spooky face and wiggled my fingers at him. "Wooooooo!" Standing up, I wandered toward the table. "You spend most of your time in Durham City or over near Middlesbrough. I wish we'd never sold *Happy Go Lucky* and I wish we'd never come up here." I paused for a moment, concentrating on sorting through that day's copious post; three bills, a letter from Charlie's school and seven pieces that looked as though they held "fantastic" deals that I probably shouldn't miss out on. I blinked rapidly as the addresses on the letters suddenly began to swim in sad water. "This place will never, ever be home."

At the beginning of April we did have one piece of mail that was actually good news. Expecting exciting books from Amazon, I was actually waiting for the postman that morning. At the sound of an engine I dragged myself off the sofa with a grin. Listening to the car pull up outside our door I frowned, that certainly didn't sound like the post van. A well-tuned engine throbbed for a couple of seconds then faded to silence. I peered out of the window at the shiny, sapphire-blue Freelander that sat on the gravel. A tall, well-built, middle-aged man climbed out, his shorts and sandals marking him as a tourist, and, straightening his multi-pocketed jacket, he headed for the door.

I beat him to it and he looked fairly surprised as I stuck my head out and grinned at his still-raised hand. "Hello, can I help you?"

He lowered his hand and gave me a charming smile.

Maybe I was wrong, maybe he wasn't a tourist, if he was selling something he was going to be sorely disappointed so I pursed my lips, crossed my arms, raised an eyebrow at him, then waited for the sales spiel to start.

"Hello," he said and gave me another dazzling smile, "I don't suppose you've lost a sheep have you?"

I stared at him as I went over his words in my head. Well, that wasn't what I'd expected at all. "Erm, no," I said, wondering if this was a new sales tactic, start with a completely mad sentence to get me on the back foot then go in for the kill. I looked over at his car and hesitantly returned the wave of the woman sitting in the passenger seat with a scruffy terrier on her lap, not a salesman then.

He continued to smile at me and I felt pressured to expand. "I don't have any sheep." I gave him an inane smile.

"Do you know anyone who has?" He was obviously a little frustrated with my reticence.

I took a moment to cudgel my brain into a semblance of working order then asked, "Have you found a sheep?" This was turning out to be a very short, succinct and slightly surreal conversation.

He nodded enthusiastically. "Yeah, it was wandering along the road all by itself and yours was the first drive I came to."

Right, that made sense. I felt I could actually contribute to the conversation now. "Well, I haven't been here long but our landlord Kevin will probably know which of his neighbours keep sheep." I nodded and smiled, yes this was definitely a problem I could palm off on someone else. "If you could tell me where it is, I'll pop round and see him and he'll no doubt do something about it." I waved over his shoulder as John the postie pulled into the drive.

"It's in the back of the car," he replied and grinned, pointing at his new, un-muddied bespoke 4X4.

"What?" I stared at the car and sure enough in the shadows of the tinted boot windows I could just make out the distinctive surprised, black and white face of a small Swaledale, male by the look of the horns, not yet very long but certainly beginning to develop that distinctive curve. "You've got it in your car?" I must have sounded a complete half-wit. "How the hell did you get it in there?"

The man frowned. "I just picked it up." He shrugged. "We've got the back all caged off for the dog so I just moved the dog and bunged him in there."

61

John joined us, a bunch of letters in his hand. "Morning." He grinned at the man, then frowned as I blubbered through a sentence that contained the words, sheep and car then stared as I pointed toward the now rocking 4X4. Its remaining passengers were beginning to look decidedly worried.

Swaledales are the local sheep, they are tough, hardy and opportunistic. Approximately two years ago I'd had a coat that, when I walked, obviously made a noise like a feedbag and I still have outstandingly clear memories of being chased for over half a mile by a very, very intent flock of these things much to the amusement of Geoff, his mother and the kids. I finally got rid of them by ditching the coat and had shivered most of the way home. Ever since then I'd been very careful to buy only silent cold weather gear.

As we all stood in silence staring at the car, the young sheep became bored and decided that, while travelling in style was great for a while, it was now time to go back to finding those lovely ladies it had obviously been searching for when this well meaning but obviously insane person had kidnapped it.

We all winced as the sheep smashed its head into the window, the lady in the passenger seat gave a short scream and the dog began to bark which only seemed to infuriate the sheep even more.

"Hey . . . HEY!" The man made a leap for his car (evidently his name was Graham, the lady in the passenger seat was now screaming over and over, "GRAHAM! Make it stop!"), I thought he was going to, sensibly, open the door and let it out. No, he ran to the window and began to hammer on it. "You stop that," he yelled as though to his dog, "stay! sit!" The sheep glowered at him and backed away from the window. John handed me the pile of letters then, gently grabbing me by the arm, manoeuvred me back toward the house. We alternated between staring at each other then back at the car which was beginning to rock with each successive thump, THUMP! As the sheep sought escape, the screams and barking from the front of the car grew in both panic and decibels.

Graham was almost incandescent, veins stood out at his temples and he continued to hammer on the window. "Pack it in you stupid animal," he screamed, the sheep just eyed him balefully through the glass. "Argh, you've pooed." He gave the window a mighty thump with his fist. "Stop treading in it," he shrieked.

John's hand closed on my arm and moved me another step into the house, we peered out through the door.

The sheep, (Ram!) jumped and closing its eyes gave the window one last bash. The lock finally gave way and the glass door snapped upward as the woolly torpedo exploded with a graceful jump out onto the gravel. John swore and grabbed the door as the enraged animal careered toward us, head down and teeth bared (or baaaaaa'd). He slammed the door shut and we both winced as the wood shuddered under the devastating impact. John grinned down at me. "He is NOT happy," he said.

Giggling, we both hurried to the window and stared out as Graham stood in shock looking at his boot door.

We watched with glee as his expression changed from anger to fear as he realised that the ram was backing slowly away from him, malice evident in its every movement. The screams and barking were now almost painful.

"I think I'd better get Kevin." John sniggered then headed off, through the house, toward the back door leaving me at the window to watch the YouTube-worthy antics outside.

I dithered, I really wanted to open the door and let the man in but I thought that any movement would attract the enraged ovine. Anyway he had managed to shut his wife up and was just creeping around the car keeping it between him and "Ram . . . bo", they seemed to have it all under control.

It seemed like an age, but was probably only a couple of minutes before Huge one and Huge two came plodding around the corner of the barn. The ram narrowed its eyes and backed up a couple of more paces. The brothers looked at each other and grinned, both stepping sideways to give the animal a couple of targets to choose from.

It really didn't take him long, putting his head down he rushed at the brother on the left. As he went past, Huge two just stepped forward and grabbed a horn in one hand and wodge of fleece in the other then spun on the spot dragging the confused animal in a circle. Legs scrabbling on the gravel, he tried to struggle but when the other brother joined in and they both had hold of his head he sighed and became as meek as a kitten.

The brothers grinned at me through the window as they staggered past dragging the now quiescent animal between them. "All right, Mrs Browne?" they nodded.

Shaking my head at their casual treatment of the evil beastie, I waved and opened the front door, the least I could do was offer these poor guys a cup of tea.

Marion, sat wide-eyed on the sofa watching Titch, the terrier, exploring the lounge, she could barely hold the mug her hand was shaking so hard. "We saw him wandering along the side of the road." She took a sip and stared unseeing into the fireplace. "It was me that made Graham pick him up; he looked so sweet and lost."

I tried to think of something comforting to say. "Well it's probably a good job you did." I smiled encouragingly. "He could have caused a nasty accident if he'd jumped out in front of a bike or a car, it was a really good thing you got him off the road." I stared out of the window and watched her husband as, with a face like thunder, he attempted to keep his boot shut with a mixture of grubby blue baler twine and pristine, unused, bungee cords.

She nodded, I really wished she would blink or something, she was beginning to make my eyes water just looking at her.

John sipped his tea and added his own pearls of wisdom. "Just be thankful he was only a baby," he commented sagely.

The woman blinked at him. "They get bigger than that?" Her face was ashen. Putting her mug down on the table she turned to me with a smile and took a deep breath. "Thank you for the tea." She whistled to Titch who was trying to climb into the log basket. "And I'm really sorry we brought that hideous animal to you." She got to her feet with another sigh. "But I'll tell you this . . ." she narrowed her eyes and shook her head as, with Titch under her arm, she headed toward the door. "If ever I can't sleep, I'm going to take a valium. I am NOT going to count sheep, ever AGAIN!"

With that she nodded and, giving us a wobbly smile, headed out to where her husband was now sitting in the driver's seat, his face still purple, (if anyone needed a valium he did).

Watching them head slowly away down the drive John and I leant on each other and howled, I hadn't laughed so hard for what seemed like years. I was still laughing even after I realised that the post he'd given me didn't contain my new book.

Draining his mug, my now favourite postman grinned. "Well, I'd better get on my way, see you tomorrow, no doubt there will be more bills . . . there always is."

I was still laughing as I waved John off then took a look at the post he'd brought me, maybe he wasn't so bad after all, there weren't even any bills, just a couple of bits of junk mail and an unexpected hand written envelope which I opened with a frown. Reading the contents I had to sit down.

Geoff's brother Philip was finally getting married; the marriage was at the end of May and was being held near Oxford. I am not a great lover of big family get-togethers for just any old reason but as this was going to give me an excuse to get closer to home I was most enthusiastic about the celebration and couldn't wait for the date to arrive.

Philip always surprised me, the first time I met him was when Geoff and I had lived in Birmingham, about thirteen years previously. I had answered the knock on the door and found myself face to face with a fairly scary-looking thug type. He's about 5'10" compared to Geoff's 5'8", with much more muscle. His short, light brown hair was the complete opposite to the long, backside length, flowing dark locks that Geoff had been so proud of in his younger days (I always tell people I married Cochise and ended up with Gandalf) and it didn't help that half this guy's face seemed to be missing, hidden under a collection of bruises, scabs and scrapes. (I found out later that he had had a run-in with a girder while doing some building work), he was also better dressed than my beloved who leans towards jeans with big holes in the knees and scruffy old T-shirts that invariably originated from either a festival or a rock concert.

"Hello," this oddball had said as I opened the door, then he stepped forward and tried to walk past me.

I had panicked slightly. "Whoa, hold it!" I had tried to stop him by standing in front of him. "Who the hell are you?" The man frowned and looked down at me for a moment. Then giving me exactly the same grin that Geoff gives me every morning, reached down, picked me up and gave me a hug, completely ignoring the squeaks. "I'm Geoff's brother," he said and grinned again, the eyes and the smile were exactly the same.

"You must be Marie, is he in?" He then pushed past me and I heard the same squeaks from Geoff as Philip picked him up and gave him a huge hug as well.

Since then he had found it hard to settle down. Unwilling to give up his bachelor lifestyle, he went through girlfriends like I go through shoes. We only really saw him at Christmas so I always bought a generic present for "a girl". We never knew who would be with him and on a couple of occasions he was actually single. However, with his good looks, mischievous nature and quick wit he was never single for long. He wandered through life, concentrating on his sports, drinking too much, enjoying himself a little too much and leaving a slightly sad trail of disappointed but still hopeful women in his wake.

Later, after regaling my husband with the tale about the ram, I picked up the invite and studied it again. "Philip's getting married." I couldn't stop my voice from heading upward in a surprised squeak at the end of that statement. "Who managed to reel him in and where has she hidden the negatives that are keeping him on a leash?"

Geoff laughed, it had always been a source of amusement to me that two children from the same parents, brought up in exactly the same environment could grow up so differently. Geoff, techno hippy programmer, spent his leisure hours reading or playing silly board games, completely teetotal. Until I had turned his life upside down, he had seemed to live entirely on copious amounts of tea and canned ravioli. Philip on the other hand, drank like a fish and played cricket and rugby, he's also connected with the local mountain rescue team.

Their attitudes to people differ as well, Geoff, at a party, is usually to be found with a cup of tea and a book, preferring not to get involved in the social hysterics that always accompany such occasions. He can, quite happily do without people at all, bumbling about, intent on his own agenda. A classic programmer, keep him in the dark, give him an interesting problem to solve and occasionally slide pizza under the door of his darkened room and he would be a happy hippy.

Philip can usually be tracked down to his local (even his mother knows that's the easiest place to locate him) he will be found in the thick of the crowd that is laughing the hardest, he knows everyone and everyone knows him. When visiting, Geoff is often treated to a wide-eyed, non-comprehending look from some of the locals — "You're Cookies brother?" They're like each other's evil twin, it really is quite baffling.

I was still slightly shell-shocked when we went to bed that evening. I had spent fruitless hours boat-hunting and had had an argument with Charlie about living conditions and why she couldn't have a puppy. "We could have one if we still lived on the boat." I had finally started using blatant blackmail to force them around to my way of thinking.

Charlie had thrown a tantrum. "I don't want to live on a stupid boat, I want to live here, but I don't want to live here, here. I want to live somewhere that's not rented, I want to live somewhere I can have a dog." And with that she had stamped up to her bedroom, I

69

could hear her ranting at her rats about the unfairness of life.

Lying in bed listening to Geoff breathing I thought again about Philip getting married, she must be some girl to get him to give up his life of decadence and self-indulgence, or maybe she just loved him the way he was and she was happy to live like that. Ah well! I would find out for myself at the end of May. There was a sudden bright light that flicked on in my head. End of May, there was something about that date that rang bells.

Quietly I climbed out of bed and went back downstairs to turn the computer on. Discovering what had rung the bells in my head, I started laughing. "Be really, really sneaky," Helen had said. Well here was an opportunity for me to be just that. Checking another couple of dates and venues I grinned then wiped all traces of my internet search from the computer, it really wouldn't do to give the family time to formulate a defence, now would it?

Smiling and happier than I had been in months, I climbed the stairs back to my nice warm Geoff-filled bed. Now I was *really* looking forward to Philip's wedding, I hoped it would be a weekend that would be a point of change for us all.

At the beginning of May, spring didn't really seem to have made much of an inroad into the winter cold at all and it was on another cold and windy day that I found myself outside Sainsbury's in Durham waiting for Charlie. Sam had been picked up from school by

Mickey and had gone to play at Aaron's house. I had some shopping to do and as Sainsbury's was just down the road from Charlie's school I arranged to meet her there at three thirty, she was late, as usual.

I felt my phone vibrate and sighed, wondering what her excuse would be this time. The text wasn't, as I expected, from my increasingly errant daughter, but from Jude at the old moorings. I read her text with an increasing amount of irritation. Just saying hello, she informed me that the weather was great and asked when we were coming down to visit, she signed off saying she had to go as Ruby, her young daughter, had just fallen over in the paddling pool.

I closed my phone with an irritated flick and looked up at the slate-grey skies, groaning as the first rain drops hit me in the face. Paddling pool! Either Jude had turned into some sort of child-abusing monster who made her children "have fun" in the cold, or they were enjoying far better weather than I hoped to see all summer.

My increasingly jealous thoughts were interrupted by Charlie arriving with a young man. Still lost in my gloomy reverie I waved vaguely when she introduced him, then, gathering up the shopping, ushered her away toward the car.

"Are you all right?" I looked up from packing the shopping bags into the boot and frowned when I saw her still standing by the passenger door. "Central locking sweetie, it's open."

"Hmm?" Charlie looked at me vaguely then nodded hurriedly. "Oh, right."

71

She fumbled open the car door and dropped into the seat with an even more graceless than normal thud. I shook my head and got behind the wheel.

"Did you have a good day?" I pulled out of the car park and headed back toward home, the sky had now turned a beautiful black and purple, I sighed, puddles up to our knees again tomorrow.

Charlie nodded and placed her hands carefully on the dashboard. "Yeah it was great, I had Geography and Sarah said that . . ."

I let her chatter wash over me and concentrated on the road ahead. It was rapidly becoming invisible in the gathering downpour.

After about five minutes I realised that she was still speaking. It was normally difficult to get more than monosyllables out of her until she had got home, got changed and had something to eat. Even then she always spent a good half an hour moaning and telling me exactly what was wrong with her day, her life, her friends, her hair, her skin and a thousand other irritants that were usually at the forefront of her mind.

I looked over at her; she was still holding onto the dashboard and had reduced her speech to a sort of constant mumble interspersed with little giggles and burps. I took a careful sniff.

"Charlie?"

"Yes?" She swivelled her head slowly and carefully toward me and stared, unblinking, in my general direction. Her too-bright eyes looked worried and unnatural.

"Why can I smell whisky?"

72

We pulled into the drive and stopped outside the house, Charlie bolted out of the door but was stopped mid flight. The house was locked up and I still had the keys.

I stood beside her at the door and sniffed again. "It's you, isn't it, have you been drinking?"

Charlie giggled then stuffed her fist into her mouth. Oh, this was no good. I wasn't going to get any sense out of her until I had sobered her up. I opened the front door and let her precede me.

At the bottom of the stairs, she turned and pulled herself very upright. "I think," she enunciated carefully, "that I have had a very hard day and would like a little nap before tea."

I nodded sourly and watched her stumble and scramble up the stairs. Following her progress overhead, I heard her go to the toilet and then stumble and crash back to her bedroom. The door closed with a thud and there were a couple of protesting squeaks as evidently she had fallen onto her bed.

I would give her an hour and then, so help me, all hell was going to break loose, I really hoped she was the type to get a hangover.

I gave her time to pass out then checked on her, she was face down, fully clothed on top of the bed, her face close to the edge, ah well if she was sick at least she wouldn't choke. I turned and with a slight start noticed three little pinched faces staring at me from the darkness of a big cage. "Hi ladies." I bent down and gave each of the rats a bit of a ruffle. "Sorry, but I think you might be missing your evening run tonight, let me know if she throws up." Covering her with a quilt, I left her to sleep and went back downstairs, I left her door ajar so that I could hear her move.

Checking on her an hour later she was still fast asleep. I left her again. Another hour and I decided that as Geoff would be home soon I had better get her up and moving. As I was walking up the stairs there was a sudden rustle of bedclothes and the rumble of running feet. She rushed past me and into the bathroom both hands held firmly to her mouth.

I waited outside as the sound of vomiting echoed around the landing. "Are you finished yet?" I stuck my head around the door, whoops no, I stood back outside the door and waited for the latest evacuation to finish.

Five minutes later a subdued young teenager staggered out of the bathroom. I decided that a sympathetic approach was not going to be in her best interests and even though she looked as though she was going to cry, I adopted a folded-arm and raised-eyebrow stance. "So are you going to tell me exactly how you got into this state?"

Charlie looked up at me, a couple of tears running down her face. "Whisky," she gasped, "at lunchtime."

I was horrified. "Do you mean you've been in this state all afternoon?" She nodded miserably. "Did you skip school?" She shook her head. "So, you were in lessons, completely drunk, all afternoon!"

Charlie slid down the wall and went for the sympathy she obviously felt she was being denied. "Mum, I think I'm dying. I feel so ill."

I grabbed her arm and pulled her to her feet. "You're not dying, this is what alcohol does you daft thing. Why do you think that your dad doesn't drink, why do you think that I only drink a little, it's because we really hate feeling like this."

"How long is it going to last?" Charlie clutched her stomach. "I've got such a headache and I think I'm going to be sick again."

I propelled her back into the bathroom and stood over her while she gagged and retched for another minute or so. "It's going to last longer than the good feeling did."

She stared up at me, her hands holding on to the edge of the toilet bowl. "How long?"

I improvised, and pretended to think for a moment. "The rule of thumb is that however long you were drunk for the hangover lasts usually twice that time, then twice again."

"Oh nooooo!" Charlie wailed then abruptly stuck her head down the toilet again.

When she had finished I urged her to clean her teeth, then helped her back to bed. It was only five thirty but I didn't expect to see her until the next morning, thank God it was Friday.

I meandered back downstairs and sat staring into the fire until Geoff was blown, windswept and soaked, through the front door.

"Wah!" he yelped as he had a short battle with the wind and the front door. "That's a bit frisky."

I nodded and shuffled down from the sofa to sit on the floor next to the fire. "I had a text from Jude today."

"Oh yeah?" he shook himself out of his soaked coat and dumped his boots into the box by the door. "Is everybody well down there?"

"I think so. She didn't say much, she had to rush off before Ruby drowned herself in the paddling pool."

"Paddling pool?" Geoff laughed, "It's amazing isn't it, that there can be such a difference in temperature over just two hundred miles?" He looked around. "Where are the horrible two? Have you finally lost all patience and buried them in a local field?"

"Sam's at Aaron's." I winced and worded it carefully, "Charlie's in bed."

"Bed?" Geoff, finally managing to extricate himself from all his outer garments wandered toward the kitchen, no doubt in search of the kettle. "Oh dear, is she not well?"

"Well, she's been sick a couple of times."

"Tummy bug?"

"No." I gave up trying to word it well. "Apparently a good dose of scotch."

Geoff stopped in the doorway to the kitchen and did a slow about face. "What?"

"Half a bottle of scotch." I grinned at him. "It seems, from what I've managed to get out of her with her head down the toilet, that she and Tom . . ."

"Tom?" Geoff came over and sat beside me on the rug.

"Friend from school I assume." I flapped a hand at him. "Anyway, they decided that drinking a bottle of scotch at lunchtime would be a good idea and then not having the nerve to skip school after drinking it, they went back and attended all their lessons."

Geoff assimilated that information for a moment then said slowly, "Oh dear."

"Yup!" I clambered to my feet and went to sit on the sofa rubbing the one arm and leg that had reached an unreasonable temperature. "I wonder if anyone noticed."

Geoff shook his head. "Is she very unwell?"

"Yep."

"But she will be all right?"

"Yes, she brought most of it back up. I'll keep an eye on her and maybe give Helen a call later."

Geoff nodded. "Always good to have a paramedic to hand," he said, "but she feels terrible?"

"Yep."

"Throbbing head?"

"Yep."

"Rolling stomach?"

"Yep."

"Thinks she might die?"

"Yep."

Geoff gave me an evil grin. "Oh good!"

I laughed and gave him a little swat. "Well at least it might stop her trying to drink at the wedding next weekend." I shuddered and winced "That could have been far more embarrassing." I watched Geoff make another break for the kitchen and decided that now would be a great time to put my evil plan in action. "Listen, I've been having a think about next weekend."

Geoff stuck his head around the door and eyed me warily. "Oh yes?"

"Well seeing as how we're heading down south what about making a weekend of it, staying in one of those family rooms at a service station and on the Sunday we could go to Crick."

He looked at me, suddenly interested. "Is it the boat show that weekend?" Geoff gave me a big grin. "How do you think the kids will take the news? They seem to hate everything to do with boating at the moment . . ."

At that moment we were interrupted by the front door being flung open and Sam, accompanied by Mickey, flounced through the door.

"Oh hi," Mickey smiled and said, "here he is, all safe and sound."

I gave Sam a hug and said to Mickey, "Was he good?"

"Oh yes, yes no problem at all." She shrugged slightly. "Well, they didn't get on very well today, there was a lot of arguing about a game they were playing."

I looked at Sam, he was slumped on the sofa, arms crossed on his chest, the very picture of wounded innocence. "Sam?" He glared up at me, angry eyes half hidden behind his hair. "What happened?"

Sam jumped to his feet and I decided that it was probably going to be a very long and involved explanation which was going to end in "it wasn't my fault", so I waved him back down again. "Tell me later," I warned him, he flung himself back on the sofa with a heavy sigh.

"I'm sure it was just one of those things," Mickey said.

"Coffee?" I glanced at Sam who seemed to be holding his lips together by dint of sheer willpower.

"Oh no." Mickey turned towards the door. "Aaron's in the car, maybe next time, but thanks anyway." And with that she was gone, blown through the door and out toward her car by another gust of freezing wind.

Sam actually managed to wait until the door closed behind her before he launched into his explanation. As expected it was long, very detailed and completely Aaron's fault. When I said to him that it sounded like it was six of one and half a dozen of the other he almost exploded.

"It wasn't my fault," he stormed, "I hate it here, I want my boat back and I want a hamster!"

"What?" The last request didn't fit at all with the rest of the rant.

"Oh forget it." Sam jumped to his feet and stamped toward the stairs. "Charlie said that you'd say no, I don't know why I even bother asking." And with that baffling statement he stomped up the stairs. At the top he paused and screamed down at us. "I never get anything, ever!" Then there was the house-shaking crash as his bedroom door was slammed shut.

A drawn-out groan issued from the other bedroom as Charlie was startled half-awake by her brother's hysterics.

"Hamster?" Geoff appeared beside me holding two steaming mugs.

"I have absolutely no idea." I shook my head and cuddled my coffee. "No whisky in this?"

Geoff shook his head but wandered off toward the kitchen. "Sorry, I should have put some in." He grinned at me. "I don't think you really need it but you should drink it as soon as possible."

I frowned. "Why? It doesn't go off."

"Well if you don't drink it, your alcoholic daughter will, and if she doesn't, it sounds like Sam might need it," he laughed.

"Oh very funny, go away!" I laughed at him and threw one of Sam's gloves in his direction, which he ducked easily and took himself and my coffee off to the kitchen again in search of alcoholic support.

I stood staring up the stairs for a moment, one kid down in an alcoholic stupor, one so angry he's almost incomprehensible, looked like it was going to be a good weekend. Well, at least next weekend should be good, I had got over the first hurdle of getting Geoff to agree to my plan for the weekend. (I have to admit it was a very small hurdle, he was always up for wandering around boats in the sunshine), now all I had to hope for was some sunshine, some people we knew and a whole dollop of nostalgia and the kids would be begging to get back to our old life. I rubbed my hands together — I love it when a plan comes together.

Once Charlie had sobered up and Sam had calmed down, Geoff and I managed to get them together for a "chat" on Saturday morning. Charlie was still suffering a slight headache and nausea, this was probably due to the fifteen-minute, very informative, phone lecture that

Helen had given her on the dangers of alcohol on an immature liver. We questioned her about her motives and she just said that it had been a stupid idea and she wasn't going to do it again. So we banned her from a party that she was supposed to be attending in a couple of week's time and dropped the subject, we were all very relieved.

Sam however was still ranting, for twenty minutes he gave us an angry monologue as to why his life was almost unbearable, this ranged from hating school, to having a friend that couldn't share and didn't know how to play computer games properly and finally ended on his biggest whinge that Charlie had her rats and he wanted a pet and the pet he wanted was a hamster. He wanted a hamster and he wanted it NOW. As far as he could see, Charlie managed to get everything she wanted and he got nothing.

Of course his accusations were wildly exaggerated. However, it was actually so nice to see him enthusiastic about something other than a computer game that we gathered ourselves together to make the trip to the local pet shop.

When we arrived at "Pet World", Geoff and I wandered through the cacophony of birds, bunnies and dog lovers, heading in the wake of Chaos and Disorder as they cut a well-known path towards the rodent area.

"Look, Mum," Charlie shouted as we approached "They have black male rats." She paused and looked at Geoff's expression. "I've got my own money, couldn't I . . ."

"No!" Geoff and I spoke together, "Not today, this is Sam's day to get a pet."

Charlie sulked. "But he's only getting a stupid hamster, it's not very interesting is it." She gave us an innocent smile. "Anyway, I don't think they've got any, we can't find them."

I spotted Sam, with an ever-increasing look of consternation on his face, peering into each cage in turn, then grabbed the nearest assistant.

"Hi." I smiled encouragingly in a way that was supposed to say the answer to the next question I am about to ask you is "yes", please say "yes" or my life is about to become unbearable. "Do you have any hamsters?"

"Yes." The young lady looked up and down the rows. "We do have one," she paused and frowned, "but I'm really not sure it's a suitable pet."

At that point Sam found his hamster. "Mum, MUM! DAD! I've found them here they are, come here quick . . . Awww isn't he sweet!"

The young assistant gave a small shudder, and I gave her an enquiring look. "We only have the one left as I said." She began walking to the cages speaking over her shoulder, "This one is a girl," she searched for a word that would convey the personality of said rodent without sending us screaming out of the door, "She's a little feisty."

Charlie became immediately interested and sauntered over to the cage where she bent down and peered at the little animal hanging from the bars of the cage. Laughing, she poked her finger toward it then recoiled quickly as it threw itself toward her, screaming loudly, the little creature's long yellow teeth tearing rabidly at the bars.

"I didn't even realise hamsters could make a noise." I stared at the swearing animal. "Wow, she's vocal isn't she?"

Realising that there was now a group of humans staring at her, the enraged little powder-puff became even more agitated and, grabbing onto the bars of the cage again, stuck her nose through the bars and started another series of strange little noises which ranged from a muffled squeak to a sort of nasal honking. Every two or three noises she would stop and stare balefully at us to see if they had had the desired effect and we had all scarpered. When she saw that we were still there she would start again, opening her little pink mouth and issuing her series of screams and vitriol. I shook my head. I had never seen a white-knuckled hamster before.

The assistant shuddered. "How about a nice rabbit?"

"No!" Sam shouted and grabbed my hand. "She just doesn't like it here, and look she's got different-coloured eyes." He stared fondly down at the incensed little creature. "She's just perfect."

Charlie and I dared to step a little closer and sure enough when she stopped screaming she unscrunched her face to reveal one black eye and one bright red eye.

"Urgh!" Charlie winced. "Demon hamster. I don't think you want this one Sam."

"Yes I do," Sam stated categorically and stretched his hand out toward the cage. "I'm going to call her Lu."

Seeing the hand approach, "Lu" took to screaming louder and throwing herself at the bars of the cage, enraged beyond all sanity.

"Yeah," Charlie muttered, "its short for Lucifer."

Geoff nodded in agreement.

Sam smiled up at us as he quickly pulled his hand back to a safe distance. "That's the pet for me," he stated.

I thought the assistant was going to cry.

It took five minutes to get "Lu" into a carry case. The assistant, who was obviously very unhappy at putting her hand into the cage had finally poked her in with a pencil. Well actually, she had put the pencil into the cage and when the infuriated creature had attacked it she had manoeuvred her, teeth still embedded into wood, into the box and quickly shut the lid on both psychotic rodent and annihilated pencil with a relieved sigh.

We spent another fifteen minutes collecting all the accompanying gubbins that a hamster needs. As it was Sam's pet he was allowed to choose her cage, toys and food. While he was puzzling over this huge decision I held the box for him. I could feel the still furious little furball throwing herself at the side, her ear-piercing squeaks only slightly muffled by the box.

"When we get this thing home," I muttered out of the side of my mouth to Geoff, "I don't think it's ever coming out of its cage again. I think it might be rabid." I paused for a moment remembering my last encounter with an angry animal. "Or part sheep."

Geoff nodded. "Maybe we can donate it to Kevin for herding cows, his dog's getting a bit ancient."

I laughed as that mental image assailed me and had to stop and look innocent as Sam whipped round with a frown.

"Are you laughing at my hamster?" he accused.

"No, no," Geoff said and, quicker than me, grabbed a particularly badly designed dog toy off the shelf. It stood about twelve inches high and was a rubber cat in a black mask, thigh boots, suspenders and a whip. "We were laughing at this."

Charlie took it from him. "Oh my God," she said, laughing, "what type of weirdo gives their dog a dominatrix cat toy to play with?" She put it back on the shelf. We were safe. Sam, his hamster's integrity intact, turned back to his cages.

Fifteen minutes later, bored and tetchy, we were still there. A young man, a woman and their large, overweight Staffordshire bull terrier came and stood beside us.

"Ahah! There it is," he shouted and grabbed the cat we had just been laughing at.

I took a closer look, he had on a tracksuit and a cap, the woman with him had, as usual, summer clothes that were two sizes too small and created overhangs of flesh that were still slightly mottled from the biting wind outside. The dog was very overweight, and wore its studded breast band and collar with a slightly embarrassed look. It was also permanently passing wind, the smell was just unbelievable. Sam began to make loud retching noises until I poked him between the shoulder blades.

"What the hell is that?" The woman picked up the cat-shaped toy.

"It's for Tyson here." He took the toy from her and began to bash the dog over the head with it. "Come on, here look at this." The dog yawned and farted again.

"Why is it wearing a bikini, and why does it have a whip?" The woman frowned (good question, we'd all like to know that).

"Who cares?" The man physically opened the dog's mouth and put the doll inside. "But I think it looks like your mum."

They moved off down the aisle, both laughing, stopping occasionally to replace the doll in Tyson's mouth as the dog spat it out every ten steps or so.

We watched them go then Charlie shook her head. "Please tell me it was the dog that smelled and not him."

I shook my head. "Not a dog that I'd want, I have to admit. Staffies always seem to be attached to that sort of person and if they're as brain-dead as their owners . . ." I shook my head. "Anyway where were we? Sam have you chosen a cage yet?"

"Yes." He picked up a box of glow in the dark hamster spaceship, all tubes and wheels. "She'll love this."

Ho hum.

Lu took about three days to settle in and bit Sam on only one occasion. It seemed he was right about her, left in the quiet with good food and water she calmed down, and spent her time wandering about the living room, happily chasing after a trail of treats, sitting happily on the back of the sofa or wandering across our shoulders.

Charlie was horribly disappointed, I think she would have been happier with the Hamster from Hell, but as usual any animal that enters our family seems to take a shot of valium and become at one with the fairies.

CHAPTER
FOUR

It's a Woman's Prerogative to Change her Mind

The wedding went pretty much as expected, the church bit was long. The photographer was intense and horribly artistic, Charlie moaned about her shoes (we had poured her into a dress for the day, I can't express how irritated she was by the whole concept), and Sam took approximately five minutes to get filthy and was annoyed that he hadn't been able to bring Lu in his pocket.

There were people there we had never met, people that even Geoff hadn't seen for about thirty years, all in all it was very normal.

Sitting in the huge old house, at a table with Geoff's very distant relatives, we tried to explain how we'd been living for the last two years. The relatives decided that we were the poor cousins and either spoke to us slowly and loudly or ignored us completely. I gazed around at the huge amount of money that had been spent and smiled as I remembered our wedding.

As I was Geoff's second wife and he was my third husband, we had decided that the wedding was going to be as tiny and cheap as possible, preferring to spend the money on a deposit for a house.

So that fateful Wednesday, May 1st 1996, Helen, who was still masquerading, like the rest of us, as an IT professional, and Philip saw us arrive, resplendent in black leather on Geoff's old Moto Guzzi California at the registry office in Birmingham City centre. Helen had dressed for the occasion in jeans, boots and a woolly hat, which was perfectly acceptable. Philip had gone far beyond the call of duty and had a suit on. I had never seen him in anything other than paint-spattered "whites" or jeans and a jumper. I noticed that he had a T shirt with a rude slogan about beer and women beneath his suit jacket and his feet rested comfortably in paint spattered, steel toe-capped boots, strangely enough he still cut a dashing figure.

The registrar had looked a little nervous as we all piled in but she did mention at the end of the ceremony that we looked as happy as she had ever seen anyone, which was nice. Outside in the May sunshine, Helen took the photographs, and then we all piled over to McDonald's for a Macbreakfast of some kind. We toasted our happiness with pale tea and after that, we all went home. My mother had baked us a wedding cake but as she was seething that she hadn't been invited, had refused to ice it which was very sweet. I had tried to explain that none of the family had been invited; it had cut no ice at all.

Poor Lillian, Geoff's mother, didn't even know we were getting married and didn't find out for nearly a year, when she did, she took to her bed with a migraine. That was one Christmas day that we won't forget in a hurry.

While I was lost in reminiscence, the dancing had started and those that had been happily imbibing for the last three hours decided that it would be perfectly acceptable to get up and jump around a bit, this was our signal that we could leave.

We had decided to stay at one of the motorway inns and I was pleasantly surprised to note that the room was large and there was a huge bath. Leaving Geoff to sort out the kids, who still had no idea of our plans for the next day, I dumped the useless skirt and painful shoes and plunged myself into a lavish amount of pink bubbling water. By the time I emerged, waterlogged and wrinkled, Chaos and Disorder were both fast asleep. Geoff actually managed to open one eye and smile before he too joined them in the peaceful darkness.

Smiling to myself as I listened to the soft snores from Charlie, the muttering and yelping from Sam and Geoff's gentle breathing. I tried to read for a while but sleep soon overcame me as well, my last thoughts were of the show that I was hoping would change everybody's minds the next day.

Just for once, those in charge of the weather heard my pleas and the morning was beautiful. Bright spring sunshine made even the motorway service buildings glow with an inner spirituality. Sam and Charlie were now asking questions. What are we doing today? Why didn't we go home?

To distract them, we introduced Sam to another spiritual experience, the Premier Inn breakfast. Seeing all his favourite foods laid out in lurid colour on the menu before him he became almost speechless: sausages, bacon, eggs, fried bread, tomatoes and black pudding (not going to bother with that, thank you very much) beans, cereal, toast and jam.

With his knife and fork poised for action and occasionally sipping his apple juice, he waited in rapt anticipation for the food to arrive, oblivious to everything around him. Over his shoulder, in the next booth along, three women and a man sat down and began talking about boats, Charlie eyed them suspiciously. Ten minutes later another set of business bods sat down in the booth behind her and also began talking boats and engines, the suspicious look deepened.

"Geoff." She leaned back in her chair, the better to hear the conversation behind her. "Where exactly are we?"

Geoff shot a look over to me and grinned, the game was up. "Just outside of Crick."

Charlie frowned as she tried desperately to remember what went on at Crick, her expression becoming one of long suffering as she put two and two together and obviously came up with 7,865.

"The boat show!" she grumbled, rolling her eyes and pursing her lips together. "It's the stupid boat show isn't it?"

Geoff and I nodded.

"I don't want to live on a boat again." She slammed her glass down for emphasis. "I like my friends, I like my school, I like living in one place, I like having space and I like a computer that works." She turned to Sam. "You don't want to live on a boat again do you?"

Geoff and I held our breath. We had found that while Sam and Charlie, for the most part, will fight like cockerels, the rest of the time they feel the need to gang together, usually against us. We had found out to our cost that once they do this they seem to make one very stubborn person and it is almost impossible to get around them.

Sam stared at his sister, then round at the rest of us and swallowed nervously. He really hated to be the one that had the final say. I could feel my heart dropping, if Sam said he definitely didn't want to live on a boat again, that would be the end of it and I might as well dye myself orange, scrape my hair back, don a fake fur and some high heels and try to fit in with my neighbours for the next ten years. I honestly thought I was going to scream.

There was a loaded silence for about thirty seconds while Sam considered his answer. (Finally he put his knife and fork down and pushed his hair out of his eyes.) "Actually," he said, staring at Charlie and shaking his head. "I wouldn't mind living on a boat again."

Charlie whipped around and went to smack him around the back of the head, this usually had the desired effect of making him fall in with her wishes, luckily Geoff was quicker and caught her hand.

"Charlie," I snapped, "you asked him what he wanted and you can't get grumpy if his wishes don't match yours." I turned to Sam who was rubbing his head. Ducking to avoid her hand he had smacked his own

92

head on a beam behind him. "Go on Sam," I continued and gave him what I hoped was an encouraging smile, "what would you like to do?"

Sam gave Charlie another wary look, his eyes widening as he saw her draw her finger slowly across her throat and point at him menacingly, he gulped, then resolutely turned away from her. "I want to go home," he spoke slowly, "I'm always cold, I don't like my school, I miss the marina and little Charlie, I liked feeding the ducks and fishing, we could have another dog if we were on a boat. Dad's always playing on the computer so I don't get to go on it, he doesn't make things any more and I miss the ducks and the fish."

There was silence for a moment which was broken by the arrival of huge breakfasts. The silence continued as we all tucked in. I looked over at Charlie, expecting her to be pushing her food around her plate as she always did when things weren't going well but to my surprise she was eating her breakfast with a thoughtful look on her face. Geoff looked thoughtful as well, "Are you all right?" I asked.

"I didn't realise I spent so much time on the computer." He stabbed a blacked piece of blood pudding. "I'm sorry love, you should have said something."

I thought back to all the something's I'd said over the last five months, then decided that discretion was probably the better part of valour and nodded at him. "Maybe I should have said more."

"I think I'm just bored," he said, "I can't work on the house because it's not ours and there's really nothing to do."

"You still enjoy work don't you?" I asked.

He shrugged. "No, actually, the boss bought a run-down nightclub and all we do is work on that." He dipped his sausage into Sam's ketchup.

Twenty minutes later and the plates were clean. Charlie hadn't said anything throughout the entire meal, preferring to ignore her family and just occasionally kicking Sam under the table. As Geoff and I were finishing our tea and Sam was on his third piece of toast (I swear that kid actually does have hollow legs), she pulled herself upright and fixed me with a frown.

"If I was to agree to move back onto a boat," she paused for effect, "does this mean we could have a puppy?"

Geoff choked slightly into his tea.

I decided that I would give a vaguely affirmative answer. "Eventually, yes." I ignored Geoff's muffled snorts and coughs. "Maybe next year, in the spring."

"Could I choose what type of puppy?" Charlie sipped her orange juice and stared at me, unblinking over the top of the glass.

"Yes, but there would be restrictions." I ignored Sam's howl of protest. "It would have to be quite small, and friendly and preferably be able to hover so it didn't bring in any mud." I laughed.

Charlie wasn't amused. "So I could have a puppy for my fifteenth birthday?"

I paused to look at Geoff who was shaking his head slightly and looking rather panicked. I chose to ignore him. "Yes."

Charlie jumped to her feet and grabbed her coat. "Come on then," she said kicking Sam in the shins yet again, "let's go and look at boats."

Once again we spent a lovely day at Crick, we wandered around, in and out of the boats, admiring the layouts, the woodwork and intricate little hidden bits that all the new boats seemed to have. Geoff and I both noticed that there seemed to be more people this year but whether that was to do with the lovely day or more people were looking at becoming live-aboards was unclear. All the vendors were doing a brisk trade and once again we gathered a huge bag of paper advertisements regarding everything from snake drives to water purifiers; it was great fun.

My only irritation of the day was with British Waterways, we were discussing the mooring issues with the young man that was manning their stall and he very loftily told us that their mooring policy was as fair as it could be. "Just check the website," he advised us, "you can see that you can tender for any mooring and 'most' of them go for far less than the advertised price."

This is true, however "most" moorings are not residential and it appears that nearly every residential mooring goes for far, far more than the guide price. This seems unfair, as many people living on boats have a fairly restricted income. But worse than that, a common moan seems to be that those that need to stay in one place, people with children or with a job, have to commit to continuous cruising. The whole system seems designed to keep families off the waterways.

Maybe we're just too messy to be considered a tourist attraction. Let's face it, there's nothing pretty about a line full of kids' pants or a winter's worth of firewood and coal parked on top of a boat, flowers and painted pots look so much better, how dare we try to actually live on these things, it's so utterly selfish of us.

Apart from my frustrations with British Waterways, the day was a huge success and once again Charlie fell silent as we pulled away into the twilight and headed back north.

"Actually," she finally muttered into the sleepy silence of the car, "even without a puppy, I think I would like to move back on to a boat."

"Why's that?" Geoff asked carefully.

"I miss it." Charlie frowned. "I didn't think I would, but I do, and if we can get a puppy as well that would just be perfect." She snuggled down into her coat and yawned, pushing Sam's arm away as he had flopped down, starfish like, to get some sleep. "But could you hurry up and get a new one please, I'd like to be back at school for the new term." Having given us our orders she snuggled further down into the back seat and as silence fell, Geoff and I grinned at each other, surely at this time of year there would be lots of boats available.

There were literally hundreds of boats for sale, but, by now, with our finances literally pouring away (usually into the oil tank of the house, or into the local garage's coffers to keep our poor little Daewoo on the road — we had long since sold the Maverick) they were well over our budget.

96

By the next weekend I had found two possible live-aboards to look at. Keeping in mind that we still would like a potential sea going vessel, I chose an old Humber Keel (Geoff was very excited by this one) and just to keep in mind sense and finances, one possible narrow boat down near Nottingham. All of these vessels were in need of some major TLC so we resigned ourselves to another two years, or more, of camping and living in a building site, the prospect wasn't daunting in the slightest. I was so excited I could barely sleep.

We had arranged to see the narrow boat on the Saturday and the Humber Keel on the Sunday, I really couldn't decide which one I was more interested in.

This particular Saturday was beautiful, with warm winds and sunshine and we rather enjoyed walking down beside the canal in our seemingly endless search for a boat called Calendula. The kids rushed ahead, enjoying the sunshine and Geoff and I wandered hand in hand through the puddles and undergrowth that had leaked out on to some parts of the path.

"Sam, Sam." Charlie was on her hands and knees beside a broken part of the canal with her head close to the water. "Look at these."

"Oh God," Geoff and I groaned together, "what on earth has she found now?" Geoff winced. "Please don't let it be another pigeon," he muttered, raising his eyes to the heavens.

As we approached, the babble of Chaos and Disorder could be heard. "Wow, they're so tiny," and, "Ew, they're really cold and slimy." That was from Sam who was kneeling in the mud, also staring at whatever had Charlie's attention. He put something back on the ground and put his hands firmly in his pockets.

Geoff frowned at me and we hurried to see what they'd found. Frogs, teeny baby frogs. Obviously these had just gained their legs and had crawled out of a sheltered bit of the canal and were desperately trying to spread themselves over as large an area as possible.

"Here's some more." Sam pointed further down the path that Charlie had taken. "And there's loads over here." Charlie had her hands full of tiny dark green frogs, "Blimey there must be hundreds of them."

Hundreds was probably an exaggeration but there were certainly a lot, they crawled out from under every leaf, across the path and were rapidly burying themselves in the undergrowth on the far side of the path. Through the bushes I could see a pond in the field beyond and surmised that that was either where they were going to, or where they had come from. Either way, we picked our way carefully through the crawling, leaping amphibians and sauntered on down the path toward a likely-looking boat.

Calendula, from the outside, wasn't particularly poor looking but she was old, and I mean really old, I don't think I had ever seen that shape of hull before, it was like an iron brick. With slabs of iron riveted in a vague boat shape (actually she looked a lot like a curved loaf tin) she squatted in the water hippo-esque, large, round and slightly overweight, I noticed smoke coming out of the chimney and figured that, like their neighbours, the inhabitants must be also be amphibian if they needed the fire on in this weather.

However, apart from her slightly elderly appearance she was well painted and blacked with a cheerful striped tiller and pots of her namesake placed carefully on the roof amid the usual assortment of ladders, coal, wood and bicycles.

"She doesn't look too bad does she?" I turned to Geoff with a hopeful smile then turned around as the screaming started behind me. "Charlie don't you dare threaten to put frogs down your brother's back."

Charlie opened the clenched fist she had been threatening Sam with, "I haven't really got a frog in it." She gave me a wounded look. "I wouldn't do that and it'd be cruel."

Sam sighed with relief. "Thanks, Charlie." He gave her a sunny smile.

"I meant it would be cruel to the frogs, Sam." Charlie gave him a sneer. "If I thought for one minute that it wouldn't bother the frogs I'd put a hundred down your back."

Sam looked hurt. Geoff and I went back to looking at the boat. "She really is sitting low in the water, isn't she?" Geoff stared at just the tip of the rudder that could be seen above the waterline. "She must be incredibly heavy with that hull. And I bet she handles like a pregnant elephant, no quick turns with this one."

I shrugged and gestured toward the boat. "Well, we're here now, shall we?" He nodded vaguely, still obviously lost in thought about the hull. As we walked toward the boat Charlie and Sam joined us, pointing out various features and generally making enthusiastic noises.

Geoff knocked on the back doors and we waited . . . and waited . . . and waited. Realising we would only have a finite amount of time before the kids became bored and looked for something "interesting" to do, I wandered down the length and tapped gently on a window. There was immediate movement inside. The shadowy figure pointed toward the bow and we all moved expectantly down the tow path.

"Hello." A tousled head appeared at a door. "Marie and Geoff?" We nodded. "Hi, I'm Dave, come on in." He looked at the kids for a moment and bit his lip, then said cheerily, "These with you or have you picked them up on route?"

I laughed. "No, they're with us, but they're mostly boat-trained."

He gave a slightly strained laugh and opened the door wider. A puff of smoke leaked out and wafted toward us before dissipating on the wind.

"Oooh." Sam sniffed and leapt toward the boat. "Incense, I love incense."

Geoff and I looked at each other, then at Dave who was sporting a rictus grin. It smelt, sort of, like incense and I can see why Sam had assumed that is what it was, but anybody burning that stuff was liable to get themselves a caution and a turn over from the drugs squad.

We smiled at Dave, I now noticed that classic airy look and the slightly soppy grin, we weren't going to get much sense out of him that was for sure.

"Just help yourself and look around." Dave waved vaguely down the boat as we stepped into the small greasy galley. Actually it was more a collection of elderly mismatched cupboards than a galley per se. "If you want me I'll just be down the other end." He puttered slowly off, carefully carving a meandering path down the boat, his long skinny legs moving in strange stilted steps. He obviously had to think about each step very carefully.

It was hard to see amid the thick, scented, smoke and I covered my mouth and nose with my scarf. Charlie stepped in through the door and nodded sagely. "Hot box," she commented.

Geoff whipped around. "That's not a term you should even know, let alone use it in context," he snapped at her.

I was confused. "Hot box?" I coughed. "What's a hot box?" Charlie grinned and grabbing Sam rushed off down the boat to explore.

"Never mind, I'll explain later." Geoff started looking around. "Let's get out of here as quickly as possible."

I listened to the giggling from Chaos and Disorder and nodded.

Ten minutes later and the giggling had grown to riotous proportions. After Sam had spent three minutes trying to explain to me why a particular stain on the side of the boat looked like a robot, I decided enough was enough and threw them out of the boat.

I had to tell them twice, they both looked at me with big owl eyes and fairly floaty smiles. In the end I took them out on the bank and parked them on the grass, among the frogs, in the hope that neither of them would try to walk on water then went back to chivvy Geoff along.

He was working through his checklist.

Engine — check, Electrics — check. Possibilities for change — check.

I noticed, as I wandered back through the kitchen, that there were no taps at the sink and no cooker, this was a little strange but some people could do without them. A little confused, I wandered out to the bow and checked the usual place for a gas locker. No Gas locker, well that could be sorted out.

I checked that Sam and Charlie were still sitting on the side of the path and made another attempt to find Geoff.

I carefully checked each door as I went down the boat and by the time I got to where Geoff and Dave were chatting, I knew what was bothering me.

"Hi!" I quipped cheerily, "how's it going?"

Geoff waved at me vaguely, the miasmic atmosphere must have been getting to him as well. "I'm just reading through the last survey."

I nodded. "And how is she?"

He shrugged and stared at me owlishly. Oh for goodness sake, I pulled my scarf closer around my mouth and nose not caring if I offended Dave. "Erm, does it say anything about the gas?"

Dave cut in. "There's no gas."

I nodded, well, that was fairly normal, there were quite a few boats around these days without gas. "What about the water system?"

Dave shook his head sadly. "There's no water."

Geoff lifted his head and frowned as he tried to bully his suddenly elusive thoughts into a semblance of order.

I nodded again. "No water tank?"

"No."

"No plumbing."

"No." Dave gave me a radiant smile. "As someone famous once said, I never drink water, fish do naughty things in it." He slumped back into the rickety, rumpled sofa and picked at the frayed ends of the psychedelic throw that was making a very poor attempt to hide the holes. He laughed quietly at his own wit.

I wasn't about to be thrown off the subject. "So, where's the toilet or bathroom, I can't seem to find it."

"Kids gone outside?" Dave sat up and frowned at me.

"Yes," I said warily, hoping he wasn't going to give me a demonstration of how he went to the loo.

"Oh good." He reached into an overfilled ashtray and extracted what looked like an oversized and slightly bumpy roll-up which he stuck between his lips and set fire to with a battered petrol lighter. "This stuff's not good for them." He nodded solicitously and crossing his eyes took a huge breath in. The burning end of the roll-up brightened and crackled, he held the aromatic smoke in his lungs, eyes watering, his lips pressed together so hard all I could see was unbroken straggly beard. Blowing out the smoke with a smile he offered the slightly soggy and limp item to me. I grinned and shook my head. "Thanks, but I need to keep an eye on the kids." He nodded sagely and offered it to Geoff who looked at it with his lip caught between his teeth, obviously happy memories from university were overpowering his common sense. I intervened. "Geoff, you're driving." He nodded sadly.

The notorious smell in the room deepened, along with the haze and trying to breathe shallowly I pulled my scarf tighter around my nose. Geoff sighed and squinted, trying to make sense of the spidery writing that covered the survey paperwork. I noticed that he had almost given up and was spending more time staring at a badly painted, fake stained-glass, fish on the window than he was on the facts and figures before him.

"The toilet," I enunciated slowly and clearly in the hope that the question would penetrate the bemusement of the man in front of me. "Where is it, do you have one?"

Straightening up, he stared at me. He was obviously finding it hard to focus, at least with more than one eye at a time. "There isn't one." He smiled and sank back taking another huge drag of the roll-up. "What you have to understand," he paused and nodded to himself, "is that, a life like this, we should get rid of all the trappings of modern living." He nodded again. Obviously this was going to be a deep and meaningful soliloquy on the meaning of alternative living. "You don't need all this rubbish like water and toilets, they're just things." He leant forward and stared at me. "They can put chemicals in the water that keep us tranquil." He took another huge drag on his roll-up and stabbed a finger down onto the table with a thud. "Well, I don't want to be 'tranquil.'"

Watching his eyes swing sideways, a pair of mistimed and bloodshot blue pendulums, I have no idea how I kept a straight face; if he had been any more "tranquil" he'd have been comatose.

Having imparted this incredibly important message, he rubbed a grubby hand down his dirty jeans. Fumbling around in his pockets he brought out a piece of red glass which he handed to me before taking another huge suck on the sad-looking roll of burning paper and dried plant life that he still had stuck in his beard. He nodded toward the glass. "Look through that." He giggled and sucked again on the now defunct, stained roll of cardboard that was all that was left of his joint. "You'll see that everything is fine, everything that they want you to see, anyway." He smiled at me, one eye wandered inward to stare at his nose then gently tracked sideways to stare vaguely out of the window, the other stared indistinctly into mine.

Just to thank him for his thoughts, I looked at him through the glass for a moment and nodding, placed it carefully on the crate he was using for a table. "Well, thanks for your time." I gently kicked Geoff in the shin. My befuddled husband swivelled his rapidly reddening eyes and stared at me owlishly. "We have another boat to see, but we'll be in touch and let you know."

Geoff, using the back of the battered sofa for support climbed slowly to his feet, smiling beatifically as he managed this extraordinary feat of dexterity. He waved vaguely to Dave then, turning unsteadily, he began to

105

make his way back down the boat toward the doors, feeling his way through the fog of happy smoke.

Once out on the front deck I pulled my scarf down with a gasp and took several huge gulps of fresh, cleansing, air. Even protected as I was, I felt fuzzy and slightly nauseous. I turned to speak to Geoff, then gave up.

I laughed as I watched him try to climb down from the front of the boat back on to the tow path, his legs, like Dave's eyes, seemed to be working independently. "Come on, let's go and find the kids." I walked back to where I'd left them.

Were they where I had ordered them to stay? No, of course they flaming well weren't. The tow path was deserted in each direction and for a moment I felt the panic begin to rise. Pushing the heart-pounding feelings back down, I took stock. If I was a slightly stoned pre-teen in charge of a slightly stoned nine-year-old boy where would I be?

Linking my arm with Geoff's to hurry him along, I pulled him down the path to where we had seen the frogs. I stood and listened. Sure enough Sam's familiar, high-pitched and strident voice emanated from behind a hedge. I breathed a sigh of relief and stood for a moment waiting for my pounding heart to subside to a normal rhythm.

Searching the undergrowth at the side of the canal I found their access hole and, leaving Geoff to stare, mesmerised, at the glistening ripples on the surface of the canal, went in search of the kids.

To this day I really don't know whether it was the second-hand smoke or just that our kids were likely to do odd things, but I will always smile at the memory of Sam lying on the grass next to a small pond, covered in a carpet of tiny green frogs. He was giggling almost uncontrollably which was annoying his sister who was trying to fill in the gaps. Sam's shaking was making it difficult for the placid little amphibians to stay on. There really are some days when I could kick myself for never carrying a camera.

"Hey guys," I called as I approached the laughing pair.

On hearing us approach, Sam tried to sit up, but his concern for the frogs kept him prone on the ground. Charlie, completely unencumbered jumped up immediately. She still looked slightly wide-eyed but obviously her sense of vague disorientation had been replaced by her normal need to gently harass her brother.

"Mum!" She stepped carefully over Sam's friends that were crawling happily around the two. "Where have you been?" She looked down at Sam then deliberately walked away from him. "I'm starving, really, really hungry, is it lunchtime yet?" Sam stayed where he was but nodded carefully and enunciated without opening his mouth. "And me."

I laughed, great, two kids with the munchies and not a cafe or shop in sight, this was going to be a fun walk back. "Yeah, come on, let's go and find an early lunch." I watched as she picked her way through the seething mass of small hoppers, waiting for her to register her brother's howls of protest at being left covered in frogs. I waited until she had reached me then physically turned her round and sent her on her way with a small push back toward the pond. "Go and dig out your brother please."

Charlie pouted, then grinned as she listened to Sam's ever-rising hysteria. "Oh I think we can just leave him there." She held up a hand as Sam howled again and went to get up. "No, Sam, don't move, you'll hurt the frogs."

Sam stiffened and held himself very still, his whole body rictus with indecision.

"Don't be foul," I said and gave her another gentle shove, "no brother, no burgers."

Charlie huffed but in a couple of minutes both children were picking their way back toward me and the frogs were left hopping about completely unconcerned by their strange morning. Well we'd all had one of those.

The kids shot ahead of me through the gap in the hedge toward Geoff who was now lying on his back in the warm grass staring up at the clouds, he sat up slowly and grinned indistinctly as we all pushed past him. Checking, I noted that his eyes were almost back to normal. "Food?" I enquired.

"Oh yes." He jumped to his feet (he only wobbled slightly) and set off down the path after the chattering kids.

As we came to the end of the path I put on a turn of speed and caught up with Chaos and Disorder. "If," I stated as I came alongside them, "when I search both of you in about two minutes, I find even one baby frog, it will be limp cheese sandwiches and water from a local garage and not rubbishy fast food." I paused to let

Geoff catch up and smiled as they stared expression-lessly at me. "Are we clear?"

I turned and walked on with Geoff and pretended that I hadn't even noticed the hurried turning out of pockets and the kerfuffle at the waterside as the kids did a very bad job of surreptitiously putting their "pets" back onto the ground.

Geoff looked at me with a grin. "You're not nice, you know." He gave me a hug. "But I love you."

Luckily just over the road from where we had parked the car was the ubiquitous set of "golden arches" and within ten minutes there was nothing but silence in which the only break was the munching and slurping of one husband and two children trying to sort out a drug-related hunger. (I'm such a proud mother.) I finally managed to get Geoff to focus. It wasn't that difficult actually, he had spent most of his university years in the same state, so the fairly vast amount of second-hand smoke he had imbibed on the boat was rapidly wearing off.

"So what did you think?" I amused myself by making horrible noises with my chocolate milkshake, allowing him to ponder for a moment.

He pursed his lips, then a look of embarrassment stole across his face and he reached into one of the many pockets on his jacket. "Whoops," he said pulling out the boat survey, "I don't think I was supposed to take this."

"Gak!" I coughed, "You stole his survey?"

"No, NO!" he hesitated. "Well . . . yes, technically, but I don't think I meant to actually steal it, I just put it in my pocket." He reached over and pulled the straw out of my mouth, obviously irritated by the noises I was still making. "Let's face it, Mr Disorientated isn't going to notice it's missing, I'll run it back to him in a couple of minutes and apologise profusely."

After wiping the spots of milkshake off my face that had been flicked from the straw, I leant over and tried to take the survey from him, but he was obviously fully restored to quick and decisive movement and whipped it out of my reach.

Replacing the straw with a humph, I concentrated on sucking quietly while he perused the document. I really don't know what they put in those milkshakes but by the time you've actually managed to get a mouthful, you have had to suck so hard your cheeks hurt.

Impatience finally won out. "Does it say anything about no gas, no water, no toilet?" I paused to suck hard again.

Geoff nodded. "But more to the point, this survey is over ten years old and it only had three millimetres of hull then." He shook his head. "If we buy this, not only are we going to have to put all the living services on, but we're going to have to have her re-bottomed." He sighed and pushed the papers toward me. "Really it's just a thin steel shell, most of which is going to have to be either replaced or re-plated." He sat back in his chair and took a sip of the greyish tea in front of him. "I wouldn't give him half of what he's asking for it."

"Well, is it a difficult job to get a boat re-bottomed?" I asked.

"Hmm, there are two ways of doing it." Geoff slipped into lecture voice. "You can either get the bottom re-plated or you can just over-plate."

I raised an eyebrow at him.

"Well, with re-plating they remove the entire bottom plate and put a new one on and with over-plating they just weld a new bottom over the old one."

"Sounds difficult," I said.

"Not really, obviously it has to be done by a company that knows what it's doing but there are enough of those around. It's just time-consuming and fairly expensive."

"Not something we want to do, I suppose," I said.

"Not if we have time constraints, no." Geoff stared at the survey. "And we can't really put it off if the steel was already this thin ten years ago, God only knows what thickness it is now. Run her aground once and if it's thin enough we could find ourselves with a hole or a tear."

I shuddered and took another long suck of milkshake as I watched Sam blithely take a frog out of his bag and place it carefully on the table in front of him.

Charlie groaned and put her head on the table. "Oh Sam," she moaned.

I got up from the table and wandered over to the counter. "Excuse me do you have a small plastic tub I could borrow?"

The young man behind the counter eyed me in confusion for a moment then nodded and passed me a white tub.

"Thank you." I wandered back and placed it on the table. "Come on, turn out your pockets and put all four-legged friends in the tub please." I gave them both the "I'm losing patience" look. Charlie and Sam looked at each other, sighed and began to turn out pockets, bags and of all things, coat hoods.

Sitting in the car and waiting for Geoff to return from his delivery of paperwork and seven small frogs back to their natural environment, I asked the kids what they had thought of the boat in the brief time they had been aboard. There was a brief pause in the argument over whose fault it was that I had found out about the frogs for just long enough for Sam to say one word "smelly" then they went back to hitting each other.

Leaving them to it, I climbed out of the car and sat on the bonnet staring out over the canal. This raised some serious questions: had we got such a good price for *Happy Go Lucky* because the prices had gone up? If that was the case, was Geoff wrong? Was that the going price for a useless lump of half-sunk steel? I sighed as I contemplated our delicate bank balance, we were in serious trouble.

We were due to see the Humber Keel the next day. Geoff was quite excited about this, I had looked into the history of the Keel and had found that the original ships came in a variety of sizes, usually between fifty-seven and sixty-eight feet long. Their sturdily built hulls had a blunt bow and a flat bottom which could navigate easily in the shallow waters that connected the inland waterways to the Humber.

112

It seemed a fairly daft design to me, great square sails had towered above these ships which, in even a moderate wind, looked as though they would have tipped over if it hadn't been for the huge Leeboards that sat like fish wings either side of the hull.

By the twentieth century the hulls had changed from oak to steel and most of the old ships were powered by steam or diesel engines. A lot of these engines were installed with the help of conversion grants at the end of the Second World War. By 1949 all but one of the original sailing keels had disappeared, the only one left has been preserved by the Humber Keel and Sloop Preservation Society who also have a Humber Sloop.

Personally I think the keel looks a little odd with sails, like an up-scaled child's toy, a brick of a ship with a big square hanky tied to the front. But they have a bulky beauty all their own, Geoff loves them and I suppose I can see why. Like Geoff, the Humber Keel has a definite air of solid practicality about it.

Built in the 1940s, this particular keel was bigger than the originals at seventy-four foot long and eighteen foot wide. She was a bit of a beast and sounded the perfect vessel to convert to an excellent houseboat. There were, however, certain drawbacks. She wouldn't be able to get through any locks and quite frankly finding a river mooring for her down south was going to be a complete nightmare but Geoff loved the idea of owning a piece of floating history.

The advert sounded promising but I had a sinking sense of déjà vu. We had looked at a barge before buying *Happy Go Lucky* and to say the viewing had been a disappointing disaster was the understatement of the year. Listing, full of water, the woodwork cobbled together by a man with a chainsaw and St Vitus' Dance and sunk up to her gunnels in mud she certainly hadn't lived up to her sales blurb.

I wasn't really holding out much hope for this viewing either. The advert showed that the Keel had no roof and someone had perched what looked very much like a Portakabin on top. Presumably to have somewhere dry and warm to live while the rest of the boat was being converted and restored, a great idea for maybe one or two of you, but for a family of four? No way. I love my children but the idea of living in a 10 x 10 space with them for at least two years just made me shudder, especially as Charlie was getting to that age where it was imperative for her to have doors to slam, no doors, then all that hormonal frustration was going to have to be taken out somewhere else: probably on me.

Personally, I was just looking forward to visiting her mooring town of Beverly. This medieval market town sounded lovely, extolled by one of the Yorkshire tourist websites as being, "perhaps one of the most beautiful towns in Britain". There was a large Saturday market (shame we were going on a Sunday) excellent architecture, great shopping and the obvious draw for tourists, the beautiful gothic Minster.

However, it wasn't really the Minster that I wanted to visit but St Mary's church which has a carving of the "jolly rabbit" inside, this is said to be the inspiration for Lewis Carroll's White Rabbit in *Alice in Wonderland*. I also wanted to take a look at the west front which is rumoured to have possibly been the influence for the Chapel of King's College, Cambridge, which was built much later.

Once again we stayed at a motorway inn which pleased Sam no end. It wasn't until the next day that we found out he had merely been looking forward to another cooked breakfast and was almost suicidal when he found out that their restaurant was closed for refurbishment and we had to go to a Little Chef. He grouched all the way through breakfast. Charlie, miserable because my snoring had kept her awake all night was snappy and short-tempered, especially with her brother who was currently pushing his breakfast around his plate with a sneer and rating each bite out of ten.

The weather wasn't helping matters. Unlike the previous day, Sunday was almost twilight in its gloom and the deep grey clouds became almost purple as we headed north-east toward almost certain nautical disappointment.

As we reached the outskirts of Beverly, the heavy grey clouds could obviously hold their contents no longer and proceeded to produce a rainstorm the like of which I had only ever seen on holidays in America. With lights on and windscreen wipers at full speed, we picked our way through tiny streets, almost invisible behind the veil of heavy rain that continued to pour from the black sky. Charlie and Sam became even more morose.

Finally, after what seemed like hours of backtracking, we found ourselves in the out of the way car park of an unnamed transport company. Geoff stopped the car and scratched his head. Peering out into the deluge, he shook his head and tapped the Sat Nav. "Well, it says that we're here."

We all peered into the running water. True, the car park did run alongside the river and we could just make out the rain-washed ghosts of various boats and barges. The visibility was down to about five foot.

A tapping on the window made us jump. Geoff, heedless of Sam's screams, rolled down the window, allowing the wind to inundate the back seat with water. He stuck his head out and shouted to a shadowy figure, that sported an interesting collection of waterproof clothing, "Hi, are you Matt?"

The figure nodded and spoke. I couldn't hear a single word as the howling wind whipped his words away. Geoff nodded and taking a moment to roll the window back up, he manfully climbed out of the car and pausing only long enough to drag his hood over his head, set off into the cloudburst.

The kids and I sat in the car and looked at each other.

"I'm not going." Charlie crossed her arms and glowered at me.

"Nor me." Sam copied his sister's posture.

I sighed. "Well I need to go, because, if I don't, I won't have the right to moan if Geoff buys the boat and I don't like it." I watched the kids glance at each other. "And I won't have the right to even have an opinion

116

about what gets done to it." I opened the door and pulled my coat around me, grimacing as an icy cold, wet wind cut through me to the bone.

Charlie and Sam, obviously also unwilling to have their opinion ignored, clambered out of the car and huddled up behind me. Sam stuck himself under my coat and holding me around the waist we paraded across the car park looking like a pantomime horse wearing a sou'wester. Charlie rolled her eyes and squeaked as the rain soaked her hair within seconds then started running down her neck.

Following in what we hoped were Geoff's footsteps, we clambered down the rickety steps that led from the car park to the Keel and, lifting the edge of the huge tarpaulin that was acting as a roof, I ushered the kids inside. Wow, it was huge. The space in which we found ourselves contained a generator, scaffolding poles, wood, power tools and there was still double the space that we had enjoyed on our narrow boat.

Charlie voiced my thoughts. "This is huge." She stared around at the space. "We could have everything in here, kitchen, dining room, lounge, bedrooms." She tailed off as she imagined it all finished and beautiful.

Sam rushed off towards his father's voice. "Dad, it's great, it's really big, can we buy it?"

I grimaced, this would be a complete rebuild, we might be able to cope under canvas for the summer but the steel to roof this and erect a proper wheelhouse would cost thousands. Following the kids through a door I found myself in another space of almost the same dimensions. This area had already been separated

117

into four sections, which obviously were going to be bedrooms and a bathroom.

"I want this one." Sam sprang out at me from a small enclosed space, laughing when he realised that he had made me jump. "Look it's nearly the same size as my bedroom in Durham." He rushed back in and closed the door.

"Mum, MUM! Look at this." Charlie's voice echoed strangely ahead of me. I pulled aside a curtain and found her in a steel-enclosed space right at the very front. "This could be our grot cupboard."

Smiling and nodding, I backed away toward the main compartment where Geoff and Matt were discussing engines. I should have left the kids in the car, I was just going to have to disappoint them. There was no way we could afford to renovate this no matter how beautiful she could be, we just didn't have the time or the money. I wandered over to Geoff. Damn it all, I should have stayed in the car, I didn't want to have to disappoint me either.

Geoff and Matt were engrossed in a large hole at the back of the boat, I joined them. The cavity was empty except for the large prop shaft. Attached to nothing at either end and half submerged in a murky concoction of oil, mud and river water, it exuded a rather self conscious air, as if, by being caught without its connections to propeller and engine, it was somehow in a state of déshabille, I nudged Geoff.

"Where's the prop?" I asked.

Geoff laughed and turned to me. "Probably at the bottom of the river," he said, grinning. "Matt here

118

thinks it may have fallen off when his granddad was taking the engine out."

I smiled but, quite honestly failed to see the humour, any prop big enough to attach to that shaft was going to be difficult to fish out. I tried again. "Where's the engine now?"

Geoff half turned toward me, distracted by the huge generator he was studying. "Hmm?" He focused on me eventually. "Oh, it's in the shed." He gave me a huge grin. "There's two dead ones we can choose from or we can probably cobble them together and make one decent one."

I gave him a tolerant smile. "Right."

An hour later we were back in the car, lost in our own thoughts. I didn't really feel like visiting the town any more. Unlike the other barge, this one was a possibility, this one had "*potential*" but only if we had the money.

The trip back to County Durham was peaceful but slightly sad. Geoff and I could both see what we could do to a boat like that, but as we were unwilling to discuss the finances we day-dreamed and plotted. Charlie caught up with the sleep she had lost the night before and Sam killed all the robots that paraded about the screen of his DS.

By the time we reached Harrogate I had given up with the scheming and plotting and the horrible reality had set in. I looked over at my silent husband. "Is there any way at all we could buy that?" I looked at him, hoping he knew about a secret cache of money that I had failed to notice.

Dragged unwillingly back to reality, Geoff clenched his jaw slightly, a sure sign that he didn't want to voice his thoughts. "We could afford to buy it, but that's about it." He started tapping vague quotes off by banging each finger on to the steering wheel.

"Ten grand's worth of steel work at least, engine fix and position, wheelhouse to set up, prop to fix." He paused. "And that's just the stuff that I can't do, that's the stuff we have to pay someone else for." Shrugging slightly he continued, "Then we have to do up the inside, there's no electrics, it all has to be insulated, walls, plumbing, floors, ceilings." He shook his head. "The list just goes on and on, it's really better not to think about it."

I shuffled down into my coat and grouched at him, "A simple 'no' would have done."

Leaning toward me slightly he gave me a sad smile, then gave my knee a squeeze. "Sorry love."

My mood matched the clouds, sullen and grey, darkening with every mile up the Al.

Back at the house and with the kids sound asleep in their beds, Geoff and I stared at the computer screen as it rolled gently and accusingly through our horrible spending for the last couple of months. When the screen finally reached the total, there was a definite collective feeling of doom and despondency. What on earth where we going to buy for that?

"This isn't good." Geoff, once more, employed his awesome ability to understate any calamity that faced us. "We could just about buy some piece of junk, and that would be small, narrow boat junk. But we couldn't

120

live in it and we wouldn't be able to afford to do anything to it." He turned with a pained look. "I'm really sorry, love, but I just don't think we can do it, maybe after the kids have left home and we can buy something smaller."

I couldn't answer him, I couldn't physically speak. I didn't want to be stuck here, I didn't want to wait another ten years. I took a breath in, desperately attempting to keep the sudden flood of nausea at bay, feeling my lip begin to quiver, I swallowed, trying to move the huge lump that was inexplicably stuck in my throat.

Geoff looked distressed and reached a hand out to give me a hug but I avoided him, backing away and shaking my head, blinking furiously to keep the tears at bay.

"I'm sorry." Geoff grabbed my arm and pulled me into a huge hug.

"It's not your fault." I blinked rapidly. "Really, it's not your fault. We just got so close, even the kids had changed their minds. You wanted another boat, I wanted another boat and now we're going to have to tell them that we've changed again." I took a deep shuddering breath. "Sam is going to be so upset."

"I know." Geoff looked almost as upset as I was. "The figures are just too horrible, I can't see a way round it."

"I'm going to have a bath." I managed to get the words out on the little breath I had left then fled to the sanctity and oblivion of warm water and a large whisky. Let's face it, if the bath became deeper and slightly salty due to a prolonged bout of crying, it would all get lost in the cheery bubbles and no one would ever have to know.

"Marie . . ." Geoff's voice followed me as I pounded up the stairs, I blew him a watery kiss and tried to smile, there was nothing he could say to make me feel better, nothing at all.

CHAPTER
FIVE

When the Going Gets Tough, the Tough Go Begging

Three days later and life wasn't really improving, Charlie had tried to cheer me up, telling me that maybe if I got a job and stopped moping about, I'd soon learn to love the place. She, very quickly, learned that there is an art to a good pep talk and she really ought to stay out of my way until she learned it.

Wednesday morning, found me standing on the river bridge in the centre of Durham. Staring out over the wide shallow river. I watched the large group of cormorants that fished from the weir. I was also enjoying a truly appalling bagpipe player who was unsuccessfully busking behind me, matching my mood note for shaky, out of tune, note. It was the musical equivalent of poking a sore tooth with your tongue.

The River Wear is only suitable for boating from Sunderland to Chester le Street — about ten and a half miles in all, so the river was empty apart from the cackling cormorants and one lone fisherman standing in the shallows. I smiled, maybe it was a good job that it was impossible to run a boat this far, the river was said to be cursed.

A particularly discordant set of notes from the busker behind me brought me back to the present with a wince and, casting a last longing glance at the sun-speckled water, I decided that maybe a coffee would do me good and anyway if I stayed here any longer I was going to need paracetamol.

I wandered back over the bridge toward the town enjoying the sunshine, maybe it wasn't so bad here, maybe I just needed to get my mind right. At that moment my phone rang and after struggling to get the wretched thing out of a tight jeans pocket (I was definitely eating my misery away, I was sure they hadn't been that tight a week ago), I managed to get to it before it went to answer phone and Amelia's voice sang out from the speaker as soon as I took the call.

"Where the hell are you?" she squawked in my ear. "I've been all over this benighted little town and I can't find you anywhere, mind you," she didn't stop for breath. "I can't find a Starbucks, only a Costa, so no wonder I can't find you."

It took a moment for all this information to sink in. "Are you in Durham, Mills?"

"Well, yes of course I am," her voice rose to match the still faintly braying bagpipes behind me. "Did you think I'd be looking for you in bloody Reading?"

I beat my brain into some semblance of order. "What are you doing here?"

"Oh nice." she huffed down the phone. "Charlie called me." She paused for a moment. "Look, meet me in Costa." There was another pause. "I think I can find it again."

124

Twenty minutes later I was suffering from severe role reversal. It transpired that Charlie, worried about my sanity and finding that my usual confidante, Helen, was away on holiday, had colluded with Geoff and called Amelia in to give me a good talking to. I personally think I would have preferred Helen, she beats me up with loaded silences and pointed looks, after fifteen years I can deal with those.

Amelia works in a different way. Like a rubber-band-powered engine, she goes at top speed, taking no breaths, her voice gets higher and higher and more and more strident, until you can't actually hear what she's saying any more but there are dogs rolling around in pain and you're in danger of being brained by the rain of bats falling around you.

"Is this it then?" she demanded as soon as we each had a drink in front of us. "Just going to give up and wallow around in self-pity for the next ten years?" She went to take a sip of her drink then, thinking of her next sentence, put it back down onto the wooden table with a thud. "You're being totally pathetic and really beginning to irritate everybody, this isn't like you, you don't give up and you've always told me I'm not allowed to give up."

I tried desperately to tune her out, and stared around at the cafe, I hadn't been into this one before, and it was quite nice, with big leather squishy sofas (all occupied by middle-aged women, staring over at us. Unfortunately, Amelia's voice can carry quite a way, especially when she's trying to be quiet), and huge

125

contemporary prints smothering the walls, it was a classic English version of an Italian coffee shop.

Amelia's voice hit the particular pitch that managed to break into my reverie about the dark, polished wooden tables. I switched my attention to the ceiling, strange how something can still be nicotine-stained even all this time after the cigarette ban.

"Mother!" she shrieked. "You're behaving like a teenager, stop ignoring me and tell me exactly what you're going to do." That was the note, about top C, I decided that I had better join in this conversation before she started breaking glasses and I had something else to pay for. I held up a placatory hand and watched as she shut her mouth with a snap.

"Hello, Amelia, nice to see you, how are you, did you have a pleasant drive up?" I gave her a big grin, and laughed when she took an obviously difficult controlling breath and with quick decisive movements smoothed the travel crinkles from her checked shirt. I liked that shirt, it definitely gave out sort of hoe-down tones, but I always felt it clashed in style with the lip piercing and the long red and black hair. I felt the thump as she uncrossed her legs in frustration then re-crossed them, the huge New Rock boots with their buckles and chains jangled as they hit the floor.

She took another deep breath. "Sorry, I was worried about you."

"Hmm." It was quite warm in here and knowing that this was a conversation that could take a while I shrugged out of my coat, then sat forward, rolling up the sleeves on my jumper, I rested my forearms on the table.

"Look." I took a sip of coffee, "Let me wallow, I'll get over this eventually and go and find something else to do." I traced sun patterns in the ring of coffee I had made on the table. "There's nothing I can do, I can't make money appear from nowhere."

"You could get a loan," she said and ferreted around in the inside pocket of her leather jacket. "Look I got you all these leaflets." She placed a pile of slightly dog-eared and brightly coloured slips onto the table.

Picking them all up I glanced through them then smiled at her. "I do appreciate it love, honestly I do, and I've considered this option." I leant back and sighed. "There isn't any way we could get a loan for living expenses and doing some knackered piece of junk up. There isn't a bank in the world that would take on that sort of flimsy nonsense." I stacked the leaflets into a neat pile and put them back on the table. "Honestly, I have thought of every stupid money-making idea I could, I even thought about *betting* what little money we have left, but even *my* sanity isn't that far gone."

Amelia grinned at me. "I bet there's one bank you haven't thought of, it's the one I try and use all the time."

I frowned. "I thought you were with NatWest?"

"Pah, I don't go to them for money, I go to Dad, the bank of Dad, good interest rates," she said, "the application process is a little scarier but it's worth it."

I stared at her. I knew she didn't mean I should borrow money from my ex-husband. Simon and I are still on talking terms but I don't think he would be too happy to see me cap in hand on his doorstep. I frowned then it hit me, the bank of Dad. True I hadn't needed it for about twenty-five years, but it was an option.

I raised my eyebrows at her. "Dad?"

She nodded and grinned back. "Granddad!"

We had a pleasant hour drinking coffee and eating cake (my jeans wouldn't fit at all if I carried on at this rate), then she disappeared to head all the way back down to Reading. She did hit me for the petrol money before she left. Obviously there is a bank of Mum as well, nowhere near as grand or as rich as the Dad but still good for the odd twenty quid now and then.

As she climbed into her little red Peugeot I gave her a big hug, noticing as I did so that those huge boots of hers made her four inches taller than me. "Thank you for coming all this way."

Amelia huffed and pushed me away with a slight kiss. "Oh poo, at least it'll stop Charlie bleating at me about how insane you're getting. As I made dinner that evening, I pondered her words, I hadn't asked to borrow money from my father since I'd had the idea that I'd like to own a travelling burger bar back in my teens. He had bought it for me, I had worked it for two weeks decided that I hated smelling of onions and loftily stated that he could take it back and sell it again. We'd had words, a lot of words.

The next day, with Geoff at work and the kids at school, I had busied myself for over two hours with ridiculous little jobs in an effort to put off the evil moment.

There is something very wrong about having to borrow money off your parents at the age of forty-five.

By forty-five you really should have sorted yourself out, you're a grown up for goodness' sake. You should have all the answers, a good job, a pension in place, a half-paid-off mortgage and some savings for a rainy day. I stared at the telephone and shuddered, just for once I wished I could be normal.

"Hey, Dad." I started out cheerily as he picked the phone up on the third ring.

"Oh, hello, you." He sounded happy and relaxed, that was a good start. "How're you?"

"We're all fine," I hesitated then, deciding that a little small talk would probably be a good thing, I added, "how're you?"

"We're fine." Dad hesitated. He has always hated "small talk" with a passion. "Did you want to speak to your mother?"

I smiled and took a deep breath then plunged in, "No, Dad, it's you I wanted."

"Oh yes," my father's tone took on a slightly suspicious edge, "what can I do for you?"

I gulped, my dad is a lovely guy, small, balding, rotund and generally genial and fairly mellow, until he starts talking money. A businessman of many years, he has owned several of his own companies and has never failed to make a profit. He views it as a game, he develops houses, owns a printing company and within one sentence the Santa-like persona can disappear and suddenly you are facing an older version of Lord Sugar. The eyes harden, the stance becomes more upright, the lips purse and one eye takes on a slight twitch. I gulped again and taking a deep breath, plunged into the fray.

"I need to borrow some money." I held my breath if the next word was "no", that was it, there would be no swaying him.

"Right." The word was long drawn out then there was silence. Argh! He really wasn't going to make this easy for me.

"I need to borrow a large amount of money," I announced and took a deep breath. "We want to move back on to a boat, we have the money to buy one, a bad one, but we don't have the money to do it up, and get us back down to Cambridge and give us time to find jobs so I need to double the money that we've got." I took another breath. "I need a loan, a proper loan. I'll pay you back the interest that you would have gained if you'd kept the money in the bank and I need it over a five-year period."

". . . " Silence.

"Dad?" I held my breath again.

"Hmm." There was a grumbling mutter down the line. "Exactly how much do you need, what boat are you going to buy, what happens if you can't pay it back. I need a business plan and a spreadsheet of what it's going to be used for." There was silence for a moment then more muttering, he was obviously speaking to my mother with his hand over the mouthpiece.

I waited until he had finished, I could hear Mum's voice but couldn't make out what she was saying.

I stood up and wandered around the sitting room, my twitchy feet and nerves needing to get rid of some energy.

130

"How much are we talking here?" Mum's voice cut across his again. I smiled, if you talk to one of my parents, you talk to both. "Twenty thousand." I gave up trying to breathe and slumped back down into the chair. There it was, the "figure" out in the open, it sounded a huge amount when said aloud.

Silence . . . then, "How much?" I could hear my mother's squeak quite plainly.

I sighed, this was our last hope, if they said no we were really doomed to stay "oop north" for ever.

"Actually we could do it." Dad sounded thoughtful. "Email me all the details, I'll talk it over with your mother and we'll get back to you." There was another set of mutters then he sighed and said, "Your mother wants a word."

I bet she did. "Thanks Dad." I breathed a huge sigh of relief, at least I hadn't been fired out of the cannon as soon as I asked him.

"Hmmm," he said again and then disappeared off the line. He was replaced by my mother.

"What are you doing?" Mum was speaking quickly and about two octaves above her normal register. I sighed, this was almost harder than talking to my dad, Mum would want every little detail. Keeping the phone pressed to my ear, wincing occasionally as I listened to Mum's list of questions, I staggered out toward the kitchen and wondered if there was any scotch left. By the time this conversation was over I was going to need one.

Two days later and I had a headache, bits of paper all over the floor, a grumpy husband, two children on tenterhooks and more quotes, estimates and bills than I had ever seen before. Finally we had managed to cobble the whole thing together, wrestle our way through Excel and had a spreadsheet that we could sort of relate to. There was absolutely no way we could afford the Humber Keel, which was a shame.

However I had managed to locate two 70ft narrow boats in Birmingham that looked as though they had potential. They weren't exactly what we were looking for, being mid-engined and definitely having a traditional feel, but as they ticked enough of the boxes we decided that we could sort out the rest of the problems. So on Friday the fourth of July, with fingers, toes, eyes and other bits crossed for good luck, we sent the spreadsheet off to Dad with a suitably grovelling letter of explanation and waited.

Of course this would have to be one of those weekends that my mum and dad pushed off to Southampton to sail their own boat around the coast so they didn't actually see the email until Monday. By Sunday night the silence was beginning to play havoc with my nerves.

Monday morning eight o'clock and Dad was on the phone.

He paused for a moment just to let me get well and truly tied up in knots then laughed. "Go on, buy your wretched boat." His voice vanished beneath my whoops and profuse thanks.

After I had calmed down we went through all the details of the loan. Fair and legal, as long as I kept my end of the bargain and one of us got a job all would be well.

When Geoff got home that night he was bounced, Tigger-like, as he walked through the door.

"Dad said yes, Dad said yes," I bellowed at him as I leapt up and down.

Geoff laughed and tried to hold me off. "We still have to find a boat, you know."

Finally leaving him alone to get his boots off I rushed over to the computer. "What about these, I know we've looked at them before but they seem to be the best of a bad bunch."

"Them?" Geoff looked up from his feet. "How many do you think we need?"

"Oh just one will do," I said airily, flapping a hand at him. "But have another look at these two, what do you think?"

Geoff wandered over and stared at the screen which showed the two 70ft boats moored at Alvechurch. Funnily enough they were very similar to the last boat we had bought, grey and red, sad and listing, I was having another déjà vu moment.

I hopped up and down on the spot while he slowly reread through the specs on both boats. Finally he turned to me and grinned. "I think you're right, these definitely have more potential than most. The engine in the middle of the boat is going to be a pain but we'll just have to be careful how we convert around it."

That week was one of the longest I have ever had to endure. We had made an appointment to see the boats on Saturday, Mum and Dad were meeting us at

Birmingham, just for the laugh, I think. They didn't really care what boat we bought but were quite enthusiastic about paddling about in the sunshine.

Thursday night we were due at a fund raising "do" at Sam's school. I had spent most of the week whinging that I didn't want to go. But, for once, Geoff put his foot down.

"Oh come on." He poked me in the ribs as I was trying to find something to wear. "You moan about these people all the time, don't you want me to meet them, maybe they're really nice and you're the one that's weird."

I stuck my tongue out at him and went back to leafing through my wardrobe, jeans, jeans, overalls (hmm I'd wondered where they'd gone) did I even own a skirt? I knew that I didn't own any shoes that weren't "functional" so boots would have to do, a little odd in July, but hey it was either that or buy new shoes and Geoff wasn't about to be conned like that.

What is it about men that they can just chat? Geoff seemed to get on fine with most of the blokes in the room. He wandered up to them, dragging me with him (obviously showing how it was done) but as the interminable evening wore on his face took on a sort of rigid smile and I noticed that he kept glancing at his watch.

"Problems?" I enquired with a grin.

Geoff crinkled his nose. "No not really, I just want to be at home checking out those boats and making plans." He looked around the hall blowing his lips out at the high ceiling, squinting in the harsh fluorescent light above the canteen hatch that was serving as the bar.

Finally, we gave up wandering about and sat down at the edge of the hall, our knees high as we perched on the kiddy-sized, metal, fold-out chairs. The PTA had made a half-hearted attempt to decorate with multi-coloured paper streamers that hung in a sort of swag over the stage. Unfortunately the heat rising from the aging band who were desperately attempting covers of eighties hits had unravelled them and they now hung in dejected limp clumps to each side. I smiled as the lead singer, who had attempted a sort of overweight Bowie look, got caught up in them as he attempted to lead the crowd in the "Time Warp".

Geoff followed my gaze and laughed as well. "That's an image that's going to stay with me for a while."

I nodded. "Why are none of these people smiling?" I stared around at the crowd, there was a sort of dogged determination to the dancers. Moving as little as possible, they swayed in one place, glaring at each other when their personal bubble was invaded. With that many stilettos on a hard wood floor the noise should have been almost deafening but the grim silence was much more worrying.

Geoff shook his head and checked his watch again.

I usually enjoy a good boogie, especially when the "middle-aged" are involved. Let off the leash of expectation, responsibility and with the smallest amount of alcohol to fuel them, older women, or at least the ones I knew, were more than happy to let their hair down. Teenagers, with their almost psychotic worries about self-image and peer perception, would be horrified at what happened at a company Christmas "do" or a forty-fifth birthday party.

To see older flesh so unashamedly on display was usually the sign of a good night out. Inappropriate shoes and skintight designer dresses that fit in front on the mirror but, after a couple of drinks and with the stomach muscles now at ease, resemble a cushion with a bungee cord around it, usually seem to be the norm. The scars and traumas of forty-plus years of life and children, are buried in an evening of bad dancing and howling laughter. Arms raised, bingo wings flapping in time to the music, dyed hair flopping, sweaty and wet over deepening crow's feet and laughter lines, the whole scene one glorious salutation to middle age. Nobody cares, everybody laughs and those under twenty decide to leave before needing to find a therapist.

But not here.

When the music stopped the dance floor came to a standstill; there was polite clapping then silence, some moved to the bar for a refill, some moved to the side to rest and some just stood frowning, waiting for the next tune. My facetious Stepford analogy took on a bleak reality.

As we sat there watching the strange, almost robotically grim, determination to not show oneself up, our reverie was disturbed by a couple sitting next to us. They were a slightly mismatched pair, he was dressed in a cheap grey suit with brown lace-up shoes, his over-long dull brown hair stuck to his head in long strands, he looked uncomfortable; shuffling his feet and running his hand over his greying moustache.

She, on the other hand, had gone to town. Bottle-blonde hair flopped solidly over one purple and green eye, the only time the completely immobilised "do" moved was when her false eyelashes caught in the fringe. She had managed to pour herself into a very pleasant dress, black with large white flowers, which fell in soft folds to just above her black-stockinged knee. With a fair amount of effort however, she had managed to cheapen it with a huge red plastic belt and matching high-heeled shoes, which caused her to stagger and totter as she headed towards the sanctity of the tiny chairs.

"Hello." I knew she was on the PTA so at least I could make conversation, "Looks like everyone's having a good time, the decorations look . . ." argh, truth or lies, truth or lies? . . . lies . . . "Nice."

She stared at me for a moment then peeling her gaze away she spoke around me to Geoff. "Hello, you must be Sam's dad."

Geoff raised his eyebrows, nodded and reached over to shake her hand. "Hi, yes I'm Geoff." He indicated me with a hug. "You already know Marie."

The woman glanced at me then smiled back at Geoff. "Hmm." She dismissed me with a lifted lip.

Geoff's eyes widened as she gave him another big smile the big, glossy red lips pulled back to reveal lipstick-stained teeth. I noticed that she stuck the tip of her tongue through a small gap in her front teeth when she smiled.

"So what do you do?" Getting up, she walked around me to sit on the chair on the other side of Geoff.

Geoff stared at her in alarm and shuffled imperceptibly toward me. "Electrician."

"Ooo," she cooed, "I couldn't work out all those coloured wires, I'd blow myself up."

Honestly, this was really too much. I snorted a laugh. Geoff sneaked another look at his watch. "It's not that difficult really." He gave her a slightly rigid smile.

Geoff was now leaning so far away from her he was almost sitting in my lap.

"You must love doing something so interesting." Wah! I couldn't believe it, she actually reached over and touched his thigh.

Geoff panicked and jumped. "Well it's not exactly my raison d'être."

I couldn't resist it and I know it was cruel, but I felt it was such an old joke there was no way she'd fall for it. However, it might remind her that his wife was sitting right next to her watching the appalling femme fatale act. At her look of confusion I interjected, "It's like an Eccles cake."

She sneered at me (dammit, I knew those old jokes couldn't cut it any more). Sliding her stony gaze up my body, she took a pointed look at my boots, long brown cord skirt and slightly baggy blouse, minimal make-up and mad spiky red hair, then, obviously unimpressed, flicked her gaze away while she smoothed her skin-tight dress. "I never eat anything with dried fruit in it," she snapped and after staring pointedly at my stomach for a moment she gave me an evil smile. "It's so fattening."

I think it was at the choking sound from my husband that I actually started laughing. Obviously this wasn't the reaction she'd expected and when Geoff joined in with a snigger, she got up from her chair, spun on her heel and stamped away, aware that we were laughing at her but not knowing why.

Geoff looked at his watch, then, pointedly gallant, he reached for my coat and held it solicitously for my attention. "Come on," he said and nodded toward the door. "Let's get the hell out of here."

I stared around at the grim-faced dancers still swaying in place, trying to get images of Hotel California out of my mind, nodded my agreement and we scarpered.

On the walk back to the car I couldn't help needling Geoff a little. "What on earth was the matter with you? Wouldn't most men have loved all that attention?"

Geoff shuddered. "I felt like a teenager again, I just didn't know what to say. It seemed rude to run screaming through the crowd."

We wandered in happy silence through the village, past the church, and down to the Chinese takeaway, and around the spa shop into the car park.

Geoff climbed into our little Daewoo Matiz, sighed and said, "I still think you're wrong."

"Huh?" I wondered what on earth he was talking about.

"They're really the same here as they are everywhere else." He started reversing the little car out of the car park. "It's not them, it's us. We *could* fit in if we tried but we want to be somewhere else and we're looking for something to blame that on."

I shook my head. "You're probably right, but if we were going to stay I'd want to move to Durham because I still think this particular village is odd." I winced as a taxi screamed up the high street. "I was talking to an estate agent yesterday, and even he stated that the people round here were weird." I shrugged. "Anyway, call me a quitter, but I'm completely unwilling to stick around and find out about it all."

Geoff peered into the dark, trying to locate the entrance to our drive. It was just at the end of a huge wall and was always difficult to find, I'd lost count of the times I'd driven past and headed towards the hills — probably some deep psychological need. "Well let's hope these boats on Saturday are something we can work with," he said shaking his head. "We're nearly out of oil and with the prices going up, the next tank full is going to cost nearly eight hundred pounds."

My stomach churned, I didn't want to hear about another wretched household bill.

That Saturday we set out early, the kids were half excited, half filled with trepidation, Charlie was particularly on tenterhooks. She hadn't been involved when we had bought our last boat as she had been living with her father at the time. She had only come to live with us when we were about halfway through the rebuild, so she hadn't actually lived through the first twelve months of camping. Cold, wood everywhere, tripping over tools and generally being as poor as church mice because every penny we had went on materials. She was trying to be positive but I could see that she was going to miss her room and certain bits of "stuff". I felt a little guilty, but after the whisky debacle I felt that she would be better back in our alternative way of life (or at least that's what I told myself).

Arriving at Alvechurch Marina I felt the tension that had built up over the last six months begin to crack, the sun was shining, creating sparkles and glints on the grey-brown water, a small paddle of ducks drifted around the boats, occasionally breaking into a quacking, splashing panic as a couple of hopeful swans, also casing the boats, flapped and hissed evil expletives at them when they came too close.

While Geoff and the kids wandered over to the Marina office in search of keys, I sat on one of the sun warmed seats and watched the meanderings of the local live-aboards, most moving around with hoses, engine parts and other various sundry items that are needed on board.

A shout broke through my reverie and I waved as Mum and Dad climbed out of their car.

"Where is it then?" Mum rushed over, leaving Dad to sort out the car, the parking, the lunch hamper? (Good grief!)

I waved a hand toward the floating pontoons that stuck out into the river, "Over there somewhere, I expect." I swivelled around as I heard Sam's voice above the sound of roaring generators and pumps. "Here come the keys now."

"NANNY!" Sam ran over to her and looked hopeful. "They're selling ice-creams in the shop." He grinned up at her and shuffled a foot. "It is quite hot . . . don't you think?"

Mum laughed and grabbing her bag from the seat beside me wandered off toward the shop, re-emerging five minutes later with six ice-creams.

Dad was quiet as we wandered from pontoon to pontoon, licking our ice-creams and guiding Sam away from the edge of the swaying wooden structures. At the end of the furthest pontoon two elderly narrow boats rocked gently on loose ropes.

"Here we are then." Geoff looked at the keys in his hand, then passed one set to me. "Those are for *Probatica*," he said and pointed to the boat on the outside of the pontoon, then pocketed the keys, "and these are for *Minerva*." He waved a hand at *Minerva* then gave me a little push. "Go on then, open her up."

Stepping over the bow and down into the front well, I firmly pushed thoughts of "Happy" away. Opening the doors before me was not going to reveal the pristine and designed interior that we had previously enjoyed. There would be no shining wooden floors, no polished mugs hanging from hooks screwed into the underside of a glowing wooden shelf on a welsh dresser, no gleaming bathroom, no beautiful fitted bedroom.

No, this was going to be damp, cobweb covered, smelly and horrible. I pushed the key into the lock and turned my wrist, grimacing as the key graunched in the lock. I kicked the door and, under duress, it finally swung open with a creak and a groan. I stuck my head through the door and clamped my nose shut to keep out the smell. Damn it, once, just once, I would really like to be surprised by something, oh yuck!

We all stepped, one by one, in silence, down into the interior of the narrow boat. Charlie and Sam wandered off down the boat, pointing things out to each other and making unenthusiastic noises.

The adults stood in silence, at the very end of the boat and stared down the long thin interior. It looked as though someone had shoe-horned a 1970s cafe into a narrow boat. Row after row of tables with benches fore and aft lined each side of the boat. Huge, greasy windows let in shafts of light which illuminated the dancing dust disturbed by our entrance.

At the side of each window, threadbare pink curtains hung in sad, uneven swags, each held back by an eclectic mixture of shoe laces, ribbons and odd pieces of material. Each curtain had undergone a certain amount of fading, the result made them look striped or patchwork. The whole thing smelt of mould, decay and ancient dust. Oh how well I remembered that smell.

"Well this isn't as bad as I expected." Geoff levered himself out of the group and set off down the boat with Dad wandering along behind him. Good God what had he expected? Mum and I looked at each other then followed mutely along behind.

There really wasn't that much to see, half the boat held tables and benches and behind those a small kitchen squatted, wallowing in its own grease and dust. There was a huge stainless steel sink, a small, two-burner, gas cooker, three sagging wooden cupboards and, for some reason, another tiny porcelain sink.

Mum and I picked our way through, trying desperately not to touch anything, there was no doubt it would leave a grubby mark. Beyond the kitchen two wooden doors barred our way, both had signs: one said "LADIES" and the other "GENTLEMEN". I frowned and turned to Geoff. "Separate toilets?"

He shrugged and opened one of the doors. "Apparently so." Stepping into the tiny toilet he turned to face us then sat down on the loo. Reaching forward he grabbed the door and pushed it closed. His voice echoed from behind the wood, "Good grief, what size person could actually use this toilet?" We could hear shuffling and knocking. "My knees are touching the door."

The door opened and Geoff stood up and began knocking on the back wall. Frowning he emerged from the Ladies and entered the Gents and began knocking again. "Dammit." He shuffled backwards towards us and stood with his hands in the pockets of his jeans.

"What's up?" I stared at the wall. It looked perfectly ordinary to me.

"Half the bloody boat is behind that wall," he replied and stabbed an irate finger at the blockage, "and that wall's really good thick steel."

"So?" I didn't understand what the problem was.

"The engine room is behind that wall, Marie." He scratched his head. "It means that to get to the engine room and the boatman's cabin that's beyond that, we'll have to cut a doorway in this wall ..." He reached

144

forward and knocked again. The steel gave off a dull "bong" "And that steel's about five ml thick."

"That means we'll have to cut through the engine room to get to the back bedroom, doesn't it?" I stared down the boat and tried not to breathe. The sunshine didn't really light up the interior but it did manage to highlight some of the more interesting features of the boat. I was particularly impressed by the miniature moss gardens that were growing around the edge of each and every window. It wouldn't have been so bad if it had just been a small green layer but the moss was so well established it was even growing long stalks, some of which had little yellow bobbles on the end. They waved cheerily at me as the draft from around the ill-fitting window sill moved them.

I wandered away from the group by the toilets and examined the "decor" in more detail, lilac, badly painted walls, a red plastic floor which was so old it had begun to perish and lift at the edges. At least the ceiling was nice, long lengths of varnished wood with small beams between each window gave the boat a cottage-like feel.

Set into the ceiling was the most fantastic thing, a recessed 5 foot by 2 foot panel which slid, on metal rails, across the roof and revealed the sky, it was lovely. The one thing about narrow boats is that it doesn't matter how many windows and doors you leave open in the summer they fill with heat and gently cook you. Opening this up would let all the heat out and create a relatively cool space to live.

Geoff and my parents clattered past, discussing the points that could be considered "potential".

"You coming?" Geoff turned to me as he stood in the doorway. "We're off to see the other one."

Fastidiously rubbing my hand down my jeans I shuddered slightly and followed in their wake.

Probatica was almost identical to *Minerva*, same state, same toilets, same wall, same moss gardens, she also had a shower and, instead of the cafe layout, had long benches set along each wall with a big gap running down the middle of the boat. She had obviously been used for shorter, day trips.

There really wasn't that much else to see, they were narrow boats, the engine bays were filled with greasy water and the battery bank was so old I couldn't actually read the writing on the sides of the batteries. Geoff and Dad did a thorough survey of what was available and working. They started up both engines and listened to them. There were comforting nods and smiles between the two of them so at least the engines were obviously acceptable.

About two hours later we had adjourned to the small pub on site and Charlie was enjoying a real ale shandy, she had asked Dad for a whisky and coke and he would have bought her one if my mother hadn't intervened. As we all tucked into various pub meals, the boats obviously became the main topic of conversation.

"So." Dad reached over and waved his fork at Sam's sausages, Sam screamed and tried to hide his plate under the table. "Are you going to buy one of the boats?"

Geoff leaned back and took a sip of tea. "Yes I think we are."

I looked up in shock, it was really out of character for him to be so decisive. "Which one was best?" I gripped Sam's arm gently, told him to put his dinner back on the table, then told Dad off for winding him up.

"It doesn't really matter," Geoff said and shrugged, "they're pretty much the same, the only difference is that *Minerva* has a Lister Canal star and of course that brilliant sun roof. *Probatica* has a much older engine." He frowned for a moment. "Hmm, I must be getting old, I can't remember what it was, another Lister but it wasn't as good."

Mum, sensing that maybe a little discussion between the two of us would be a good idea, ushered Dad and the kids out in search of more ice cream. I watched them go and hoped they'd buy me one, or failing that a bottle of gin would be welcome.

Geoff stared at me over his cup of tea. "Are you ready to do this all again?"

I really hate it when he speaks my thoughts. I hesitated for a moment thinking about all the work that would be ahead of us and just for a moment wavered horribly, was the village of the damned really so bad?

I shuddered, yes it bloody well was, all I wanted was to be back at home and if it meant that I had to spend another two years in a floating building site so be it. "Yes, I think I am, how about you?"

Geoff stared into his tea. "I'll have to give up my job, I haven't got another to go to and we're going to be horribly broke because we have to pay your Dad back so we're going to have issues with both time and money." He paused, shaking his head slightly and took a gulp of cold tea. "That's if I can even get a job, we're taking a hell of a risk." He looked worried.

I bit my lip and stayed quiet, I couldn't manipulate this decision, to make this right we both had to be committed to the job. Actually I think we both needed to be committed, or at least sectioned.

After a couple of minutes Geoff nodded to himself and decisively set his tea cup down with a slight clank, then standing up he extended a hand to pull me to my feet. "Shall we buy a boat, dear?"

I let out a huge whoop which startled the poor man behind the bar. Then flung myself round the table to give my husband a huge hug. "Are you sure?"

Geoff nodded decisively. "I suppose we'd better have a final chat with the kids and if they're enthusiastic we'd better hope your dad has his cheque book on him."

Stepping out into the sunshine, we found the rest of the family happily sitting under an umbrella eating yet more ice cream. Plonking ourselves on some spare chairs, we managed to get the kids attention. "This is your last chance to say no." I prodded Sam as his attention wandered to the ducks still circling the marina. "Do you want to stay in Durham or are you happy with a new boat and we go back to our old life and do up another boat?" Much as I wanted them to agree, they had to know how it was going to go for the next year. "It'll be cold, smelly and we're going to have to rip most of it out before we leave just to give us some space."

Charlie frowned.

"We'll have to camp in the wretched thing while we're travelling and it's going to be a little crude for a while."

There was silence. Finally Sam nodded and said, "I want to go home, I want to go back to my old school."

I grinned at him. All eyes turned to Charlie who was still frowning at the table. "What about you Charles?" I reached over and gave her a small prod. "You must say what you're thinking; we all have to be together on this, if it makes even one person sad it's not worth doing because it's going to be really, really hard work."

Charlie looked up at me. "Can we have a dog?"

I nodded. "Yes, we'll get one when we get to Cambridge, but we can't have one while we're travelling, it's just not fair to any animal to introduce it to a new life like that. Actually the animal would probably be fine, I'm just not sure that Geoff and I would cope, but when we get home we'll look into it."

Mum looked aghast and rounded on my youngest daughter. "A dog?" she yelped, "All this change and all you're worried about is can you have a stupid dog?"

Charlie grinned. "I really, really want a dog." She gave her ice-cream another decisive lick. "And . . ." she shrugged with a slightly embarrassed look ". . . I have missed it, but I'd made such a fuss I didn't want to say that I'd changed my mind, School's all right here, but I don't think that my friends and I want the same things, I'd like to go home as well."

Half an hour later we were back on *Minerva* again. The cheque had been paid and we had decided against a survey. That was probably a stupid decision but we had neither the time nor the spare money to commission one. I watched as Geoff drew out the dimensions and then joined the kids in saying goodbye to Mum and Dad as they headed for home.

Sitting on the front deck I watched as Charlie stared at the water, her facial expression changing from happy to sad then back to happy again as she processed all the information. Eventually she nodded and looked over at the ducks with a smile. Standing up she stretched then, quick as lightning, thumped her brother and shot off up the gang plank with him in hot pursuit. I laughed, it looked as though she had finally considered all the options. It was great that she'd worked through it in a positive way, that sort of attitude might just cushion her against all the horrors to come.

I leaned back on the bow, wincing as my backside came in contact with the edge of the gas locker. It was so nice to be back aboard; I closed my eyes as the sun beat down. Well it was too late now, the cheque had been passed over and *Minerva* had been taken off sale. Trying to ignore the slow churning of my stomach, I determinedly imagined what she'd be like when she was finished and tried to ignore the journey we'd have to undertake to get her in that state.

CHAPTER
SIX

Déjà Vu

The next two weeks were an absolute whirlwind of activity. Geoff gave in his notice on Monday, the kids went off to their last week at school very happy and I set to packing with a will. We also commandeered Helens big van and every third night we filled it with boxes and Geoff travelled the six hundred miles to dump the wretched stuff into storage and then return home. Once again I listed all of our furniture on eBay and watched happily as the furniture left the building and the money rolled into our PayPal account. It wasn't very much to be honest but with every item that left the house I felt lighter and more free, I hadn't realised that our possessions weighed so heavily.

At the weekend, while sadly packing up all our books, I heard a car roll up and two minutes later Helen stuck her head round the door. "Anyone home?" She stepped into the echoingly empty lounge and stared around, ignoring me as I tried to shove a thousand books into boxes designed to hold about seven hundred and fifty.

She stared about the empty room and shook her head. "I hope you haven't packed the coffee."

Wandering past me she deliberately and nonchalantly knocked over one of my teetering piles of books, then ran away laughing maniacally.

I ducked as the books cascaded around me, then, realising I wasn't going to get a lot of packing done I clambered to my feet and headed for the kitchen.

"Thanks for that." I rubbed my arm. "What are you doing here?" I accepted a hug with an ungracious glower.

Helen laughed. "I've come to help, you grumpy cow."

"Excellent!" I smirked at her. "All I have left to do is empty the loft and I could do with a hand."

She sighed and said, "Great, leave the best till last eh?"

I laughed and turned to fill the kettle with water, coming to a halt as another knock came at the front door.

"Expecting someone?" Helen asked.

"Don't think so." Plugging the kettle in and turning it on, I picked up a tea towel then wiping my hands we headed through the lounge toward the still open front door.

A tall woman stood on the doorstep. With her coiffured blonde hair and deep blue suit, high heels and blank expression she looked like a health inspector. She stared through the open door into the living room.

"Hi." I threw the tea towel over my shoulder and grinned at her. "Can I help you?"

"Marie Browne?"

I nodded, she sounded very severe and a small knot of worry began to materialise in the pit of my stomach.

"I'm from the estate agents." She pulled a leather document file from beneath her arm and opened it with a frown.

The small knot of worry disappeared, she must be here to do the moving out inspection, it was a little early as we weren't leaving for a week, but at least we'd get our deposit back and that would be another £600 to add to the coffers.

I smiled at her. "Oh hi, I'm not sure we're really at inspection level, but you can see that no damage has been done to the house."

She stared at me blankly, then a look of comprehension appeared on her face and she gave me a thin smile. "I'm not here to do your exit inspection." She hesitated then smiled widely, obviously this was a woman that enjoyed her job. "Mainly because you're not going to be erm . . ." she searched for the word ". . . exiting."

"What?" The spinning knot was back with a vengeance, I could feel sweat beginning to form on my forehead and palms.

"You signed a new tenancy agreement for a year and that was only four months ago." She held out a piece of paper to me. "I'm afraid you can't leave for another eight months," she hesitated, "well, actually, you can leave but you'll have to pay for those remaining months." Having delivered her coup de grace she took a step back and waited for my reaction.

153

I stared at the paper in my hand then watched it leave as Helen whipped it away to study it.

"I thought you'd gone on to a month by month contract," Helen said as she read through the contract.

"I did." I racked my brains, thinking back to that day in the estate agents office. "Or at least, I thought I did, that was certainly what I asked for."

Taking the paper back from Helen I handed the contract back to the woman on the doorstep. "This can't be right, I renewed the contract but it was supposed to move to a month by month."

She shrugged. "Well, obviously a mistake's been made, but this is the contract that's been signed and now you're stuck." She raised her eyebrows. "Eight months isn't that long, we'll make sure we get the right contract signed next time. Oh, by the way," she said giving me that shark-like grin again, "I've already told Kevin and Val that you'll be staying so you don't have to bother squaring it with them." She looked past me into our bare room. "I hope you can get your furniture back." With that she turned on her heel and strutted back toward her car.

Resisting the urge to throw my coffee at her, I slammed the door in her wake then sank to the floor. Helen bit her lip then rushed out to the kitchen to make more coffee.

"So what are you going to do now?" Two minutes later she broke into my dark reverie and handed me a steaming mug of sanity.

I took a sip of coffee then, placing the mug carefully in the fireplace, sank my head into my hands.

"Look at this place, we can't live here, the boat's been bought, Geoff's handed in his notice, the kids are booked into new schools and I am this close," I held up my thumb and forefinger about an inch apart "to getting out of here and back to my life. There is no way I'm staying here for another eight months."

Helen looked up from opening a packet of chocolate digestives. "So what are you going to do?"

Smiling happily, I took a deep breath and picked up my coffee. "Something I never thought I would have to do at the age of forty-five." Grabbing a couple of biscuits I dunked one into my coffee and watched as the chocolate melted from the surface and slid slowly into the cup. "We're going to do a runner."

Helen spluttered, coughed and spilt her coffee onto the carpet. "Whoops sorry," she muttered and stealing the tea towel that was still resting on my shoulder, tried to mop up the spill. "A runner, really? But what will happen when they catch you?"

Taking the towel away from her I threw it back over my shoulder. "Don't worry about that staining, I'm not going to get my deposit back anyway, not now." Staggering to my feet I reached down a hand to pull Helen to hers. "Look, the way I see it, we have the moral high ground here. I know what I asked for and it wasn't another year's flaming contract on this place." Picking up the coffee mugs I moved toward the kitchen. "Yes I should have checked the contract but they're obviously unwilling to negotiate on this so phooey to them. I have done everything I should, I've paid on time, I asked for the right thing, I sent in the letter telling them we were leaving and they, quite frankly, are just messing with me." I set the mugs down on the kitchen counter and turned to Helen with a big grin. "Nothing's changed, the plan remains the same."

Helen frowned, she's an inherently law-abiding person and this idea didn't sit well at all. "But what if they catch you?"

"Do you know the best thing about living on a boat?" I rinsed out the mugs and set them to drain. "No address: once you get into that boat and turn on the engine you are, essentially, untraceable." I turned to Helen and grinned. "Don't get me wrong, people can be found but it takes far more effort, a boat could be on any one of a hundred waterways."

Helen shook her head dubiously. "I'm not sure this is the best way to handle this," she said, then she sniffed and laughed, "but it doesn't matter what I say, does it?" She shrugged. "And I suppose you have done everything you could to sort it out."

I leant back on the draining board and sighed. "Look, I know it's not the 'right' way to deal with things but I can't think of a way out of it, we've bought the boat, we now owe my dad a huge amount of money which we have to start paying off next week. If we stay here even another week, we need another tank of oil and that's going to cost us the equivalent of eight weeks payback to Dad." I shook my head. "If we stay, we're bankrupt and my family never talks to me again, if we go, the worst that can happen is that I'll never again be able to rent a house from that particular estate agents."

Helen sniggered, "Well if you put it that way, maybe we'd better go and sort out the loft."

I laughed and pushed away from the sink but as we walked up the stairs I couldn't quite get rid of the nagging little feeling that I was planning something very, very naughty and the feeling was making me quite nauseous.

Exactly eight days later, at three o'clock in the morning, I found myself marshalling the troops. The last of our possessions, those we needed with us to take *Minerva* down to Cambridge, had been squashed into Helen's van.

The last week had been a bit of a nightmare. Geoff hadn't been happy with the idea of "doing a runner" and had made his objections very clear. But, after twenty-four hours of denial and some rather intense conversations with the estate agents and the owners, he had also decided there was no other way and had joined me in my surreptitious packing and moving habits. We loaded the van in the middle of the night and crept around keeping things as quiet as we possibly could.

The pressure had built and built until finally the fatal day had arrived and I was almost beside myself with trepidation and anxiety that, as we left the house, Kevin, accompanied by Huge one and Huge two would come strolling around the corner of the barn with a shotgun and order us all back to our beds.

As I crept around in the darkness, opening cupboards and drawers, throwing any final forgotten things into a black bin bag, all I could hear was my heart beating. My palms were sweaty and I could feel my chest tightening as the adrenalin surged around my panic-stricken body threatening to cut off my breathing entirely.

Eventually, we were all assembled in the empty living room, the van and the car were packed to the point of bulging and we were finally ready to leave.

"Now listen," I hissed at the kids. They stared back at me in silence, their big eyes showing the amount of discomfort all this creeping around and late night activity was causing. "We're leaving, so I need you to walk out of that door in silence, get into the van in silence, stay silent until we are on the main road and that will be it. After that you can scream and jump up and down as much as you like because I know that's exactly what I'll be doing."

Both Chaos and Disorder nodded. "What if I have to cough or sneeze?" Sam grabbed my arm and looked worried.

"Hold your breath." Charlie pinched him gently.

I nodded. "Come on then, all aboard; let's get the hell out of here."

I felt a bit guilty as I watched them holding each other's arms and heading (in relative silence) toward the van. Geoff nodded to me as they got in and I gathered up the last bag and headed out through the door. Carefully and silently locking the door behind me, I posted the keys back through the letterbox. As I turned toward the car some night creature streaked across the lawn and set off the security lights on the barn. Caught in the sudden blazing shaft of light, I felt sick. I could almost hear the howl of wind up sirens and the shouts of the guards.

Argh! It was ridiculous. My limbs locked and I stood in full floodlit glory, a black bin bag in one hand a small desk lamp in the other. It was the final straw, my breathing stopped entirely. Swivelling only my eyes I could see Geoff, Chaos and Disorder as they all pressed their faces up against the van windows. They looked confused, Geoff rolled the window down. "What the hell are you doing?" he enquired. His calm and normal voice breaking into my strange Colditz-type fantasy.

Trying not to move my lips I hissed, "The lights." I remained standing stock-still in the middle of the drive.

Geoff heaved a sigh and just stared at me, I could hear Sam asking, "Why is Mum standing there like that, has she got her foot stuck?" Charlie just hit him on the head with a gentle fist.

As the lights went out I darted to the car and fumblingly started the engine. After checking that Geoff had managed to get the van running I pulled out into the driveway. It was now 3.45 a.m. As I passed the entrance to the main farmhouse I checked the drive and was horrified to notice a light come on in the upstairs window, a dark figure moved behind the curtains.

For a moment I panicked then, realising it would take a fair while for anyone to get downstairs, and he was probably only going to the loo anyway, put my foot down and sped toward the road and freedom. I turned right on to the main road with only a slight squeal of tyres then headed toward the A68, the lights of Helen's van large in my rear view mirror, the lights from the farmhouse rapidly fading into the distance.

It must have taken about twenty minutes for my heart to slow, my palms to dry and my breathing to ease, but as I headed through Barnard Castle for the last time and turned toward the M6 I couldn't stop grinning. I felt as though I had got away with a bank robbery. As I passed the turning toward the museum I had a momentary flash of sadness, It had been lovely seeing Helen so often, God only knew when I'd see her again, but the grin soon returned, we were out of the twilight zone that was the village of the damned and heading south toward normality again. No one could find us. From the moment we were out of the drive we were free; free of bills, free of that horrible house and completely free of the strange half lives that inhabited the village, I honestly couldn't remember a time I'd been happier.

At seven o'clock in the morning we pulled into Mum and Dad's drive. Mum had offered to look after the kids for the weekend while we tried to make the boat at least clean, if not really habitable. With the maximum amount of noise, Charlie and Sam clambered out of the car. Sam was carefully carrying Lu in her cage, as he walked, he made little cooing noises that he hoped would calm her down. The long bumpy ride in the car, the noise and the smells had made her completely insane again and she was currently running backwards and forwards throwing herself with piercing screams at the bars of the cage. Charlie wandered over to the car

160

to check on her rats but they were all fast asleep, all that could be seen was a selection of little pink feet and a ball of long tails; she shrugged and left them to it.

Mum opened the door and stopped mid yawn as she caught sight of Sam's package. "What the hell is that?" She peered into the cage then took a sudden step back as Lu launched herself toward her face, screaming incoherently. Mum shook her head then ushered us all into the kitchen where she had been making a full cooked breakfast. Sam was ecstatic and the worries of our sneaky getaway faded as he tucked into sausages, bacon and beans. Charlie was far more blasé about the whole thing and insisted on telling Mum every nuance of our late night adventure. The more she talked, the more anxious my mother became and the more anxious my mother became, the more creative Charlie became. I pushed Geoff to hurry his breakfast, I really felt we should be off toward the boat before the questions became too searching. Dad just laughed and shook his head.

By ten o'clock the sun was beating down upon my head as I sat on a bench with an ice cream. Waiting, once again, for our new boat to make its first appearance away from the sales pontoon. Geoff brought her around and threw me a rope so that we could moor her up near a skip. The marina had been fantastic and had agreed that we could use their repair dock for a couple of days while we sorted ourselves out.

"So, what's the plan?" Having tied her safely to one of the large concrete bollards I stepped aboard dragging with me a huge bag of cleaning materials. I dumped

161

them onto the front deck then went back for the hoover, the mop and bucket, Geoff's bag of electrical tools, a hammer, a lump hammer, a sledge hammer and a crow bar. I wasn't entirely convinced that we needed quite so many weapons of mass destruction, but Geoff had assured me they were essential so we'd brought them along.

He helped me load everything on to the boat, then stepped inside. "I think the easiest way to deal with this is pure violence." He grinned and pointed toward the stern. "Leave those last two dinettes in place, as they'll provide beds for the kids." He held up an electric screwdriver, gun style and gave it a bit of a whizz. "Take all the rest out, however you can and we'll sort ourselves out from there."

"Right." I grabbed another electric screwdriver and slotted it into the first of the screws I could see that appeared to hold one of the bench sets together. "1 . . . 2 . . . 3 go!"

Five hours later, Geoff and I were both lying on our backs in the sweet-smelling grass outside the marina shop and breathing heavily. After about twenty minutes of attempting to remove screws with the appropriate tool we had given up trying to get the wretched and ancient fixings out the proper way and had resorted, as Geoff knew we would, to more violent forms of DIY (Destroy it yourself).

I had become almost expert with a crow bar and Geoff's muscles had been very useful when wielding a sledge hammer. The bangs, thumps, cracking of wood and swearing had drawn quite a crowd which scattered, like pigeons before an oncoming car every time we threw another piece of annihilated wood out of the boat.

After a while we had a fairly clear path down the boat and the pain had set in. Throwing our tools to the floor we had staggered out into the afternoon sunshine to have a drink, examine and nurse bruises and apply antiseptic to some of the larger scratches and cuts, the painful product, of flying debris.

I levered myself into a sitting position and groaned, "Ow, I hurt all over."

Geoff, sensibly, stayed flat on his back. "You know, I don't think there's a single part of me that isn't bruised or cut or damaged in some way." He rolled over on to his front and groaned into the grass. "I don't think I can get up and we still have to move all that stuff into the skip. He pointed vaguely in the direction of the sprawling pile of shattered timber, bent metal and torn soft furnishings that littered the wharf.

"Great!" I flopped back down. "Maybe if we just go back to Mum's and leave it, the jetsam fairies will come and take it away for us during the night?"

"Urgh!" Geoff heaved himself to his hands and knees. "Nice thought but I doubt it." He staggered upright and held a hand out to me. "Come on, let's get this stuff in the skip then we can get home in time for tea." His eyes glazed for a moment as he realised that Mum would be cooking, then snapping back to reality he moved with a far more willing gait, my mother's cooking can have that effect on a hungry man.

Another two hours hard graft and we were finally back in the car. As we headed through Birmingham, Geoff was ticking jobs off his list as I drove the well-remembered roads. Chatting about the boat and tomorrow's jobs we didn't really notice where we were until Geoff pointed out the old Rover works.

"Wow, that's changed a lot." I stared out at the dilapidated site, quite sad to see the remnants of the once proud company reduced to a miserable mass of rubble and dust. The buildings that hadn't been demolished stood empty and grey, broken windows and trailing wood illustrated only too well how quickly something vibrant and working can die and decay.

"I wonder what we'd be doing now if Rover hadn't gone into receivership," I mused at Geoff, "I mean, let's face it that was our undoing. If Rover hadn't gone down owing us so much money, we'd never have sold the house, never have bought the first boat. Would we still be happy mooching along with our 'normal' life?"

Geoff shrugged and then winced as one of his minor injuries gave a twinge. "I don't know." He paused and stared at the site as it rolled slowly past. "If you could go back, knowing what you know now, would you change anything?"

I concentrated on negotiating the roundabout that would take us to the M5. "Of course, I would." I watched as Rover receded into the distance behind us. "I'd make sure you retrained while we had the money to do it, I'd still buy *Happy Go Lucky*, but I don't think I'd sell her or maybe I would have bought a Dutch barge or a wide beam."

Geoff nodded. "Let's hear it for 20:20 hindsight eh?"

I laughed. "Well we could all do with a bit of that. But quite honestly I wouldn't change anything, not the really big stuff, I'd still prefer living on a boat to a house, and I would have avoided village life." I shuddered theatrically, "Actually that little period I would definitely change. I'd never have gone past the Manchester ship canal if I'd known what the last year and a half was going to be like." Geoff opened his mouth but I cut him off. "And I don't care what you say, I'm never crossing it again."

The evening passed pleasantly enough. Mum had taken one look at us as we'd staggered through the front door and thrown us straight into the shower, stolen all our clothes and put them into the washing machine, all the time pleasantly tutting and fussing. The kids had hardly looked up as we fell through the door, both of them completely mesmerised by the huge flat screen plasma TV that was Dad's pride and joy. *Star Trek* takes on a whole new dimension when it's being fed, electronically, straight into your brain.

After a huge dinner, Geoff and I retired to the parents' Jacuzzi, he had a cup of tea, I had a glass of wine, we were also equipped with his and hers tweezers. We spent a fairly unpleasant hour pulling out all the splinters that we found embedded in fingers, hands and arms. By nine o'clock we were both asleep on the sofa much to my mother's disgust. By ten the kids had taken themselves to bed and Dad poked us awake to do the same.

165

Awaking to the sound of the alarm the next morning, I forced open my eyes then panicked. "Geoff! Geoff!!"

"Wha?" Geoff huffed, then groaned, "I can't move, I think I'm paralysed."

I tried again to lift an arm, the pain was unbearable. "Argh! Everything hurts."

Geoff sniggered, "Feeling a little sore are we?" he muttered, then lifted himself with effort into a sitting position. "Ow!" He rubbed his shoulder and pulled a pained face. "Do you think your mum has any pain-killers?" He winced and rolled his shoulders. "Ow, ouch, ow!"

I managed to sit up, I honestly felt as though I had been run over. "Oh God, I hope so. I can't believe we've got to do it all again today."

Geoff shuffled around so that he could sit on the edge of the bed. "Well, look on the bright side, all we have to do today is cleaning then we have to create some sort of living space, we pretty much destroyed as much as we could, I don't think there's anything left."

Staggering to my feet I held on to the window sill for support, my thighs felt twice their normal size (and that's no mean feat). "Do we have to do it today?"

"Yep!" Geoff, finally managing to gain his feet stretched, I swear I heard something go "twang!" as he did so. "We have to move her tonight, they've put aside a pontoon for us but, really, there isn't much we'll be able to do there apart from actually move all our stuff on board and try and get the kids settled. We really have to do all that we can today, especially things that need that skip."

He smiled as he picked up his clean and lovely-smelling clothes that Mum had placed, carefully ironed and folded just outside our door, bless her. "Why can't you be this sort of wife? I could get used to this sort of attention to detail." Unluckily for him, his protesting muscles stopped him from moving as quickly as usual so, for once, I actually managed to hit him with a well thrown hairbrush. After another day of cleaning, tidying, de-moulding and general maintenance, the boat looked almost, if not entirely, liveable. Standing in the doorway with a well-deserved cup of coffee it occurred to me that dirt was relative and transferable, the cleaner the boat became so the dirtier Geoff and I became.

I looked down at myself and grimaced, my jeans were covered in oil, cobwebs, mould, moss and other more unidentifiable things. My T-shirt, once white-and-blue, now had an interesting design of red splashes down the front, I hoped it wasn't blood as I couldn't actually identify whence it had originated. My hands were spotless, after spending a day elbow deep in buckets of hot soapy water they were pink, wrinkled and sore-looking, my nails shone and not a speck of dirt could be seen beneath them.

All the hard work had been worth it. We had cleaned and scrubbed every surface and moved in a huge rug which fitted perfectly wall to wall. On top of this we had placed a small sofa, futon thing, our television sat in the corner of the boat on a bedside table that was currently being utilised as a TV stand and DVD cupboard. The kitchen had been scrubbed till I could actually identify wood beneath the years of grease and the sink, now devoid of its growing, glowing, green plughole warmer, shone with hygienic innocence.

I smiled as Geoff staggered through the front doors and flopped down on the sofa. "Can we go home now?" he gasped. Apart from helping me to move in some of the larger items of furniture, he had spent the whole day in the engine room, pumping out the bilges into big containers, checking the electrics and the engine and other such mechanical and baffling tasks. He staggered to his feet again. "Here, come and have a look at this." He led the way out on to the wharf again.

"What the hell is that?" I stared at the sodden pile of material that was draped, in a still leaking heap, on the grass.

"I think it's a sleeping bag." Geoff prodded the squelchy thing with his boot.

I shrugged, what was so significant about a drowned sleeping bag? Unless of course its recent inhabitant was still in it.

"Unlike last time, we don't have a prop cutter on this boat." Geoff shook his head, "I think we're going to miss it, I found this wrapped around the propeller."

"Oh yuck!" I stepped away from the sodden thing.

"I'm quite relieved actually." Geoff put on a pair of gloves and started dragging the soggy item toward the skip. "I just thought that she handled really, really badly." He hoisted the material into the opening of the skip above his head, shuddering as a slimy green rain pattered down onto his face and shoulders. "I can imagine that she'll have a lot more power now."

I processed all this information for a moment. "So when were you going to tell me that she handled badly?"

Geoff had the courtesy to look slightly embarrassed. "You didn't need any more bad news." He rubbed his head with a towel. "And I figured I could fix any problem before you got round to driving it."

Well you can't really be angry at that sort of announcement can you? I laughed and went back inside to put the kettle on.

After a last night of luxury at my mother's, we were ready by eight o'clock the next morning to leave for yet another new home. After a round of goodbyes and the gentle acceptance of a picnic hamper from my mum we all piled into various vehicles.

Just as we pulled out of the drive Sam suddenly screamed, "Stop, STOP!! I've left Lu behind!" I slammed on the brakes and Geoff stopped just behind me. Sam leapt out of the car and grabbed Lu's cage from my laughing father. Lu had become quite happy at Mum's, especially as Mum kept feeding her biscuits and cake and so she started screaming almost as soon as she left my father's hands. I considered suggesting that Sam and Lu swap with Charlie and they ride with Geoff (his hearing isn't as good as mine), but finally decided that it was more important to be on our way. So off we went for the final time with Lu screaming all the way.

At the marina Charlie sauntered over to check on her rats. "What's happened to them?" she shouted at me angrily. I looked into the cage and discovered that all

169

the rats were huddled into one corner, shaking and looking decidedly upset.

"I don't know, they were fine half an hour ago." I looked around the car "Maybe they pulled something through the bars of the cage and ate it?" I really had no idea why they were all upset. At that moment, Lu seeing Charlie and I so close to her cage began screaming and swearing again. The effect on the rats was immediate and extreme. As one they all laid their ears back and climbed on top of each other in a huge effort to get as far away as they could from the lunatic in the next cell. Charlie laughed. "So much for evil, rabid, dangerous rats." She peered into the cage. "You should be ashamed of yourself, it's only a flaming hamster; for normal rats that's classed as 'dinner'. Oh for goodness' sake."

Unable to bear her darling pets being upset, she dragged the huge cage out of the car and staggered with it over to the van. Placing it carefully into the passenger seat she pointed a warning finger at the rather embarrassed looking vermin. "There, the nasty scary hamster's gone now." She shook her head and wandered off toward the office, following Geoff and Sam.

I stared at the enraged hamster. "You've got flaming Napoleon complex you have." Then shutting the door on Lu's screaming I followed the rest of the family.

The children were much more enthusiastic about the changes to the boat than I could ever have imagined. Charlie immediately claimed the boatman's cabin but stated that she wouldn't sleep in it until we reached

170

Cambridge. But at least it was a place she could store her rats. Lu was brought in and positioned on a table in the kitchen. Her screams, amplified by the mostly empty shell, echoed down the boat, she lasted about twenty minutes before she was relegated to one of the toilets where we could shut the door on her. I really hoped that she'd calm down fairly soon.

By the evening we were all unpacked, clothes had been carefully stacked into big plastic boxes at one end of the boat and we were all huddled on the floppy sofa watching telly, the kids were relaxed and happy watching some loud cartoon; Geoff was making lists as usual and I was desperately trying to stop Lu from burrowing into the back of the sofa.

It seemed all so normal and cosy that I couldn't stop smiling, in fact I was so happy to be out of the house and back on a boat that the children finally asked me to stop grinning as it was beginning to un-nerve them a bit.

At about ten o'clock, exhausted after a day of unpacking and rushing about, we packed the kids off to bed and managed to get ten minutes to ourselves to review Geoff's numerous lists of "things to do". I have to admit they did seem a little extensive.

"So how much of this do we have to do before we can actually leave?" I poked the piles of paper with a finger. "Surely we can put a new fire in when we get to Cambridge, can't we?"

Geoff looked up from the laptop where he was job-hunting, pricing fires and desperately trying to get his head around the plumbing that should be put in when installing a log burner with a back boiler.

"I need another couple of days to have a good check on the water system." He paused and picked up one list that had a lot of red marks on it. "And I need to dismantle the heating system, but honestly, I think it's completely defunct, I've never even seen anything like it before."

I have to admit our heating system was a cause for concern. When I had first seen it I had thought someone had strapped a bomb to the back wall of the engine room. It looked ancient and was made by a company called Wallace.

Completely unlike our last heating system which executed the normal process of running hot water through radiators, this thing blew hot air through huge silver ducts that ran along the floor of the boat, opening occasionally in little grills set into a shelf at ground level. It was a right pain as it took up at least six inches either side of the boat, I had tripped over it on numerous occasions and was hoping that we could get rid of the wretched thing at the earliest opportunity.

Geoff grinned over at the snoring children, each secure in a little dinette sleeping compartment. "Charlie's sleeping on the diagonal in that thing," he said, shaking his head. "Really, the sooner we get home and she feels comfortable and safe enough to sleep in her bedroom the better, at least she'll be able to sleep straight."

I yawned. "Maybe we ought to get some sleep as well?" I yawned again. "Those kids are going to be up at dawn tomorrow."

Geoff nodded and dragged himself to his feet. "OK, come on let's get this wretched bed together."

Our bed was actually a futon and doubled up as the family seating. It was going to be irritating to change the thing from sofa to sleeper every night, make it up with sheets and duvet as a bed and then put the whole thing away again in the morning, but it was either that or sleep on a blow-up mattress on the floor. The thought did occur to me that the one thing I was going to miss about a house was the ability to just throw myself into bed as soon as I was tired. It also occurred to me that maybe I ought to talk to someone about this need to make my life, and the lives of those around me, as difficult as possible; I had no doubt that any therapist would have a field day.

I woke up the next morning with a huge groan. Two days of hard manual labour and a night sleeping on something that resembled a collection of wooden pallets had done nothing for my aches and pains. Geoff woke at the noise and then joined me in the pained moaning. Charlie's sleep-tousled head appeared over the top of our bed.

"What's the matter with you two?" she asked, "You sound like a couple of old hippos in a territorial scrap." She laughed and sauntered past with a big bowl of munchies and fruit, obviously off to feed her rats.

Geoff stuck his tongue out at her as she passed, then pulled himself slowly upright with another moan of pain.

It actually took us nearly two hours to get ourselves together, by that time, Sam and Charlie had helped themselves to breakfast, trashed the kitchen while doing so and had rushed off out to explore the canal side in the sun, taking most of our bread with them. (Ducks get fed so well, I'm not sure why I have to do without toast so that they can get fat.)

In the quiet, Geoff and I sat comfortably on the sofa and alternated between sipping tea and taking pain-killers.

With his aches and pains finally deadened to the point he could move, Geoff sauntered off to his engine room to have a look at the heater and I was left in the sunshine, in blessed silence, to unpack some more boxes and make a futile attempt to turn this heap into a holiday home that, even if we couldn't actually live in it, we could camp in for a couple of weeks.

An hour later I had my head in the last box and was happily singing along to Radio GaGa by Queen at the top of my lungs. The kids were kicking up a row of their own outside, they had absconded with the next door neighbour's dog and there was a huge scrum of kids, dog, sticks and balls going on outside the window and Geoff was beating some sort of large piece of metal into submission in the engine room. With all the noise, I only just heard my phone, I caught it on the very last ring before it went to answer phone.

"Mum?" Amelia screeched in my ear. "You took your time answering, where are you?"

I panicked for a moment. I had told her we were moving hadn't I? I racked my brains, trying to remember the conversation; yes I had definitely told her we were moving this weekend.

"We're at the boat, where are you?" Oh please, please don't say you're standing outside a deserted house I thought.

"Reading." Her voice became even more tetchy. "Where did you think I'd be?"

This was not an Amelia in a good mood, I decided to take a huge leap and change the subject entirely.

"So what are you up to?" I smiled down the phone and hoped she would calm down a little.

"Looking for somewhere to bloody well live," she yelled at me.

I sat down with a wince, I knew immediately what she was going to say. "Have you and Huw finally split up?"

There was silence for a moment then a little sniff which deteriorated rapidly into a sporadic, sniff- and gurgle-punctuated, tearful rant.

"We had a row." Sniff, gurgle. "It hasn't been good for ages." Sniff. "I walked out." Sniff. "Nowhere to go." Gurgle. "All my stuff." Sniff. "Need somewhere to live . . ."

Oh dear. I took the phone away from my ear and holding a hand carefully over the mouthpiece counted to ten. Then taking a deep breath I brought the phone back to my ear.

"Better come home." I stared around the boat and wondered where the hell I was going to put her.

"Really?" Amelia took a deep shuddering breath and there was silence as she gathered her thoughts. "Erm, Mum?"

"Yes, love?"

"Where the hell are you?"

After I had given Amelia directions to the marina and had made a placatory cup of tea, I went in search of my obliging and loving husband.

"Geoff, are you busy?" I held out the big mug of steaming tea.

Geoff stared at me, his hair was sticking up in oily tufts, his face was covered in mud and grease, and he was currently beating seven hells out of a particularly sticky panel on the side of the bomb-shaped heating system. I winced and listened carefully for any sign of ticking.

"No dear, not at all." He glared at me and then aimed a particularly vicious kick at the heater. "This is me doing very little, I am, in face, having a most relaxing bloody DAY!"

"Good." I decided to ignore the sarcasm. "Amelia has split up with Huw and is coming down, is there any chance we could get the boatman's cabin ready for her to sleep in?"

Geoff gave me an absolutely incredulous look. "Are you completely bonkers?" He ran two black, oily hands through his hair, they left streaks, he now looked like a terrified badger. "Where are we going to put her and how long is she staying for? This really isn't a very good time."

I held my phone out to him. "Tell you what, you give our lovelorn and weeping daughter a call, and tell her that we don't want her either and that it's really inconvenient that she's found herself homeless at the moment and could she put it off for a couple of weeks until it's more convenient for us to deal with."

Geoff sighed and staggered to his feet, giving the heater a final kick he wandered off toward the back of the boat to start unloading all the bits and pieces that had been carefully stacked into the back cabin.

Watching him stamp away, I sighed, I really hoped that Amelia didn't mind sleeping with rats then laughed, there was a joke about boyfriends there somewhere but I doubted whether she'd laugh right at this very moment.

I sidestepped quickly as Sam, Charlie and borrowed dog came hurtling past me, then headed for the boxes stacked carefully in the one toilet we had designated as storage, intending to hunt out some bedding for Milly.

I had only managed to unpack three boxes when the lady in question flung herself through the door trailing Charlie, Sam and dog in a bewildered line behind her.

"What's the matter, Leelee?" Sam, empathic as ever, wandered over and patted his big sister on the head. That was all it took to set her off and watching her face crumple, I rushed over, putting the kettle on as I went past and handed her a box of tissues, then ushered Charlie, Sam and stolen dog outside. With only a few complaints they went, but sat on the side of the bank in a huddle staring with big worried eyes through the window, the dog, (evidently its name was Capri), unable to understand why all the games had stopped, looked sadly at Charlie and Sam. They made a mournful little group.

We sat for a while, waiting for the water overflow to stop, I made tea and gave her a big hug. We must have sat in near silence for about twenty minutes until, eventually there were no more tears to cry. Amelia gave her ravaged face a final wipe. It's a fact of life that pale-skinned blondes do not cry prettily. Sniffing a decisive sniff and tossing the tissue into the growing pile on the saloon floor, she looked so young without all the black make-up and the Goth outfits that she normally wore.

I raised my eyebrows at her, not quite trusting the reaction to an actual "spoken" question.

"What am I going to do, Mum?" Her voice broke slightly on the question, she coughed, then pursing her lips together shook her head and got to her feet.

I watched her heading over toward the kettle. "I don't know, love, but you know you can come with us."

She stared around. "Mum, this place is tiny, where would I sleep?"

I acted nonchalant. "There's a cabin at the back and we'll make do."

She shook her head. "No, I have to go back to Reading, I have friends there and a job." She hesitated then turned slightly red, her eyes dropped toward the floor and she sucked on her lower lip. "There are other reasons as well." She concentrated as she put teabags into mugs.

"What exactly did you and Huw argue about?" I asked.

Silence . . .

"Milly?"

She gave a huge sigh. "Huw decided that I was seeing someone else."

"Hmm mmm." Again an unspoken question.

She looked down at the floor, "I'm not actually seeing him," she sniffed again, "It's this bloke from the pub."

"Hmm mmm?" I raised my eyebrows at her and waited.

"We're just good friends." She raised her eyes and stared, unseeing out of the window.

"Hmm mmm?" I tilted my head toward her and waited.

"Huw and I have had issues for ages, we've just grown apart, I think." She shrugged. "I can't see the point of arguing with him about Chris, because I think if the opportunity arose I probably would and if that's the case and that's how I feel then it's obviously over."

"And how does this Chris feel about it all?" I sighed. Oh great, another useless bloke that worked in a pub, at least Huw had a decent job. I frowned and gave myself a mental slap, that was a completely hypocritical thought, here we were desperately trying to stick two fingers up at conventional society and with one weeping daughter I had fallen straight back into the "What's best for my child" mode.

"I think he's interested." Amelia gave a small smile. But I think I need to sort myself out before I explore that option, don't you?"

"Hmm," I replied, nodding, "more tea?"

Two hours, a big lunch, more tea, a packet of chocolate biscuits and four phone calls later and she had worked it all out. In fact she had found somewhere to live, decided to go back to college and was full of plans for the future. Charlie and Sam were relieved that she was smiling again. Geoff had merely sighed and put the boatman's cabin back as it was. The dog had been fed with leftover dinner and was asleep on the sofa, (who owns this flaming thing?). As we wandered back towards her car I tried to make sense of all the sudden changes.

"So let me get this straight." I frowned as I ticked all the points off on an imaginary list. "You're staying with some bloke called Mick in his spare room, you're going back to college in September to study Sociology and Psychology, you're going to find a part-time job and you and Huw are definitely over, is that about right?" I wondered if I'd missed anything. "And you're sure you want to go and sort this out tonight."

Amelia gave me a huge grin. "Yep." She juggled half the contents of my larder cupboard, a couple of pairs of shoes that she'd nicked off me and her car keys, then sighed as she looked at her car. "Hmm I'm not sure I can fit this in."

I laughed as I looked at her car overloaded with all her possessions. "Welcome to my world."

Amelia stared at me for a moment. "I used to think you were mad for moving around like this." She opened the back door and unceremoniously shoved all the stuff she was carrying on top of the pile that was already there, then quickly slammed the door shut before it could all flow blob-like into the car park. "But I feel great, I've got somewhere to go and a plan." She smirked. "Sort of."

Wandering over for a hug she shook her head again, "But it doesn't matter if it changes does it, or if something else goes wrong because I can always just change how I look at things and change the plan."

I hugged her and laughed "Yep, that's the way it goes, duck any major trauma and call what happens "the plan" then it doesn't matter what goes on in life you are always sticking to 'the plan', you can't go wrong really."

Later that evening as we were all sitting around enjoying a moment of peace and a late tea in the final glow of the slowly setting sun a small, elderly man with a can of beer in hand wandered down the tow path and stopped with a smile at our boat. He glared at the kids. "Ah, there you are, you young reprobates," he said.

"Oh God, what have they done now." I got ready to apologise and fetch the cheque book.

He laughed and shook his head. "I think they may have enticed my dog into a more rowdy way of life."

I gasped, Capri was still asleep on the sofa, he was only small and I had become so used to having a nondescript hairy, smelly terrier around from when Herbert, our last dog, was with us on *Happy Go Lucky* that I had completely failed to remember that he wasn't actually ours.

"Oh, I'm so sorry, I forgot he was still here." I turned to Charlie and Sam. "Go and get the dog, guys." Sam's lip quivered and I intervened quickly, "I said you could have a dog but we'll get one in Cambridge and you have to choose one of your own, you can't just pinch someone else's."

The kids sighed and trooped off to entice our guest out of the boat. I turned to apologise again but the man held his hand up. "Don't worry, he'll have had a fine old time playing with those two today and I was keeping half an eye on him." He laughed and accepted a chicken sandwich. "Truth is, it's nice to see him rushing about again, neither of us move very fast these days and after a day like today, he'll sleep for a week, poor old thing."

I shook my head. "I can't believe I forgot he was there. It does seem strange without a dog on the boat."

Geoff rolled his eyes. "I think it's quite nice," he said hopefully.

I laughed and got up to put the kettle on again. "I know you don't want another pet but I think you may be out-voted on this one."

The kids came out with a sleepy terrier cuddled up in Charlie's arms, they both gave him a lot of fuss as they handed him over. Capri's only response was to give a huge yawn and a slow wag of his tail. Michael (Capri's owner) smiled as he accepted the hairy package. "Right, well, thanks for wearing him out and feeding him." (I had admitted that he'd had a fair amount of chicken casserole at lunch time.) Managing to get one hand out from under the dog he gave us a wave and headed back towards his own boat. Capri's eyes fluttered closed as he walked and we could hear the sonorous snores that grew with every step.

"He was a nice dog, but I think I'd like a puppy, one that had a bit more energy," Charlie said.

Sam nodded; Geoff groaned; I laughed and went to make more tea.

CHAPTER
SEVEN

Banjos and Beer

Another couple of days' hard work and we were almost ready to go. The boat had been transformed into a sort of luxury floating camping thing, no real rooms but a lot of cushions and curtains and general goodwill made it exciting and good fun, the sun shone, the birds sang and the holidaymakers laughed and waved as they swished past in warm, beer fuelled, waves that rocked us and bashed us gently against the side of the canal.

Geoff had finally beaten the engine into submission and had fixed the gas water heater but the heating system had completely scuppered him. He announced that it was too warm to worry about a heating system, and, as we had just had our log burner delivered, he really couldn't be bothered with it and would take it apart when we got to Cambridge. Seemed like a good idea to me.

After the departure of Michael and Capri, another boat had taken their place. The lone occupant of this one had become a complete side show for Charlie who was completely in awe of this guy's musical talents. Having never heard a violin played like that before she would sit for hours listening to him play, picking up on his rather rude songs. Luckily Brian didn't mind being stalked by an impressed young teenager and cheerfully went about teaching her some of his more "colourful" creations. She could often be heard on the top of our boat with her guitar singing about people "who aren't like me".

Brian also renewed her passion for real ale which was a little unfortunate as she now, at fourteen, decided that she was old enough to drink and we had long discussions about the function and collapse of the young liver and why she wasn't allowed to sink herself into two or three bottles of Fursty Ferret or Old Peculier. These conversations usually culminated in her stamping off with a small glass of ale to the front of the boat where she would make up songs about the injustice of youth and the ridiculous rules of adults.

The boat in front of Brian's had an almost abandoned look. It had been there for our entire stay and we had yet to see anyone enter or leave it. Painted in waves of different colours with tinkly things hanging in the windows, the kids often went down and looked at it and tried to decide what sort of person would live in it. Sam actually became quite adept at imitating Lloyd Grossman and would stand outside the boat saying with a wonderful drawl, "Here we have imaginative paintwork, mismatched curtains, a skewed chimney, now who would live in a boat like this."

The morning before we were due to leave Sam rushed into the boat. "Mum! MUM!!" he grabbed my hand and pulled me toward the door. "There are people on the boat and they're . . ." he stopped and shook his head, trying to think of a good descriptive word, "weird."

Charlie looked up from the book she was reading with an interested look. "Weird?" she asked, "What's weird about them?"

Sam was hopping from one foot to another desperate to get someone to come and have a look. "The lady has really fat hair."

"Fat hair?" Charlie looked confused. "How can you have fat hair?"

Sam frowned and huffed. "Oh I don't know, it's like snakes, come and look."

Charlie jumped to her feet then grimaced as I shot in front of them and held out a hand to stop them. "Hold on a moment, you can't just go and stare at people, at least have a little courtesy and try to be surreptitious about it." I held out a bowl. "Go and pick some blackberries, there are some really good ones down by their boat."

The kids nodded and grabbing the bowl, rushed off to pretend to pick fruit. I, as usual, put the kettle on then settled back down with my book.

It must have been about an hour later when I realised that they'd been gone a rather long time. I expected them to be back with about five squashed blackberries in less than ten minutes. So draining my mug of the horrible cold coffee I had been drinking, I put my book down and headed out to find the kids.

Geoff was messing about on the roof, trying to work out the best position to cut a hole for the new flue.

I handed him a new cup of tea, which, like the previous one, he would probably completely ignore. "Have you seen thing one and thing two recently?" I stared down the empty canal path. "They went off to pick blackberries and spy on the neighbours."

Geoff scowled at the roof and taking a sip of his tea poked at the metal. "Why were they spying on the neighbours?" He poked again at the metal and his frown deepened.

"Sam said the woman had fat hair, so they went to see it."

Geoff looked up at me, confused for a moment. "Fat hair?" He suddenly grinned. "She had long purple and black dreadlocks," he said and laughed, "fat hair! I like it, they were pretty impressive actually, she had all these things like beads and bones and little silver tinkly things in them."

"Oh no." I suddenly thought of Brian and his violin. "I need to go and find the kids now."

Geoff looked really confused. "What on earth's the matter with you? They didn't look like child molesters or anything, she was really nice when she was chatting to me and her other half is a big beardy hippy type, he was fine as well."

"Don't be silly, I know there's nothing wrong with them, it's Charlie and the hair." I turned and headed up the path toward the multi-coloured boat. "I'll explain later, I've got to go."

Geoff shook his head, shrugged and turned his attention back to the roof.

I found Sam and Charlie about half a mile down the tow path and as I feared they were with the new neighbours, chatting away for all they were worth and, having filled the bowl I had given them, were now helping to fill a bucket with the succulent shining berries for the neighbours.

I grimaced and wandered up to them. "Hi!" I turned toward the woman, Geoff was right those locks were really impressive. "I'm Marie, owner of these two horrors."

"Oh, hi." She gave me a huge smile and swung round to shake my hand. "I think we met your husband earlier. I'm Sara and this is another Geoff." A tall and heavily bearded man looked up from where he was holding down a branch for Sam to reach the berries. "Hi there." The voice that emanated from behind the huge beard was surprisingly gentle for such a big man.

"I'm sorry, we seem to have stolen your children," Sara said and flopped down onto the ground with a huff. "They've been really great, though, we've picked twice as many berries with their help." Folding her long purple skirt over her legs she kicked off a pair of ancient Birkenstock clogs and began rootling around in a gigantic striped beach bag. "Anybody want a drink?"

"Yay!" Sam squeaked and rushed over to sit down. She gave him a big grin and passed him a small bottle of elderflower presse and a rather squashed piece of carrot cake. Charlie followed at a more dignified pace, her smile at the drink and cake fell rather as she watched me being offered a bottle of ale.

I looked at it. "I don't think I really deserve this, I haven't been doing any work with the blackberry picking."

Sara laughed. "No your tiny minions have been doing it all for you." She waved the beer at me again. "Go on, it's great beer, our friend makes it in his garage."

I took a sip, she was right, it was good beer. "He must have a hell of a garage."

"Well, we call it 'the garage' but really it's a proper small brewery, it's good, isn't it?"

I nodded then smiled up as Geoff (her Geoff not my Geoff) sat down with us, he gave me a big grin that only just showed as a flash of white between the hairs on his face, he tousled Sam's hair then began rootling around in the copious bag for his own beer and cake. "Your son picks a mean blackberry." He laughed then poked Sam gently in the cheek. "But it seems to be one for me, one for the pot, two for me, one for the pot."

I laughed, Sam's face below the nose, was indeed dyed purple with the juice from his spoils.

"And that one," he continued, pointing at Charlie, "climbs like a monkey, there was some early apples and she was up the tree and picking them so fast we had to rush to catch them as she threw them down." He gently kicked Charlie in the foot. "You ever think about joining the circus?"

Charlie blushed.

"She does seem to have a knack of getting into places others wouldn't bother with."

We sat for about an hour chatting, they had just returned from a music festival where they ran kids' clubs in circus skills, both could juggle, Geoff could breathe fire and swallow swords, Sara could ride a unicycle, and did strange things with something called poi, they were both utterly lovely. Sam got bored after about twenty minutes of chat and went back to the boat to get in his dad's way, but Charlie and I were quite happy to sit and swap stories with these two.

As the sun began to set, we gathered up the bowls of fruit and Sara's big bag and headed back toward the boats. Waving goodbye I looked down at Charlie who was deep in thought. "I'd like dreadlocks," she stated.

"That was why I rushed off," I said to Geoff later as we were washing up after tea, "I knew that she'd take one look at that hair and want hers the same."

About an hour later we were all relaxing in front of the telly, various pets were mooching about the boat (although Sam was always irritated that Lu had to be relegated to the table because she scared the rats) when there was a sudden scream from Charlie.

"Beans!!" She rushed over to the telly and stuck her hand down amongst the wires. "Beans!"

"Get her out," Charlie was shouting at Sam who, after putting a rather stuffed Lu back in her cage had wandered over to see what all the hubbub was about.

"I can't," Sam shouted back, "she's gone behind the wall."

Realising that something was going on, I put my book down, drained my mug and wandered around to the small group of family that was clustered around the television. "What's up?" I enquired.

Sam turned round. "Beans's gone behind the television," he moaned.

"Well, just leave her alone and she'll come out," I peered over the back of the TV cabinet. I couldn't see anything. "Are you sure she's down there, I can't see her."

Geoff, who was scrabbling around in the wires stood up with a look of consternation on his face. "She's gone into that hole," he announced, "we have to get her out of there, there's a gap behind there that goes under the floor. If she gets under there she could get anywhere and we might never get her back." He stood up and wandered out of the front doors. "And apart from that there's a lot of wires down there; if she chews those she'll be one frazzled rat and we'll have no electrics."

"Great, decomposing rat in the bilges, just what we need," I snapped. The kids looked around at me, twin looks of horror on their faces and I backtracked quickly. "Just making a very bad joke," I said, "don't worry, we'll get her out."

Within five minutes Geoff was back armed with a fair range of tools of destruction. "What on earth are you going to do?" I was alarmed at the sight of the hammer, screwdriver and crowbar that he'd brought back.

"Don't panic." He set about moving the TV cabinet. "I'm just going to take that section of wall off and get her out." He started undoing screws. "I can't take the risk that she squirms through one of the little gaps and gets under the floor." He paused for a moment to stare at the wall. "If she gets through there, we'll have to take some of the floor up."

"Come on kids, time for bed," I sighed.

Both Sam and Charlie put up strenuous arguments about wanting to see the outcome of the great rat trap, but I managed to convince them that she would be far more likely to come out if it was peaceful and quiet. Sam's suggestion of putting Lu on a little string harness and feeding her through the wall as bait was firmly quashed and with only slight sulks both kids headed off for bed.

Two hours later and Geoff had found that our insulation behind the walls was nowhere near as good as it could be, the wiring was a mess, the walls were damp and the windows were very badly fitted. What he hadn't found was a rat.

Dangerous Beans wasn't the brightest of rats, she was certainly getting on a bit and was the oddest thing to look at. Beans was a naked, dumbo rat, the dumbo part of her name being more a comment on the size of her ears than her IQ, the naked part meant that she was entirely hairless. Charlie loved her to bits and I have to admit she certainly occupied a certain soft spot in my heart as well, even if she did look a little like a slightly quizzical oven ready chicken. Her huge ears made her look permanently surprised and if she got cold she would shake and make a beeline for the inside of your jumper, climb up into the warm hollow between your breasts and make soft whuffling noises. I really would've hated to lose her to anything other than old age.

Later, we sat and studied the devastation over yet another cup of tea. I couldn't stop yawning; it was now well past midnight and the boat looked as though a team of bad builders had been through it. The wall sections were stacked against the sofa, there were bits of polystyrene insulation everywhere and the whole place smelled of dust and mould.

"I just don't know where she could be." Geoff studied his handiwork and frowned. "There's no way she could have got past the metal supporting strut in that wall. I can only think that she's managed to wedge herself between the wall and the floor."

We both stared in silence at the devastation and I wondered where I could get another gentle, ageing, naked big-eared rat at very short notice.

As we both sat in silence there was a very faint scuffling from beneath our feet. "Listen." Geoff got down on his hands and knees and put his ear to the rug, I joined him and sure enough there was another set of scratching and chittering sounds.

Geoff rubbed a hand over his face. "Well at least she's still alive." He shook his head and stared down at our 6ft by 10ft rug that covered the whole floor. "There's no way I can get under there without moving the sofa, the rug and taking half the floor up."

"Well, we'd better get started then." I downed the last half inch of cold tea.

It took us an hour to move all the sections of wall down the boat, another hour to move the sofa out on to the tow path and roll the rug up then about twenty seconds to lift a section of floor and lift out the bedraggled, miserable and oil-covered rodent from between the floor struts.

"Got you, you little miscreant." Geoff reached in and made a grab for the panicked rat as she tried to back away down the boat. He dragged her out by the scruff of her neck and placed her, greasy and covered in cobwebs into my lap. Enraged, cold, confused, and upset Beans promptly dug all her claws into my hand and then bit my finger. Her normally pink-and-white skin was smeared with dust and other dirt. She hissed and spat as she twisted and struggled in my hands.

"Ouch! Blimey." I did the only thing I could think of, and grabbing a tea towel wrapped the rat in it so that only her head was in the open air. Sucking my bleeding finger I pouted at Geoff. "She bit me."

He just chuckled and carried on moving the wall segments back into position.

By the time the birds had begun to sing, the walls were back in place, the rug was back down and the sofa had been dragged back in from outside and everything had been swept and cleaned. Dangerous Beans had been washed in baby shampoo (she didn't like that either) and had been placed in a nice large box with a big woolly sock and a hot water bottle to sleep on and was now out cold after her adventures. Geoff and I were leaning on each other over a last cuppa.

When the kids got up about eight that was exactly where they found us, we hadn't even managed to open the bed up before falling asleep.

At about ten Sara and Geoff appeared, they had just popped around to say goodbye and presented us with a magnificent apple and blackberry cake thing, I don't know how she made it but it tasted wonderful, probably not the best thing for breakfast but everybody enjoyed it, especially the rat who was enjoying being fed food she wasn't normally allowed and having Charlie coo over her. She hadn't suffered any lasting harm and was now leaping around as usual. It was a shame the same couldn't be said for Geoff and me.

It's odd, over the last three years I had probably taken, and given, at least ten addresses but we never seem to keep in touch with the people we meet on boats, you sort of pass a little time together have fun then move on. I suppose if we permanently toured and weren't heading for a particular place we would meet them again, have fun again, swap stories and then move on again. I wondered if this was something Geoff and I could look forward to when we didn't have to work, the kids were grown up and doing their own thing. I must admit it's a nice way to meet people and it's also a really good way to leave behind those you never ever want to see again.

Charlie watched Geoff and Sara wander off hand in hand toward the marina. "I want a dog and I want dreadlocks." She turned to look at me. "How do you get dreadlocks?"

I really had no idea how they were created. "Why don't you set the computer up and see if you can find out." I placed a hand on her arm as she nodded and headed toward the table where we usually set up the laptop. "A dog I'm quite happy with." I made sure she was looking me in the eye. "Dreadlocks . . . well, not so much, I think the school would certainly pitch a fit."

Charlie frowned.

"Look," I continued quickly before she could start listing the reasons why she should tie her hair in knots, "I have no problem with you having dreadlocks, I think they look great but the school is going to go mad if you turn up with those, why don't you find out how it's done, then decide if you really want it." I paused, thinking about it. "Honestly, Charlie, they look like they take a huge amount of work to keep them clean and sorted out, it would be like having another pet, let's just sort out the dog first, then maybe at a later date you can turn your head into a small furry animal and look after that as well, eh? Just as long as you promise me one teeny tiny little thing."

Charlie stared at me for a moment, then muttered, "What?"

"That if it leaps off your head and hides in the walls we damn well leave it there to die." I laughed, honestly I'm so funny sometimes.

Charlie glared at me (obviously not as funny as I thought), shook her head and stamped off toward the laptop. I winced slightly at her expression then, crisis averted for the moment, sauntered out to find out how Geoff was getting on, I was quite anxious to be under way.

It was about midday when we pulled out and finally headed, once again, toward Cambridge. Not having had a chance yet to steer her, I elected to drive, Geoff happily agreed and pottered around in the engine room.

Happy Go Lucky, our last boat, had had a fairly modern engine situated at the very rear of the boat, contentedly and tidily ensconced beneath nice clean boards in a small engine room that was clean and fairly quiet. With the engine running you could look over the side and watch the (very small) eddies of smoke erupt from the exhaust and there were never any problems.

This thing wore its engine like a medal, the huge green monstrosity reared boulder-like from the very centre of the engine room, the floor around it sticky with oil, old water and various bits of machinery, both new and ancient, it was all a bit of a mish-mash and poor Geoff, with his obsessive-compulsive need to have things orderly found it a little unsettling.

When the engine leapt into life, it would do so with a coughing fit that a retired, asthmatic miner would be proud of. It wouldn't have been so bad if it had then settled down to a steady working throb, it didn't. Huge clouds of black smoke would billow from the exhaust that was situated like a small chimney on the top of the roof, throwing small smuts and sooty particles high into the air. With every cough and hack the engine created another small black cloud of indistinguishable "things" which would be shot into the air.

Geoff had decided that as long as the engine was actually running, he wouldn't take it apart until we had reached Cambridge. I could understand why, to revamp that engine room was going to be a huge task and with Geoff's need to "get things right", once he started he wouldn't be able to stop until the engine was purring like a kitten and the engine room was sorted, polished and catalogued.

As we pulled out into mid stream, I could feel my face reddening with each successive cough and bellow from the engine, honestly the wretched thing sounded like it was on its last legs. (It could have been, I wouldn't have known.) It was actually incredibly easy to ignore what must have been astonished and disapproving looks from those enjoying a canal side walk as the huge cloud of smoke from the exhaust was streaming right into my face, I honestly couldn't see a thing.

I couldn't understand how Geoff could drive this thing. I couldn't breathe, I couldn't see, my eyes watered and every lungful of air I tried to take burned as though I was standing next to a bonfire, and the smell was quite appalling. Eventually I gave up trying to breathe through the horrendous effluvium and pulled the neck of my jumper up over my nose. With this barrier in place I then leant as far out over the river as I could, allowing the stream of noxious gasses to pass by my left ear.

By the time we had covered the three miles to the entrance to Wast Hill tunnel I was in agony. Bent at uncertain angles, my back was straining and complaining. However, if I stood straight in an effort to ease the pain I couldn't breathe and to cap it all, as I slowed down at the approach to the tunnel, a small red light on the start-up panel began to flash insistently. Worried about small flashing red lights, I slowed further; the light stopped flashing and just pulsed redly at me. I pulled her over to the side and screamed for Geoff.

At my second shout Geoff emerged from the engine room and made his way carefully along the gunwales to where I was standing.

"What's up?" He stared along the roof toward the entrance of the tunnel. "Why have you stopped?"

He turned to look at me and his enquiring look turned to one that alternated between concern and amusement. "What the hell happened to you?"

"What?" I put a hand up to my face. "What's the matter?"

"Never mind," Geoff said, grinning at me, "so what's with the stop?" He seemed to be having trouble keeping a straight face.

I pointed to the red light that was now just flat red. "What's that mean? It says 'oil', is that bad?"

Geoff stopped smiling "Oh crud." He stared at the light. "I think we may have a problem."

He climbed over the roof and gathering a rope as he went, leapt onto the bank and tied *Minerva* to a tree. With another two ropes in place, he clambered back aboard then disappeared to go and sort out the infernal engine.

Getting in and out of the engine room was a huge pain. Because the engine was so exposed and needed so much ventilation, double doors had been built into each side of the boat, these needed to be open when she was running just to allow enough air flow around the engine. You could also gain access via the boatman's cabin at the back, but that tiny space was so full of "stuff" that it was easier to just swing yourself in via the doors. This was fine as long as you remembered that there was a fairly long drop down to uncertain footing. I mostly stayed out, Geoff always remembered, but I usually either fell into the engine room or managed to fall over when I was actually in there.

While I was waiting for him to do whatever magic was required to make the engine functional again I indulged in a huge coughing fit in an effort to rid my poor lungs of all the yuck that I had inhaled. A couple walking their dog on the opposite side of the canal heard me coughing and looked over. I waved a hand at them which was sort of intending to say, "Hello and don't worry I have neither emphysema nor pleurisy however I sound."

The couple stared at me for a moment then looking slightly startled they rushed off. I shook my head, surely my coughing couldn't have been that bad?

Geoff chose that moment to stick his head out of the engine room. "Turn her on again."

I shrugged and hit the start button. *Minerva* shuddered and coughed into life within a cloud of smoke, but wonder of wonders the red light stayed off.

"Yay!" I gave Geoff a thumbs-up. "You fixed it, what was wrong?" Geoff held up one finger telling me to hang on a mo and disappeared from sight again. When he returned he was carrying a length of steel pipe and a small mirror.

I eyed the pipe suspiciously. "Where did that come from?"

"It's not really important where it came from," he said as he slid past me and out on to the bankside gunwales. "It's much more exciting to know where it should go." Reaching into the thick cloud of smoke he slid the metal pipe down on top of the small exhaust that stuck some four inches out of the roof. The thick smog cleared almost immediately as the short pipe extended the chimney to about two foot which effectively channelled the smoke and fumes over my head and away up into the trees.

"Sorry about that." He clambered back down to me and handed me the mirror. "I thought you knew about the exhaust extension, you take it off if you're going under a low bridge." He tapped the mirror then, looking at me, he pointed to my face. "You may want to go and have a wash."

Bemused, I looked at the mirror then gave a little scream. I looked just like a bad rendition of one of the old black and white minstrels. My forehead, cheeks, and between my eyes were completely black, where I had squinted against the smoke there were small white lines all around my eyes, set off beautifully by the long white tracks that had been made by asphyxiated tears. There were a couple of beautiful muddy smudges where I had dragged the back of my hand over my eyes in an effort to get them to stop watering; this had had the added effect of blackening my ears and dying the surrounding roots of my hair. The whole thing faded to grey below my nose where the neck of my jumper had created a fairly useless barrier against the smoke.

It was no wonder those people had looked surprised and worried: along with the coughing I looked exactly like an escaped coal miner on his last legs.

Geoff had the grace to look a little embarrassed. "Erm, I probably should have told you about the chimney."

I pushed the tiller toward him and glared. "You think?" Shaking my head I hurried back into the boat to have a good wash, all the time wondering if Swarfega was going to be classed as a good skin product. Sadly, probably not.

By the time I returned to the back of the boat, clean and sparkly, Geoff had got the engine running again but the little red light was back.

"So what's the verdict, oh great mechanic?" I quipped as I clambered up onto the back deck.

Geoff was staring at the little red light with a certain amount of irritation, as I stepped aboard he gave me the same look. Whoops, not the time for blasé jokes and gentle joshing about his engineering skills then.

"I'm not exactly sure." Geoff tapped the little red light, obviously hoping it was an electrical problem, he was far happier when it was an electrical problem.

"Oh dear." I joined him in staring at the little red light. Maybe both of us staring at it would give it enough positive energy to go out without us having to do anything real about the problem.

"Look at this . . ." Geoff moved the throttle forward and the engine coughed and spluttered a little faster. The red light began to flash.

"Wah." I made a grab for the throttle. "Turn it off, turn it off!"

"No, no," Geoff said and slapped my hand away from the throttle, "flashing is better than glowing."

"Oh." I stared at the steadily blinking light. "Really?"

Geoff nodded, then upped the revs a little more. The light went out.

I reached forward and tapped it. "What did you do?"

Geoff slapped my hand away again. "Nothing, that's the point." He lowered the revs again and the light came back on, then he moved the throttle forward and the glow became dark.

"As far as I can see . . ." Geoff said and shook his head, ". . . and I'm no mechanic, I need someone like Andy to verify this." He paused for a moment to think.

I waited for him to finish thinking. He didn't have much chance of getting that help. Andy and Sarah, long-standing friends of ours, were currently cruising around Reading on the Kennet and Avon.

"Look," Geoff said and stepped around the tiller and headed toward the engine room along the gunwales. "I've checked the level of the oil, it's fine and the oil pump seems to be working as far as I can see and everything seems to be in order." He stared up at the chimney still attempting to blow chunks of smut into the stratosphere. "Well, mostly," he amended.

I followed his gaze. "We really ought to think about either moving or shutting down the engine, that tree's beginning to turn black."

Geoff waved a dismissive hand. "We'll go on." He took a deep breath and squatting down on the gunwales

203

stared into the noisy engine room. "I think that when the engine drops below a certain amount of revs there just isn't enough ..." he paused for thought ". . . oomph to get the oil round." He stood up again and stepped backward on to dry land. "Just keep the revs up, don't slow it down too much and we should be fine." He grinned.

"Are you sure?" I dropped the throttle back to idle and grimaced as the red light started flashing again.

"Nope!" Geoff began to untie the ropes. "But it's the best I can come up with."

As he jumped back aboard I eased *Minerva* into gear and watched with a certain amount of trepidation as the red light flicked off again. "So what you're telling me . . ." I said, easing her nose toward the entrance of the tunnel, "is don't slow down, go faster."

"Yep!" Geoff laughed. "But not too fast, or with this engine we could end up with a big bang and bits of unidentifiable coggage and stuff sitting on the bottom of the cut."

"Great!"

By the time we had eased our way through the fairly long tunnel it was getting on for about four o'clock. I'm normally quite wary of tunnels, the dark and the cold, coupled with the sounds of water dripping and the reverberation of the engine all serve to disorientate me hugely. Halfway through any longish tunnel I usually begin to hallucinate, especially when the entrance has vanished behind me and the exit has yet to make an appearance. I hear footsteps, odd splashes; imagine that things are looking down at me from the dripping roof.

At one point during a trip through Braunston tunnel, I was completely convinced that something has reached up from the water and stroked the back of my leg.

This time however, I was so completely focused on that little red light I didn't notice anything else and it seemed like only seconds before we emerged out of the other end of the tunnel back into bright sunlight.

If I hadn't been so paranoid about that little light it probably wouldn't have taken me so long to notice that it was, without doubt, the most beautiful day. Geoff, who hates navigating tunnels with his poor eyesight, came to take over the steering which left me nothing to do but sit at the bow and watch the world go by.

Classic English countryside grows on the far side of Wast hill, willow, hazel and beech grow both sides of the canal, allowing only the occasional flare of sunlight to hit the murky brown water. When this happens the tops of all the little ripples glow and glisten and, in the wake behind the boat, it looks like a a trail of fire. Looking back down the length of *Minerva's* roof I could see Geoff's eyes hidden by the rim of his big hat, grinning teeth flashing in the sunlight from between the hair of his short beard. It really was idyllic.

Minerva chugged along at a steady pace sending up short puffs of smoke to mingle with the buzzing gnats that swirled and danced in small clouds around Geoff's. At one point, after a particularly foul emission, I swear I could hear little coughing and choking noises from amongst the clouds of insects. Finally getting the message that being around Geoff's hat was bad for their health they all swirled off to bother some walkers who were seriously lacking in smoke.

The kids came out and joined me and for the next hour, we sat happily watching the world go by. Sam leaning out over the gunwales managed to break the mood entirely.

"Mum, MUM! Look," he shouted pointing into the water, "look at that, it's a dead badger and it's all puffed up and swollen, oh yeurch!"

Ho hum, time to go and explore the cupboards in search of dinner then, is it?

We moored up for the night about an hour later. This time we knew what we were supposed to do so it was an easy mooring, we all leaped about, banging in mooring pins, tying the boat up and shutting windows in an effort to keep out the ever-hopeful bugs.

The next morning we all gathered around the breakfast table each sleepy-eyed, a little confused and very itchy, we obviously hadn't managed to keep out all the bugs.

"What happened to all the electrics?" Sam had tried to turn the telly on but had been thwarted by the complete lack of power. "It was working last night."

Geoff shook his head. "I don't know, the batteries should have been well charged yesterday." He took a last swig of his tea and got up from the table. "I'll go and have a look," he said and with a big sigh, signifying how irritating he found all this, he meandered off back to the engine room. "I do wish we hadn't had to leave so quickly," he said, "I really needed more time to go through all this lot."

I shrugged, we really didn't have a lot of choice if we were going to get the kids to school any time soon.

About half an hour later he returned with some bad news. "Quite frankly, we have two problems, the alternator's too small, it must only be putting out about 10 amps, the two batteries are 100 amp hours each so it needs twenty hours running time to charge the batteries so we could do with a nice 40/50 amp alternator. I have a horrible feeling that those batteries are also completely totalled so even if we could put in a huge amount of charge they wouldn't hold it."

"We're just going to have to run on the generator," he muttered and frowned, obviously remembering that he had packed the generator in the back cabin under a large cage of rats and behind our nice new log burner. He looked hopefully at the kettle. "Tell you what, make us a cup of tea and I'll try and unearth the genny, but we'll have to find somewhere a little out of the way to moor if we want to use it, it's not quiet."

I stared out of the window, we were currently moored just past the Brandwood tunnel, there were a fair number of houses around and I couldn't see that we were going to be able to use our generator around here, it was far too built-up. I started gathering up the coffee cups. The kids were going to be upset, they were in for some early nights.

Travelling that day, through the outskirts of Birmingham, I felt uneasy, the tow paths were no longer frequented by joggers and walkers but by small gangs of kids, who lounged, smoking and drinking, under the bridges on the left-hand side of the canal, they either shouted abuse at each other or at us as we chugged slowly past.

Just after a long sweeping turn we came upon some woods on the right side of the canal, a shadowy figure lurked among the trees. With an androgynous style of hair, clothing, and body shape I really couldn't tell whether it was male or female. The figure was squatting on the stones and gravel at the water's edge poking at the water with a stick. As we approached I could make out that it was a young man of around 16–18 years with what appeared to be the worst case of acne I had ever seen.

As his features became more and more defined I realised it wasn't acne at all but a rather large amount of plasters that were stuck on his face. One side sported a beautiful black eye, his nose was swollen and just to complete this picture of pain, his lip was cut and puffy on one side. With his long hair and grungy clothing, he really looked the picture of unloved dejection.

Looking up from whatever he was poking with the stick he noticed me watching him and standing up sauntered backwards into the tree line, where he stood half hidden in the shadows watching *Minerva* cruise slowly past.

I jumped as Charlie joined me at the window. "I'm soooooo bored," she whinged, "there's nothing to do and I'm hot." She looked over at the trees obviously following my line of sight. "Mum, MUM! What are you doing,"

I looked down at her. "Just watching the trees."

208

Charlie looked over at the little copse, if you looked hard you could just make out the figure still standing amongst the shadows. "Well that's boring."

"Why don't you read a book?"

"No, they're all boring."

"Paint?"

"Boring."

"Watch a DVD?"

"Oh blah!"

"Do some cooking? We could make a cake or something."

"Do I look like bloody Gordon Ramsay?" Charlie raised her eyes to the ceiling and stood in that amazing "young" position of one hip up and one hip down, her whole body stance calculated to irritate any parent within two hundred yards.

"Don't swear."

She rolled her eyes again. Obviously I couldn't get any more irritating if I tried. I had a sudden idea, Geoff would kill me later but it was better than being teenaged right at this moment. "Tell you what, go and see your dad and tell him you need to learn to drive the boat."

I held my breath, either this would be a brilliant idea or it would be shot out of a cannon so fast my head would spin.

Charlie narrowed her eyes at me, then grinned. "That's a brilliant idea, thanks Mum!" And with a sudden hug and an unexpected kiss she rushed off down the boat screaming, "Geoff, Geoff, Mum says I can drive the boat."

I took a breath ready to shout to Geoff that that wasn't exactly what I'd said and then let it out again. Oh let them get on with it.

Sam, listening to the conversation, watched Charlie shoot past, then putting his book down sauntered down toward me. "Can I learn to drive the boat?"

"Sorry, love." I leaned down to give him a hug. "You really need to be able to see over the roof."

He frowned. "Can I do some cooking then?"

I looked down at my youngest and gave him a big grin. "Chocolate or vanilla cake?"

"Chocolate." He stared down the boat after Charlie. "She doesn't like much any more, does she?" He looked sad for a moment. "And she doesn't want to play games with me any more."

I gave him a cuddle. "Don't worry, tomorrow she'll change her mind and it will all be different again."

For the next hour, we made cake. Well, I made cake, Sam licked the bowls and the spoons, covered our pathetic excuse for a kitchen in flour (it actually made it look better), dropped one of the eggs and ate most of the chocolate but we had fun and that was the main thing. As the resulting pale brown mush went into the oven Sam scampered back to his book, thoughtfully giving me space to tidy up. I had just finished when the phone rang.

"Hey, Mum."

Aha! Child number three. Sticking the phone between ear and shoulder, I put the kettle on. "Hi Amelia . . ."

I didn't get time to say anything else before she was off, giving me all her news and as usual talking nineteen to the dozen.

"I got in at college, I've left work, I've got a job at the local pub, I'm moving again and I'm taking my motorcycle test."

Grinning at her excitement, I settled down at the dinette to await the kettle boiling, I had a feeling this bout of change was going to take some time to explain and from past experience it was better to just sit still and let her blather.

Later that evening with all the kids asleep, Geoff and I were curled up on the futon with a last cup of tea. After talking to Amelia there had been thirteen locks which, for once, we had managed to do as a family. Charlie and Sam had both put on inches since the last time we'd attempted a lock so had been most useful at the gates. Geoff and I had had almost a peaceful passage watching the children bound on ahead to set the water level. I did have the feeling that while they enjoyed today they might well have a very different view after the next one hundred and twenty-four locks that we had to face before we got back to our mooring. I could see that Geoff and I might well have to enjoy it while we could because either tomorrow or maybe the day after the children were going to be conspicuous by their absence.

CHAPTER
EIGHT

Off the Beaten Track

Arriving the next day at the Hatton locks, we stopped very early in order to visit Hatton Country world. Any place that offers shopping, rides, a soft play park rigging thingy, a pub and animals was really good for all of us. Checking out Google maps it looked as though it was only one field away, an easy walk, so putting our best foot forward we hit the English countryside.

An hour later we had worked out that Geoff was very good with a compass, Charlie was really, really unlucky with prickly things and Sam could be counted on to find every rut and pothole then fall down it. However, spurred on and succoured by the idea of shopping and a hot lunch we persevered.

Hatton Country world is a strange little space, there are lots of little sheds that sell crafty type items, shoes, clothes, danglies, pictures and all that sort of thing. Further on there is a farm park with rides, animals to pet, sheepdog displays and other exciting things such as a Guinea Pig village. There is also a large pub situated between the two areas, a huge generic pub, not unlike a Wetherspoon, the meals aren't great but they're adequate and the beer is, well, nothing special to be honest, but it lives up to your expectations of a place like this.

By the time we had shopped, eaten, played on the rides, laughed at the guinea pigs, been terrorised by the goats and done all the things that were available, we were exhausted and the day had slipped away. Loaded down with all sorts of goodies we weren't really happy to contemplate the cross-country trek back to *Minerva*.

Halfway back Geoff decided that he was unsure of his bearings and asked Sam if he could look at the compass just to make sure we were heading in the right direction. A blank look came over Sam's face. "Compass?"

"Yes, Sam." I poked him gently. "You wanted to carry it, you promised that you would look after it, you said you were going to put it somewhere safe." Sam continued to look blank so I tried again. "Did you put it in your pocket?"

Sam shrugged unconcernedly. "I haven't got it."

I stared around at the area where we were standing. Tall grass surrounded us on all sides serving merely to hide from view the vast expanse of featureless fields that stretched into the distance. I squashed a sudden desire to turn Sam upside down and shake him until either a compass or some sort of brains fell out.

"Right." Geoff grabbed Sam's arm. "Come on, you, up on my shoulders, have a good look over the grass and hedges and see if you can spot the river."

Sam nodded and Geoff hoisted him aloft.

"Can you see it?" Geoff winced as Sam grabbed his hair.

"See what?" Sam laughed, he was enjoying the height immensely.

Geoff gritted his teeth and staggered slightly. "The river," he said, "look for the tops of chimneys or painted boats or anything."

Sam stared vaguely back the way we'd just come and then shouted cheerfully, "Nope can't see a thing."

"Oh for God's sake." Charlie put her bags down and yanked on Sam's leg. "Let me have a look, honestly you couldn't find your own arse with both hands."

"Charlie!" I put my bags down as well, the handles were beginning to cut into my fingers and I was sure I just felt a spot of rain. "Don't be so rude."

Geoff swung Sam back down to terra firma and hoisted Charlie up. "So what can you see?"

At least she was looking in the right direction.

"Nothing, the hedges are too high, can I stand on your shoulders?"

I intervened. "I'm not sure that's a good idea, you'd be ever so high."

Charlie gave me an airy wave then, after kicking off her trainers, she pulled off her socks. "I'll be fine."

Geoff gave a strained shrug and held his hand up for her to hold on to; I wandered over and held up a hand for her to hold as well. I have to admit I'm always quite impressed with her dexterity, within seconds she was standing on Geoff's shoulders, grabbing either his hand or mine as she wobbled backward and forward. Poor Geoff had broken out in a sweat despite the rapidly dropping temperature.

"Oh I see the river." Charlie pointed, her sudden movement causing Geoff to stagger sideways. "It's just beyond that hedge."

"That's great, come down now." I held up my hand for her to hold on to, with luck it would create some stability in Charlie's trapeze antics.

Ignoring my hand she settled back down to sit on Geoff's shoulders again. Once again the movement caused him to stagger away from me, as he did so his left foot slipped on a rut in the field and he started to fall.

There were screams and a certain amount of swearing as Geoff and Charlie both ended up in a pile on the floor, Geoff was fine, he'd landed on Charlie, Charlie on the other hand was horribly winded and had landed directly on her bottom so had some blossoming bruises to contend with.

After picking her up and dusting her down we headed in the direction that she had indicated. The gentle rain picked up pace causing us to do the same and eventually we pushed through a section of hedge that had obviously never been intended to be a door and staggered out on to the tow path.

By the time we got back to the boat we had been bitten by unidentifiable flying and crawling things, scratched, grazed and grated by hedges that objected to our forcing both ingress and egress. While shouting at Sam for falling a short distance out of a small tree, I had stepped backwards and fallen down a tractor rut and had twisted my ankle, Charlie's bag of "interesting farmhouse chutneys and jams" had split, spilling the contents into long grass, forcing her to scrabble around in an effort to locate them all.

We made a sad little sight as we got back to the boat, me, limping and leaning on Geoff, Sam bending down every other step to scratch at his insect bites and Charlie, one leg and an arm covered in mud, bringing up the rear. She was desperately trying to keep all the preserves in a sad scrap of plastic that was once a carrier bag and looked very much like a woman trying to put an octopus into a string bag. All of us were soaked to the skin. Coming in the other direction were a couple we had had a quick chat with while waiting to get served in the restaurant.

"Hello," the woman (I think she'd said her name was Mary) took a long look at our dishevelled appearance, "you look like you've had an exciting time."

I looked down at myself. Covered in dust from walking along dry fields, the rain had created muddy streaks and run down my legs and arms (I had no doubt my face was equally creative). "Hmm, we decided to take the cross-country route home from Hatton World." I shrugged and grinned. "We only got slightly lost." I winced as my injured ankle gave a twinge. "And slightly damaged."

"Wow, you're brave." She pointed back along the path. "We thought we were taking a chance walking along the nature trail."

"The Nature Trail?" Charlie peered around me to give Mary an ominous stare. "What Nature Trail?"

"There's a nature trail that runs between Hatton Locks and farm world." Mary made a wry face. "Oh dear, I take it you didn't know."

Charlie dropped the jars and the sad, broken bag onto the floor. "No we didn't know." She glared up at me. "Fancy that, a nice saunter from there to here, with signs and flat path and all that sort of thing." She gave a jar of Ginger and Rhubarb jam a vicious kick sending it off into the bushes. "And even if we did know we wouldn't have used it because that would mean you wouldn't be able to torture us with a walk in the bloody wilderness." Pushing past me she stamped on up the towpath toward *Minerva*.

We all stood in a group in slightly embarrassed silence. Sam, bless him, broke it with a quote from a film that he had enjoyed. "Teenagers." He nodded sagely. "They're all completely mental."

There really wasn't anything left to say after that so nodding our goodbyes and gathering up our errant conserves we wandered off in Charlie's angry wake.

She was waiting for us as we arrived, as *Minerva* was locked there was no way she could have got inside, as we opened the doors she stepped in and with a certain air of controlled fury walked over to the box that contained all the animal food, grabbed some treats for her rats then picking up the keys on route headed back out. We watched her as she walked back along the path toward the back of the boat. Nothing was said.

It occurred to me at the time that keeping a wild animal in an enclosed space required a fair amount of specialised licensing and wondered whether a teenager suffering from demented mood swings should have the same consideration or at least a heavily fortified cage.

The next morning it was cold, really cold, the sun had disappeared and grey clouds hung heavy over our little travelling party.

Geoff watched me unearth woollies and socks for a moment while drinking his tea. "Just for once," he said with a grin, "I think I'm going to pre-empt what you're going to say."

"Oh yeah?" I forced my head through the neck hole of my thick grey fleece.

"Hmm." He stared out of the window, the canal wandered off through the dew-covered trees, a dull brown ribbon cutting off toward the distance. "Isn't it about time I started to get that fire in."

I studied my socks, then began to force them over ice-cold clammy toes. "We've obviously been married far too long and need to get an immediate divorce."

"Tell you what." Geoff gave me one of those grins that tells me something horrible is coming. "You and the kids run her today and I'll build the fireplace, what do you reckon?"

"I knew there was going to be a catch." I laughed and wandering over to the cooker began to boil water for a thermos of tea.

Actually we didn't really have a bad day at all, Charlie had decided that being a sulky angry teenager was far too much trouble and spent the day leaping around the locks with Sam, the sun came out at about one and Geoff emerged carrying a picnic and more tea. It was a lovely day but by the time we moored up near Lapworth junction north we were all very tired.

Geoff however hadn't been a slouch and had built a nice plinth, painted it, covered the plinth in tiles and had backed the whole corner in fireproof board.

It looked a little odd without a fire in place.

"I don't think we'll go anywhere tomorrow," Geoff said. He looked up from the computer where he'd been checking the weather, "I think I might want to put that fire in."

"Really." I frowned over his shoulder. "Why so quick?" I stared at the screen. "Oh dear, that's not going to be good, is it."

The weather site he was looking at showed a huge black band of cloud coming in, there seemed to be no back end to it.

"Oh dear," I muttered again, wondering where we'd stored the waterproofs. "When is that due to hit us?"

"Well, this is a long-range weather forecast." Geoff shook his head. "The temperature's going to drop really quickly as well."

"Yes, but when?" I clasped my hands around my nice warm mug.

"A week maybe." Geoff frowned. "You know what these things are like, it could be tomorrow if it speeds up or next week if it slows down, you can only really rely on the weather forecast for today and you really might as well just look up at the sky to see what it's doing."

The next day gave no sign of the weather changing and we woke to clear blue skies. Geoff began to doubt. "Maybe we ought to push on," he hemmed and hawed.

"No, I've told the kids we're staying here today, and while you're fiddling around drilling holes in the roof, we're all going out for a walk along the path and seeing what we can find." I looked up from packing yet another picnic. "Besides which, they'll go mad if they have to stay in this hot boat, let me run some energy off them while we still have good weather."

Geoff tilted his head and listened as, outside, Sam screamed at Charlie and Charlie screamed back, it was a good job there wasn't anyone parked near us. He nodded. "Maybe you're right." He looked out of the window. "And it's a good place to run the generator. There's no one around for miles."

"Sorted." I hefted the bag. "Do you want help with anything before I drag the horrors away?"

"Actually," Geoff said as he rolled a shoulder and winced, "could you help me drag the fire out of the back cabin and around to the front deck."

I sighed and put the rucksack back down. "Of course, darling." I gave him a bright smile which didn't fool him for a second, "I'd love to."

A cast-iron log burner filled with firebricks, grate and other bits and pieces, weighs a lot, an awful lot. Between us we managed to inch it off the back of the boat, on to the tow path and carefully walk it the seventy foot to the front of the boat.

We stared at the raised sides of the bow. This was not going to be easy.

"How the hell are we supposed to lift it over the gunwales then down into the front deck?" I stared at the high sides before me.

Geoff frowned, then his expression cleared. Wandering over to the fire he began to dismantle it. Out came the firebricks, the grate, the riddling ring thing that allows all the ash to fall through the grate. Out came the ash pan, these and a few other little bits and pieces soon made a small pile on the gravel.

The kids were given stern instructions to not touch any of it then we headed, with a not significantly lighter lump of iron toward the boat.

It was decided that Geoff should stand in the front well and reach over the side, this would allow his greater strength and reach to pull straight up and all I would have to do was push and guide.

While Geoff climbed on to the boat I leant the fire on my knees, it was standing half on and half off the bank. After a couple of moments my knees began to feel the strain so reversing the tilt I leant the top of the fire against the boat ready for Geoff to hoist it aboard.

"Oh hang on a mo." Geoff stepped through the front doors and into *Minerva*'s dark interior. "I just want to get some gloves, I've got really slippery sweaty hands and I wouldn't want to drop it."

I nodded and leant on the fire. The day was definitely warming up and I glared up at the sky. I was hoping to be walking around some woods by now, there were some listed on the map and they looked a good place for a cool picnic.

Lost in my reverie I didn't notice when the boat first started to move. It was only when I felt the fire move beneath my hand that the first panic-stricken jolts of adrenaline started racing through my body.

The mooring lines were far too long and with the weight of the fire pushing her, *Minerva* moved gracefully out toward the centre of the canal and at the end of her tether there was just enough space for the fire to topple slowly and elegantly into the cut. I tried to stop it, I really did but once it passed its balance point there was absolutely nothing I could do. Without the heavy weight of the fire pushing her outwards Min moved slowly back to bump into the moorings again, she covered even the ripples that the falling fire had left behind. It had all happened so slowly there hadn't even been a significant splash.

Geoff emerged back on the sunny deck flexing his muscles in a Popeye fashion. "Right," he said "I've had my spinach, let's go." He looked at me with raised eyebrows. "What's up."

I pointed down toward the water, I really didn't know whether to laugh or cry. "Fire." Was all I managed.

Geoff's grin faded. "What?"

"The fire fell in the water." I could feel my stomach begin to churn.

Geoff leaped over the side and on to the canal path. "Fire? Water? What?" He stared at the side of the boat.

I explained what had happened and watched my poor, put-upon, husband sink down on his haunches beside *Minerva* and began, very gently, to bang his head on the side of the boat. I winced with each dull thud.

When he had finished driving my burgeoning guilt firmly home, he stood up with a large, false smile. I noticed there were little bits of weed and grit stuck between the ever deepening wrinkles that had appeared over the last few years and winced again.

I tried to make light of the situation. "Look, it can't be very far down, it's a canal they aren't very deep are they?" I laughed and clapped him on the shoulder. "It could have been worse, I could have dropped it in the river.

Geoff swivelled his head toward me and just stared "No." Geoff gave me a long look with absolutely no expression on his face at all. "No they aren't deep, but we now have to get into the water, find the fire, pick the damn thing up and get it back on to dry land. We then have to dry it out and hope that it hasn't landed on something awful in the water and cracked."

"What do you mean we have to get in the water?" I stared down into the chocolate-coloured murk. "I'm not getting in that, can't we just reach in and pull it out, get a rope round it or something?"

Geoff glared at me. "We've got to find it before we can get a rope round it, unless of course you have a huge electro-magnet somewhere about your person."

By this time the raised voices had alerted the kids that something interesting was going on and they wandered up to "help".

"You dropped the fire in the river?" Sam looked horribly confused. "Why did you do that?"

I sighed. "I didn't do it on purpose, Sam, it was an accident." I continued to glare at the water.

Charlie was much quicker to catch on and sat down on the bank to get a good view. "And now Sam," she said laughing, "she has to go in and get it. You know the rules, 'you broke it, you replace it', 'you messed it up, you clean it'." She gave me a great big grin. "You dropped it in the river, you go get it. This I have to see."

I shuddered. "I'll give you twenty quid to go in for me." I sighed as she shook her head still grinning like a maniac.

"Have you got to go in the water, Mum?" Sam stared horrified into the cut. "Oh yuck, it's all brown and slimy."

Geoff gently moved him out of the way. "Yes, thank you, Sam, I think your mother has realised that and she can see that it's really horrible in there."

"Yes, yes, thank you, all of you." I stared at the river. "Can we all shut up about it now?"

I have always prided myself that I would do anything it took to make a situation right, but this really was a step too far and I could feel myself beginning to panic. I couldn't go in that water, the footing was going to be all slimy and slippery and if I took my shoes off the sludge at the bottom would squelch between my toes. I felt sick.

Geoff gave me a hug. "Don't worry." He kissed me. "I'll go in for you."

I stared at him, really very tempted to take him up on the offer, but I couldn't. If the children hadn't been there I would have given in immediately and let him jump in twenty canals for me; let's face it, a husband has to prove how much he loves his wife on occasion and he owed me one after the coal in the stocking incident at Christmas. I sighed and shook my head.

Rules were rules and they applied to everybody, there was no way I was going to be the parent exposed as a complete hypocrite. If I shied away from this I was going to open myself up to a whole world of pain and argument from the two horrors over every little thing they didn't want to do. "No, I dropped it and I'll fetch it. Anyway we need you on the bank to hoist it up." I turned toward the boat, "Let me just get my wellies."

Charlie stared over the side. "Mum, I think it's deeper than your wellies."

I ignored her. I knew it was going to be deeper than my wellies but at least they'd fill with just water and I wouldn't be able to feel the yuck at the bottom.

While I was wasting time getting into an old pair of jeans and putting my wellies on, Geoff and the kids moved the boat back about ten foot, giving me a free fire-finding-point. Sam stood with a stick in the water to mark the place the fire fell in.

Soon I was standing on the bank staring into the water. There was no going back now, sitting on the side I dangled my wellied feet into the murky water. Then with Geoff hanging on to me just in case it was deeper than Sam's stick said it was I dropped into the water.

Argh! Good God it was cold. Ha! It only came up to my knees. OK my wellies were full of water but really, it wasn't that bad at all. I turned around to grin at my worried-looking family, took one step backward and fell off the fire that I had obviously landed on. With flailing arms and a huge scream I measured my length in the canal. Cold water closed over my head and for a moment I panicked and thrashed. Suddenly a big strong hand grabbed my shoulder and pulled me upright.

My hero! For a moment I stood staring at my husband as I spluttered out a mouthful of muddy water and used my hands to push my wet hair out of my eyes. Then hearing the cheers from the bank as the kids leapt up and down, I started to laugh, Geoff looked confused for a moment then started as well. We must have made a mad sight, two middle-aged loonies standing hip-deep in the cut laughing like hyenas with baby hyenas baying from the bank.

"Ah well." Geoff finally managed to get his breath back. "At least we know where the bloody fire is."

After half an hour of pushing and shoving we were no nearer to getting the fire ashore than when we started. We could get it up the side of the canal but even with Charlie pulling from the top and Sam shouting encouragement, we just couldn't lift it above chest height to get it on to the bank. Despite the warm sun, we were both beginning to shiver.

Two men and a retriever wandered along the footpath, they stopped, uncertain, next to the boat. They couldn't see the fire, all they saw were two cretins standing in the water.

"Need a hand?" one of them enquired hesitantly.

As soon as we had explained what had happened they rushed over and pulled the fire out as we pushed from the bottom and within seconds the whole soggy, muddy, affair was thankfully a thing of the past and with continued help (I have to admit we were definitely playing the pathetic card now), we managed to get the sopping fire on to the front of the boat.

Having beautifully averted a prolonged disaster the gentlemen and their dog continued their walk warmed by the sun, our gushing thanks and a huge amount of karmic wellbeing. We took ourselves inside to have a wash, then, warm and dry (but still smelling faintly of mud), we dragged the picnic out on to the towpath and ate it on the grass.

By about half past twelve we had finished cleaning out the fire and the kids and I did manage to take the walk we had been promising ourselves, leaving Geoff behind, we spent a happy afternoon among the trees.

By the time we came back, tired, hungry and slightly sunburned, Geoff had managed to cut a hole in the roof and had placed the flue through it. He had set the fire on its plinth and as we entered was happily sealing around the top.

Charlie stared at the fire and then out at the still blazing, setting sun and shook her head. "And this day happened because we obviously needed a fire so badly."

Geoff frowned at her. "Hmm, I can see that it's a stupid idea." He paused for effect. "Let's see, we could do it your way. We should have waited until the weather turned, and then sat on the roof in the freezing rain and howling wind trying to get a hole in the roof. Then, while we were cold and wet waiting for the sealant to dry we could have started the fire and sat around the five small fires you need to create to get the thing running and burn off all the awful new fire smell." He raised an eyebrow at her. "So this way, the fire's in, we'll have the small fires and then when we need it, it will be ready to go, all installed correctly and just waiting for the right moment to light it." He shook his head sadly. "Stupid way to go about things but there you go, that's the old for you."

Charlie narrowed her eyes at him then flounced off up the boat.

"One of these days," I said, watching her grab the laptop then turn her back to us to plug it in, "your sarcastic gob is going to get you in a whole heap of trouble."

Geoff just laughed.

"Is it ready to go?" I looked at the fire sitting proud on its new plinth. "And this is probably entirely the wrong time to tell you that I hate those tiles, isn't it?"

"Yep." Geoff grinned. "You chose 'em, you're stuck with them, and no we're not quite ready to go, I've run out of heatproof sealant, but that's all right, we should be at Midland Chandlers the day after tomorrow. Let's hope the weather holds out until then, eh?"

For the next two days we puddled along, locks, locks and more locks; it did occur to me on more than one occasion that it might be nice to do a trip where we weren't under time constraints but I supposed that would have to wait until Geoff and I actually had some time to ourselves. Staring out of the window I gave a wry smile, about ten years then.

We reached Midland Chandlers at about 4.30p.m. on a Thursday afternoon. The weather, for the last three hours had certainly begun to threaten that proposed change. The sun was still shining but a strong wind had blown in and was pushing us gently backwards and forwards as we tried, with increasing desperation, to get our seventy-foot monster on to the moorings by the Chandlers. As there was another boat already there we had to leave *Minerva*'s bum sticking out into the river and make a huge jump on to dry land. The kids and Geoff managed it without any problem at all but I dithered and shuffled up and down the gunwales trying to find a good launch point.

"Oh come on, Grandma." Charlie held her arms out. "Jump! Don't worry I'll catch you."

Geoff picked her up physically and moved her aside. "How about 'I' catch you." He laughed.

I really don't know what happened, wet gunwales? A strong gust of wind? Vast natural incompetence? It really could have been any of them or all of them but as I jumped I sort of twisted and completely failed to lift my feet up so I kind of fell forward with yet another scream.

To give him his due Geoff did actually catch me but the only way he could stop me from face-planting myself into the gravel of the car park was to throw himself gallantly beneath me. Consequently we both ended up in a dusty pile on the ground.

Charlie stepped over us shaking her head as she did so. "The idea of jumping, Mum," she said, "is to actually go 'up' before you come 'down'. You jump like a ninety-year-old."

"Or an elephant," Sam chimed in. "Look, you jump like this," he demonstrated by jumping up and down on the spot. "Did you know the elephant is the only animal in the world that can't jump?"

"That's not true." Charlie poked him. "The elephant is NOT the only animal that can't jump."

Sam frowned. He really hates it when his "interesting facts" are challenged. I remember that he was upset for over a week because a little girl at school told him he was stupid for believing that there was a particular crab that can climb trees (it's called the coconut crab). Consequently his voice rose, "The elephant IS the only animal that can't jump, Charlie."

"No, no." Charlie grinned at his outraged expression. "The elephant can't jump and neither can Mum. So that makes two animals doesn't it?"

This logic stumped Sam for a moment then he laughed. "Elephants and mum can't jump," he said.

Finally managing to extricate myself from on top of my poor flat husband I groaned as I brushed the dust and muck from my jeans and T-shirt. Sticking my lower lip out for sympathy, I watched as a dark stain spread around a rip near my knee.

Charlie stared at it as well. "Mum, you're bleeding."

"Yes, thank you, I realise that." I pulled the ripped material aside and winced at the hot tingle of pain which ensued.

"Wow," she said, staring at my knee, "I haven't had scabby knees since I was about six, even Sam doesn't have scabby knees any more."

Geoff, having finally got to his own feet, linked his arm with mine. "Come on, gimpy." He pulled me limping and protesting toward the door of the shop.

"They're going to be closed in about fifteen minutes and I think that we might need that fire pretty soon."

The Chandlers were actually closing their doors as we approached but, as usual, they were welcoming and polite and gave us the extra twenty minutes that we needed to load ourselves up with goodies.

I love chandlers, I always have. They are like huge Aladdin's caves of stuff, amongst which I could furtle for hours. Tiny baths, fridges, cookers and fires take up one side of the shop while down the centre are ropes, couplings, gas fittings and all other manner of bits and bobs with which to make all your in-boat systems work.

To the right was a selection of lights and "pretty stuff" with which to adorn your living area. I became completely enamoured with a selection of "Tiller Pins". *Minerva's* was a completely standard brass pin that looked like a tiny poker. It wasn't very fancy and I decided that the only way my life would be complete was to purchase a brand new pin. There were swans, boots, dogs, all sorts of things, each with its own attraction. The only problem was that I couldn't decide between one shaped like a witch and one in the shape of a Buckby Can, which is the classic boatman's water can, you often see them decorated in the classic Rose and Castles design, standing proud and tall and full of flowers on the top of some of the more ornate boats.

Finally I decided on the witch. She stood with her broom held between her hands, her hat crumpled and tilted to one side, her long cloak fell in folds about her back, she was lovely. I felt Geoff smooch up behind me so held her up for him to see.

231

"Look, I'm thinking of getting her, what do you think." I refused to look at his face knowing full well how he feels about "useless frippery".

"Hmmm." Geoff began to tick items off on his fingers. "New water tank, new floor, heating system, paint, wood, diesel and . . ." he paused for a moment to let his tedious list sink through my haze of consumerist hope, ". . . NO JOB."

As he wandered off toward the till, his hands full of functional items, I pulled a face at his back, then replaced the witch back into the display. I really hated it when he was right but surely isn't it nice to buy something that is just "nice"? Does everything have to be for a reason?

Sighing, I began to make hand signals to the kids who were examining a bath, "Come on you two, time to go." I stared at my witch one last time. "I don't want you anyway." I poked her in the hat. "You have a really big nose."

Getting back on to *Minerva* was much easier. The other boat had gone and we pulled her close to the mooring and I just stepped aboard.

That evening, parked up just past Braunston Marina and with the fire and flue now sealed to within an inch of its life we lit our first fire then sat outside, sheltered from the wind by a huge hedge as the fire gave off horrendous "first fire" smells.

It seemed utterly ridiculous to have the fire burning bright and warm inside while we were all sitting outside, freezing our bits off and huddled under a blanket while we waited for the stink to burn away.

I stared up at the sky. For the previous two weeks we had been able to see nothing but stars, now, however, the stars could only be seen occasionally as the clouds scudding across the sky broke and frayed, spun about by the rising winds. Autumn was coming, there was no doubt about it, and I contemplated the long winter we'd have to face before we could really start any major jobs. It was all a bit daunting really.

Pulling myself together, I pushed aside the slight feeling of foreboding. We chose this, I in particular pushed hard for this lifestyle, I had absolutely no right to worry about it now. Shaking off the feelings, I got to my feet. "Come on, time for bed." I poked Sam who gave me a sleepy grin from where he was slumped on Geoff's lap.

Later that evening Geoff and I were snuggled up in bed when the first drops of rain began their inevitable tattoo on the roof. I smiled, this was what I liked best. The fire, having given up stinking, had a few feebly glowing bits of wood which gave off a faint red light. This was what I remembered about living on a boat and snuggling down, I fell asleep listening to the gentle sounds of rain and being rocked to sleep by the still-rising winds, I didn't know why I'd had that moment of being maudlin earlier in the evening, everything was going to be fine.

Waking up the next morning, I yawned then snapped awake. I was freezing and completely wet through. Leaping out of bed with a yell I woke the rest of the family, who finding themselves also wet and cold soon joined me in adding to the rapidly expanding litany of complaints that, for some reason, we all aimed at poor Geoff, as though it was his fault we were wet, our bedding was soaked and under each window a large semi-circle of damp stained the floor.

Geoff, seemingly deaf to all our moans and whines, moved from window to window, his expression darkening with each examination he carried out.

An hour later the sun had come out and we had decorated the tow path, the hedge and the top of the boat with every wet item we could find. Geoff had dug out two huge canisters of sealant and was currently smearing the sticky substance around each and every window.

"So what's the prognosis?" I handed him a cup of tea and frowned as he touched my arm with a sticky hand. "Yuck, that stuff's horrible. Do you think you've managed to get all the leaks?"

Geoff shook his head. "I honestly don't know, I hope so." He took a huge gulp of hot tea. "I won't really know until there's more rain, so we just have to hope that the next rainfall is heavy enough to test the sealant but short enough that if I *have* got it wrong, we have time to seal it again." He shrugged and then fumbled in his pocket as his phone rang.

Great, I wandered off to check the slowly drying items that were still strewn around the area. With the weather threatening more change, short sharp rain showers weren't really on the cards, it was far more likely that it would start to rain and wouldn't stop for hours.

"Hey." Geoff had finished his phone call and was wandering down the tow path toward me. "I've got an interview."

I felt a sudden rush of relief. It was like suddenly letting out a big breath that you didn't really realise you were actually holding in.

"Great," I said, giving him a hug, "which one of the three hundred jobs you applied for finally came through?"

Geoff frowned at me. He hates, really, really hates and abhors exaggeration.

"I've only applied for about six." He shook his head. "It's that printing company in Cambridge that wants an in-house maintenance electrician."

"And is it a job that you really want?" I didn't feel confident about the look on his face.

"It's a job," he said and shrugged, "and we 'want' money coming in so I 'want' this job."

I nodded. "OK, and when is the interview?"

"Next Thursday."

I counted up on my fingers. "So we have six days to get somewhere that we can stop for the day, we have to get a car to somewhere useful and then we have to be able to get you to the interview and back again."

Geoff nodded then, as my phone rang, he mooched off to continue sealing the windows.

"Hey Mum!"

Amelia's strident voice shrieked at me out of the earpiece. "Hey you," I replied, grinning, "what are you up to?"

For the next half an hour Amelia gave me her potted plans for the next three years. Dismissing most of it as potentially, and probably, changeable, some of it within days, I concentrated on a name that kept cropping up: Chris.

Waiting for a gap in the lifestyle monologue that covered: work (now working at a pub in Reading and enjoying it enormously); education (had just got her acceptance to Reading College and would be starting in September); living arrangements (Amelia and Tallulah her pet gecko were currently occupying a friends spare room, but she was looking for something more permanent.) I finally managed to get a word in edgeways. "So how's Chris?" I asked in a deliberately casual tone.

There was silence, a small cough and then a slightly squeaky, "He's fine."

"Hmm mmm?" I waited, knowing that Amelia's innate need to fill a silence meant that she'd have to tell me probably far more that she had originally intended to. Sure enough, after a split-second she launched into a detailed description of his looks, his personality and his mental capacity. All, of course, entirely perfect.

When she had finished, or at least paused for breath, I leapt into the conversation. "So when do we get to meet this paragon of virtue, gorgeousness and intellectual prowess?

There was a giggle from the earpiece. "Soon, I should think." There was a pause. "But I think I need to prepare him to meet you lot." She laughed again. "Let's face it, I don't want you frightening him off with all your weirdness and it doesn't matter how much I pretend to be normal, they say if you want to see how your girlfriend turns out you look at her mother."

"Hey!" I bleated down the phone. "I'm completely lovely."

She laughed again. "Yes, you are. But let's be honest, Mum, any new boyfriend walking into the hell you call home had better be the forgiving type."

Hmm, she was probably right. I looked down at myself, the only thing I could find this morning that hadn't been soggy was a pair of Geoff's long khaki shorts and a puffy flannel shirt, which I was finding a bit warm so I'd rolled the sleeves up and opened all the buttons to show the lime green vest thing I was wearing beneath. This fetching ensemble had been finished off with some accessories (Gok Wan says that accessories are vital to an outfit), a really scraggy pair of Birkenstock clogs which I was wearing with a pair of merle grey fluffy walking socks and a bad tatty old straw hat which I had picked up from a folk festival.

Geoff, trophy husband that he was, complemented my sartorial elegance by sporting the grizzled, sticky-tar-and-sealant-spotted, not-shaved-for-days look. Together we made a right pair, with the contents of our life strewn, drying, across the vicinity it was no wonder that walkers hesitated before they walked past and I can see how my eldest might hesitate before introducing us to an unsuspecting new boyfriend.

"I promise we'll scrub up before we meet him."

"Good." Amelia's tone changed. "Anyhoo, got to go I'm due at work in about half an hour. Oh, before I forget, I'm coming down to see you, I have a day off next Friday, where will you be?"

"Just you?" I asked hopefully.

"Yes, Mother." Amelia became stern. "Just me, Chris is working. Text me where you'll be and I'll see you about lunchtime. Speak before then. Byeeeee!" And with a click the phone became silent.

With the disappearance of my oldest I sat and contemplated this wonderful young man that she seemed to have found, but it was no good, I couldn't imagine him at all; I was just going to have to be patient and wait until she delivered him up for parental assessment. I sighed, I hated being patient it really wasn't me at all.

CHAPTER
NINE

Nothing's so Scary Second Time Around

Later that day I found out that Braunston tunnel hadn't changed at all. It was still drippy and horrible and, being a Saturday, there were a lot of boats making a run for home territory before the weather changed for good. We met four boats coming the other way, one in particular, was a little trying. A hire boat with a group of twenty-somethings aboard. Drunk twenty-somethings, guiding a large narrow boat badly through the dark was a bit worrying. They came haring through the tunnel going far too fast, their lights were off and the only way I knew they actually even existed was by the echoes of screaming and yelling that drifted to me on the tunnel air flow, so luckily I had slowed down, confused by the fact that I couldn't actually see any lights.

I finally worked out that, to frighten the girls on board, one bright spark kept turning off the tunnel light and plunging them into darkness. This made the girls scream and must have made the macho intellectual feel great.

Slowing right down I hugged the tunnel wall, I could see the light flashing on and off but couldn't really work out how far away they were, so to give them a good idea of where we were I hit the horn, hard.

There were more screams but from the sound of the engine they didn't bother to slow down and as their lights flicked back on I could see that they were about twenty foot away and heading right for us.

Laughing at all the screaming, the driver swung the tiller over and then began to panic as he realised it wasn't having much of an effect. Up to that point their speeding boat had only been required to go in a straight line, now being asked to turn in a confined space and at speed it was behaving as a normal narrow boat does and ignoring him completely.

His facial expression changed from one of fairly drunk amiability to sheer panic and he hauled the tiller over as far as he could. Luckily, and I still think it was a mistake, he grabbed the throttle and poured on more power, I think it was a mistake because he only did it for a moment before he screamed and then pulled the throttle back, killing the engine completely. Luckily that burst of power turned the nose just enough, enabling the boat to skid down the side of ours. Knowing how this works, I grabbed the top of the roof and just held on.

For a moment there was nothing but the sound of scraping and grinding metal then they were gone, their screams and shouts echoing back down the tunnel toward me. I waited until silence was regained and a normal heart rate was restored then, taking a deep breath, I began to think about continuing down the tunnel.

240

Charlie leapt out onto the gunwales and tottered across to the back deck where she proceeded to scream things like "Morons" and "Slow down you drunken Twits". (I think she said "twits".)

Geoff stuck his head out of the other side door and was obviously confused when he came face to face with the tunnel wall. "What happened?" he shouted back at me.

"Holidaymakers," I shouted back, "drunk."

He shook his head and helpfully pushed off against the wall of the tunnel with the handle of our broom. "You all right?"

I looked ahead and was relieved to see that the opening of the tunnel was just visible. "Fine, we'll be out soon."

Going into the tunnel we had left behind bright sunshine, we emerged into what can only be described as dank gloom. A light rain had started, the type of rain that you don't really feel the individual drops but within half an hour every single item of clothing that you have on is soaked through, it has to be my least favourite type of rain: insidious.

Stopping for the night just outside Bugbrooke, we headed again for the village. Last time we had visited the village shop in a desperate search for a can opener. This time we were fully stocked with can openers (we had three, all in different colours).

We knew that we had to face the Rothersthorpe flight and hoped that we'd be able to get to Northampton as soon as possible. With Geoff's interview looming, we'd

241

decided that our biggest problem was moving a car so he'd have some transport to get to Cambridge that Friday. Our cunning plan was to stop over at Northampton for the day, the kids and I would go and do some much-needed shopping and laundry, Geoff would take the train back to Birmingham, pick up the car from there and would drive to Rushden & Diamonds football ground near Irthlingborough. He would then catch a bus back to Northampton where he would rejoin the boat and we would all head for Irthlingborough to pick up the car. Simple really.

After a ridiculously early start (I'm sure that Sundays were never intended for early anything), and having battled down through the Rothersthorpe locks, we seemed to be making good time and pulled up on the Northampton Wharf to go shopping at Asda at about two o'clock in the afternoon.

Organising the children to go shopping before Geoff could look at his watch and decide that we could perhaps get a little further, I decided that maybe now would be a good time to stock up on all those little items like jumpers and warm socks. The long sunny days at the start of this journey now seemed like a distant memory and I was becoming used to the rain clouds suddenly looming up and pouring their contents over me. There seemed to be a constant cold wind as well and I was beginning to miss my thermals.

After the shopping trip we loaded all our packages back aboard and started to make ready to leave. We were only heading for the water point which was just a little way down the river, so we were all being pretty relaxed about the whole thing. Charlie, who had been staring out of the window, crinkling her nose at the concrete and steel wharf of Northampton's main boat parking facility, suddenly frowned and pressed her nose to the window.

"What's he got in that cage?" She stood up and sauntered down the length of the boat and stood staring out of the double doors at the occupant of the next boat along who was currently sitting on one of the benches talking to a large black bird that had emerged from the cage resting on the seat beside him.

"Look, he's got a crow." Charlie dithered, unsure whether she could go and talk to him.

"Go on." I nodded toward the figure on the bench. "Go and ask him about it, I'm sure he won't mind and if he does you'll soon know."

She nodded and leapt off the boat with her brother only inches behind her. Watching them go, with Geoff a couple of paces behind them, I decided that it was no wonder Charlie was so interested in this particular pet. A couple of years ago she had attempted to tame a wild crow and had actually managed to get it to take food from her hand. The only problem was that while Charlie was at school, Eric (the crow) had taken out his frustration at Charlie's absence by ripping open all the bin bags of the other boaters. A couple of them had asked her to stop inciting the wildlife to riot and Eric had been firmly ignored until he went back to foraging in more normal crow-like places. Charlie hadn't been happy about it at all.

I had just finished putting the last of the shopping away when the thunder of not so tiny feet trashed the gentle quiet of the boat. Charlie threw herself on the sofa. "He's had him since he was tiny," she announced, frowning at her feet. "He found him and looked after him." She stared into the water the circles made by the sudden onset of yet another shower mirrored the shape of her thoughts. "I wish I'd kept Eric."

"Eric wasn't really a baby though was he," I said, smiling as I remembered the huge black bird, he wouldn't have looked out of place stunt doubling for a raven in an Edgar Allan Poe poem, the way he looked at you, all speculative intelligence and controlled malice still made me shudder a little. Nothing that bird did would have surprised me, but even with all his horror-film connotations I couldn't deny that he was incredibly beautiful.

Charlie shook her head. "No, he was too old to properly tame," she said and gave me a sudden grin, "hey, there's loads of crows around the old mooring, maybe next spring I can find a baby."

Argh! Quick, which way to handle this? If I disagreed she would almost certainly find one and if I agreed she would also find one. I decided to settle on gentle apathy so I gave her a distracted nod and a muttered "maybe" then sauntered off down the boat in an effort to lose this particular conversation.

The next morning Geoff was off to the train station bright and early, he was due to bring the car back to the car park across the road for the night and then we would all take off and go our separate ways tomorrow. I was a little tense about running *Minerva* without

244

Geoff's wonderfully steadying presence but we were only due to meet him just down river. There was a lovely little mooring just before the first lock and we'd decided that we would park there and take a walk to the health food store "Daily Bread" which was a nice walk along park-way and cycle paths. True, it wasn't as peaceful as it might have been, due to the six lane A45 that runs alongside the river, but it was still a nice walk.

We spent a happy day shopping in Northampton. Charlie managed to get her hair cut and Sam managed to talk me into buying him yet another version of the card game Munchkin. I didn't really mind, we'd spent a lot of riotous evenings playing this ridiculous game so another addition to the set wasn't a huge hardship. As the rain began again we slogged through Beckett's park, juggling purchases and polystyrene trays of fish and chips.

Charlie had only recently purchased a little model of a narrow boat, it was beautifully painted and very sweet and she had looked a little sad as we'd taken it to the post office and posted it off to her friend Louise, who still lived in Durham. "Do you think we'll ever have a normal summer holiday?" Charlie threw a chip to a rather fearless squirrel that had been shadowing us for the past ten minutes. Squirrels on land, swans on water, it occurred to me there was always some creature harassing you to share your dinner.

"Sure." I laughed as another squirrel shot down from a tree, stole the chip and vanished with a flick of the tail. The muggee screamed useless chattering threats at the mugger then doggedly followed us again in the hope of some more dinner coming his way. Sam quite happily gave in to his request. "Next year you'll be bored as anything, nowhere to go, long days of sunshine and mowing the lawn, you watch, you'll be begging us to take a boat trip before the second week is out."

Charlie was silent for a moment and carried on throwing chips at the squirrels (there was now a little gaggle of them and they were beginning to appear quite threatening). "I bet I bloody well won't," she muttered.

I pretended not to hear her.

Geoff turned up that evening, tired and irritated. Tired because he had basically been travelling since eight o'clock that morning and irritated because public transport, in his opinion, is unreliable and the other road users are just out to get him.

Snuggled up in bed that evening I shuffled over to give him a hug. "What time's your interview on Friday?"

"Three o'clock," came the short reply followed by a long yawn.

I took the heavy hint and asked no more questions.

By ten o'clock the next morning we were all ready to go our separate ways. The kids and I began untying the boat and Geoff waved us off before he headed toward the car. We weren't going far, about a mile down river where there was a nice mooring next to a lock. We had decided that while we waited for Geoff to transfer the car to the football ground then catch a bus from Irthlingborough to Northampton then walk along the towpath to the lock, we would visit Daily Bread which was an interesting little shop about twenty five minutes' walk away.

There are two Daily Bread co-operatives, one in Cambridge and one in Northampton; they are lovely shops which I try to visit as often as possible. Selling healthy and wholesome food, they are trying to walk that fine line where they are a supplier of products which are good value for money and offer a positive benefit to the customer and the environment. Based on some sound trading principles of profit without greed, fair trading and responsible retailing they stock things like nuts, flours, breads, fruits and a whole list of other things that it is difficult to get elsewhere or at least, difficult to get in bulk.

Back in the boat Charlie and I were attempting to find a dry place to store 5 kilos of rice when Amelia rang.

"Hey mum," she panted at me (she always sounds like she's running a race), "right," she didn't even give me time to say hello, "coming down on Friday."

"Oka —"

"Shhhh." She shushed me. "I need to remember all this or I'll forget to tell you."

"Oka —"

"Shhhh . . . now is it OK if I hand over the kids' Christmas present?"

"What?" My head spun a bit. "Isn't it still September?"

"Well, yes," Amelia huffed, "I ordered and paid for it when I still had a proper job and now it's turned up I need to get rid of it as quickly as possible, I think my living space is even smaller than yours."

247

"I doubt it." I looked over to where Charlie was trying to stuff the rice into a cupboard and making up swear words while she attempted the seemingly impossible.

"Anyway, is that all right?" Amelia pushed.

I sighed, "Yes I suppose so, what the hell is it anyway?" I stared over to where Charlie was gazing out of the window with her hand over her mouth.

"Never mind, it's a surprise." Amelia laughed, "I'll see you on Friday, OK?"

My attention shifted, Charlie was now banging for all she was worth on the window shouting, "Get off, get off."

"Amelia sweetie, I have to go, your sister's threatening something outside."

"I can hear her," Amelia was silent for a split second then said, "never mind, tell me all about it on Friday. See you, byeee." And she was gone.

Placing the phone in my pocket I looked over at the middle child. "What are you doing Charlie?" She took no notice just carried on banging on the window and screaming. I raised my voice over the din, "CHARLIE!"

Turning a distraught face toward me she pointed out of the window. Following her gaze I spied a short, squat black and tan dog holding something down with his paws. "What's he got?"

"A squirrel." Charlie banged on the window again, the dog looked toward her with a happy grin. "Stupid dog."

We watched as the dog, tail wagging, took a step toward the boat. Taking the opportunity to escape, its rather ruffled victim shot out from between its paws and straight up the nearest tree where it disappeared into the leaves.

"I really don't like those dogs at all," I said and shook my head, "new rule, when we decide to get a dog you can have anything but a staffy, I really don't know why so many people like them."

Charlie nodded vigorously.

"Hmm." I stared out of the window, then had a thought. "Mind you the squirrel can't have been very bright being caught by one of those lumpets, I mean let's face it they aren't exactly streamlined and they certainly can't climb trees.

Charlie raised her eyebrows as she considered that. "Good point," she finally conceded, "maybe the squirrel had suicidal tendencies and threw itself out of that tall tree in front of a dog that has fairly bad eyesight, a complete lack of speed and agility, and very little brain. Good grief, it must have been desperate."

I nodded. "Do you think it had to jump up and down for a while, wearing a sign saying 'I taste like chicken' before the staffy noticed it?"

Charlie nodded sagely. "Probably jumped out of a tree while blowing a horn."

We watched for a while as the dog meandered about at the bottom of the tree, finally I couldn't stand it any more and, knowing that there was no way I would leave a lost dog alone, I went outside, trying to ignore the kids staring worriedly out of the window at me. "Careful, Mum," Charlie shouted, "he's quite big, he may be a pit bull."

"Great," I muttered to myself, "that's exactly what I needed to hear."

I meandered over toward the dog, stopping only when it noticed me and whipped around to stare, its stocky body held entirely still, tiny, golden eyes unblinking as it watched me. I was slightly relieved to notice that its tail was slowly wagging. I slowly put my hand into my pocket and brought out a little packet of cheese cubes, taking out one I put it into my mouth and chewed slowly.

The effect was instantaneous: the dog broke into a run and came at me, jaws flapping. Knowing there was no way I could outrun it I stood still and looked determinedly away into the distance. The bite never came. I looked down to find a pair of eyes fixed on the cheese packet and the dog sitting at my feet in a perfect begging position. Paws up, eyes open, mouth hanging wide open in a pink grin, he was so cute and looked so expectant I couldn't resist giving him a pat as well as a piece of cheese.

We sat there for a couple of minutes, him performing tricks for cheese, he could sit, beg, hold out alternate paws and lie down. Once the cheese was finished he came and sat on my lap and attacked my ears with his tongue. I was just about to look for a telephone number on his collar when a deep voice pulled me up short.

"Oh, sorry, is he being a bother?" The dog leapt off my lap with a happy squeak and rushed over to a tall man who was holding the hand of a small blonde girl.

"Hi, no, not at all," I looked over at the dog who was jumping around the child. "He was on his own so I came out to see if he had a name tag."

The man smiled down at the dog and clipped on a lead. "He's usually very good but one of the squirrels did a fly-past right under his nose and he took off after it."

"He caught it." I grinned down at the dog.

"Really?" The man looked surprised. "Oh no is it, erm, demised?" He gave a nervous look at his daughter.

"Oh no, no," I assured him, "it escaped and ran up that tree."

"Thank goodness for that." He smiled with real affection down at the dog. "One squirrel saved from being licked to death." He held his hand out for the little girl to take and then passed her the lead. "Anyway, thanks for looking out for him." He gave me a wave then turned to the family, "Come on then, Emily, do you have Tosca's lead held tight this time?"

The little girl nodded and they all moved off down the path.

I turned to find Charlie standing behind me. "He was quite sweet actually," I informed her.

"Oh, Mum, you worry too much." She stared at the backs of the departing family. "I always knew that type of dog would be fine, it's just the owners, not the dogs."

She gave me a big grin and disappeared back into the boat leaving me with my mouth open, I really couldn't think of anything to say.

By the time Geoff returned, the rain was coming down in sheets and I have to admit it took a fair amount of willpower for us to struggle into our waterproofs and get out on to the back deck. Within a couple of hours Billing Aquadome floated past on our left and we headed off toward Wellingborough.

The rain obviously wasn't going to let up at all and Geoff, finally unable to take the gibbering, jittering, moaning thing standing next to him at the tiller (me), sent me inside to light a fire. Before I left we decided that although we actually had the time to get to Rushden & Diamonds we would stop for the night in Wellingborough and take a run across the park to Tesco, treat ourselves to something naughty for tea and settle down by our fire and watch Doctor Who while eating something sticky and horrible.

Pulling into Wellingborough at about four-thirty, I helped tie us up then went back to gently feeding wood into the fire. There was no way I was going outside to chop the wood into fire-sized pieces, so had rolled back the rug and was chopping it on the floor by the fire, much to Charlie's disgust.

"You never let me do that," she griped, "I always had to go outside."

"Hmm," I agreed, "that's because armed with a small axe you have the tendency to become a close relative of Attila the Hun and attack everything within a three foot radius." I paused "You're a danger to yourself and everyone around you."

Charlie watched me miss the piece of wood I was holding completely and bury the axe half an inch into the wooden floor. "And of course, you're so much better at it than I am." She flounced away to complain to Geoff about parental double standards, leaving me to hurriedly cover the chop marks in the floor with another piece of wood and arrange my facial features into something suitably innocent.

Watching the torrential rain outside, it had been decided by vote that we'd watch *Dr Who* first then with luck it would have eased off a little. Geoff was feeling in a good mood as it seemed that most of the windows had stopped leaking and we now only had two that were still letting in water, they had a bucket each to stop the floor from rotting away beneath them.

"Has anyone seen my lighter? I know I had it here a minute ago." I scanned the area around the fire. That was very odd, I had just been using it to re-light the fire for the third time. With it being so new, we were only supposed to place small fires to allow it to expand and contract, we'd had about four now and I was getting heartily tired of not being able to put some coal on and have it banked for the night.

Nobody even looked up, they were all mesmerised by the Doctor's antics. I have to admit I adore David Tennant but the lack of my lighter meant that the fire was cooling rapidly. "Come on guys, don't ignore me. Who's got my lighter?"

Geoff silently stuck his hand in his pocket and handed me another one. "That's not mine." Looking at the rapt faces I gave up. "Oh never mind, I'll use this one."

Pilling handfuls of woodchips around a single fire lighter I set fire to a spill of paper and started the whole thing going again. When the initial tinder was burning brightly I used both hands to round up as much of the wood shavings and chopping bits that I could find, then, placing them on the fire I began to layer on kindling.

"Do you think we could put some coal on this tonight?" I asked Geoff while staring longingly through the glass at the tiny little fire, "This rain is just getting heavier and my feet feel like little blocks of ice . . ." I was interrupted by a "WHUMPH!!" noise, the fire sort of shuddered and smoke puffed from every joint, hinge and glass plate. Throwing myself backwards, away from the fire, I crashed at the feet of those sitting on the sofa, sending cups of tea and glasses of lemonade spiralling away under the sofa. Charlie jumped to her feet, one hand over her mouth to protect herself from the clouds of smoke that had billowed from the fire and were now lurking above our heads and the other holding tight to Sam's arm (I don't know what she thought she was protecting him from). "What the hell was that?" she screamed at me.

Hoping that it wasn't going to do it again I gingerly crept forward and opened the glass door. The short sharp explosion had scattered the fledgling fire and even as I opened the door the glowing bits of wood were already dying away.

"I have no idea." I poked around in the dying embers then, deciding that it would be easier to clear the whole fire out, I riddled it hard and dragged out the ash pan.

There in the centre of the ash pan, glowing red hot, was the remains of my lighter. It was quite sad really, all that remained was the now scarred and dented metal cap, the wheel and a small piece of melted plastic. The rest of the gas container had obviously blown apart and then melted in the fire. I stared at it for a moment. "Erm . . . ah!"

254

Geoff peered over my shoulder and shook his head sadly. "Well at least you found your lighter."

Charlie caught on really quickly. "You threw your lighter on the fire?" she laughed.

Sam joined in. "Wouldn't that cause an explosion?" he asked without taking his eyes off the telly.

"Well, duh, Sam," Charlie sneered, "what do you think that big bang was?"

"I dunno," Sam muttered, "would you get out of the way please, look, the Daleks are on."

I sighed, obviously my son was one of "that" generation who felt that science fantasy and made-up stuff was far more exciting that an explosion in your own home.

For the next hour I dithered, coming up with excuses not to relight the fire just in case it went bang again, (or whumph!) Finally Geoff decided that we needed to go to Tesco and, as there was a slight break in the rain, we decided to make a dash for it, then light the fire when we got home.

Getting two children into waterproofs and out into a dark night to walk across a deserted park met with more than the normal amount of resistance. Heading for the lights of the supermarket, Charlie and Sam stayed unusually close to us. I could see their point. Empty parks are quite spooky, swings moving in the wind howling across the open spaces, and although I muttered comforting things to the kids even I was a bit freaked out and pleased to step on to the tarmac of the main road.

After an hour in Tesco, we were completely loaded up with shopping — UHT milk, bread — staring at all the tins and packets I decided that it would be a really, really good idea to sort out a fridge. I was fed up with my coffee tasting like it had chemicals in it and I had already lost two large slices of Brie when it had turned into Brie soup in the afternoon sun. I was devastated, I had really been looking forward to eating it.

But a fridge would have to wait, our electrics were temperamental and our bank balance was laughable. So we hoisted our bags and stepped away from the bright "come hither" lights of the supermarket and headed towards the park, heads down and hoods up in a desperate attempt to keep dry.

The wind and the rain, which had stopped just long enough for us to get to the supermarket, had returned with a vengeance and together they made walking an arduous slog. We staggered across the park only occasionally glancing up to make sure we were going in the right direction.

It was nearly impossible to see more than about five feet ahead so when a figure, accompanied by what appeared to be a dead rat on a piece of string, leapt out of the gloom right beside me I couldn't stop a little scream from escaping.

The figure stepped closer and a pair of glittering eyes peered at me from beneath a plastic hood. "Sorry, love, didn't mean to scare you."

Taking a deep breath in order to calm my racing heart, I grinned at him. "Don't worry, my fault, I had my head down against this wind and didn't see you." I struggled to talk as the screaming wind and rain kept sweeping my voice away over the river.

"Yup, it's a bit larey tonight." He laughed. "But I have to make sure that Joe here gets his walk." There, in a rapidly expanding puddle sat the saddest little dog I have ever seen. It was probably a Yorkshire terrier, but it was tiny and so completely soaked that it resembled a badly wrung-out dish mop in a plastic bag. Either unwilling or unable to buy it a proper coat, its master had purloined one of those elderly lady plastic rain hats, cut four holes in it for Joe's legs and tied it up under his stomach. The bright yellow daisies that decorated the clear plastic didn't really make it look any better, and the peak which sat around his neck like a vampire's fantasy collar just caught the rain and channelled it down poor Joe's back. The unfortunate animal sat on the floor, little legs akimbo and alternated between sneezing and licking the drops of water off its nose.

"Loves his walk does Joe," the old man said, "can't go a day without a walk. It wouldn't be good for him, so here we are out in all weathers." Joe started to shiver.

"He does look as if he's enjoying himself." I managed not to laugh as the poor little thing crept closer to his master's foot and settled under his long mac, then began sneezing again.

"Well, he can go on for hours, but it's definitely time for me to get back to my kettle and fire." Giving me a wave he turned away. "Come on, Joe, time for dinner."

Joe perked up an ear at the word dinner but unfortunately didn't manage to get out of the way of the swinging coat and got himself knocked face first into the wet grass. Completely oblivious to the plight of his pet, the old man sauntered away across the field dragging Joe on his back, he was now completely tangled in his long thin lead.

I contemplated running after him and extricating the poor animal but as they disappeared into the storm I noticed that Joe had managed to get all his legs under control and was once more up and walking. (And dripping, and sneezing, and coughing and limping.)

Shaking my head at the wretched animal's plight, I looked around for the rest of my family. They had, as expected, completely disappeared. Hurrying off in the general direction of the river I noticed that the park seemed even wilder when you are completely on your own. I silently thanked the local council for the lights they had installed on the waterfront. I have no night vision at all and without them I would have been almost completely blind.

Finally making it back to the boat, I noticed that the river had risen significantly and it was quite a hop to get back on to *Minerva*'s front deck which, devoid of drainage holes, now held two inches of water. As I opened the door a small fall of water cascaded over the door stop and down into the boat landing on a towel that Geoff had obviously placed there for just such a situation.

"Wow! It's quite scary out there." I stepped into the warm boat with a shudder. "I'm definitely not going out again and the river's coming up quite fast."

Geoff nodded around a large chocolate muffin. "Hmm, it is a bit wild. Well at least the weather forecast was right."

I wandered over and put the kettle on. "I think I would have preferred it to be wrong."

The kids sat silent and wide-eyed on the sofa. "What's the matter with you two?" I asked.

Charlie looked up at the ceiling. "Is it safe?"

I was confused. "Is what safe?"

"If it gets any heavier are we going to sink?" she said, huddling back under her blanket.

"No." Geoff was very firm (he has a good "firm voice"), "and it's definitely time for bed. When you wake up tomorrow morning the sun will be out and we may be a couple of inches higher than we were, but one night of heavy rain really won't make any difference."

Charlie and Sam nodded and headed off to brush their teeth before bed.

"Really?" I whispered to him, when I was fairly sure they were out of earshot, I was a little bothered by his noncommittal shrug.

"I've no idea," he whispered back, "the boat should be fine, we've been through heavy rain before, but as to how far the river's going to rise, I really don't know."

As I lay in bed that night I told myself it was Geoff's snoring that was keeping me awake but I knew that really it was the rain. I told myself I couldn't really feel the boat rising on the burgeoning waters but it really felt as though I could.

Geoff, as normal, was right. I awoke to bright sunshine streaming through the windows. With the fire on and banked for the night it was as hot as one of Dante's rings inside and there appeared to be an in-boat fog, I assumed it was just the heat drying off the wet floors and it was probably a good thing, but then rushed around opening doors, windows, hatches, and roof slide anyway. Once the heat had an escape route the temperature quickly returned to something a lot more tolerable.

The river was definitely higher and seemed to be flowing a little faster but it wasn't too bad, so with the sun shining and the birds singing we set off toward Rushden & Diamonds.

As the day progressed, the sky became more and more overcast. The wind, only this morning a summer zephyr, now howled around the boat, pushing us toward the far bank. Huge grey thunderheads loomed ahead of us and the shrinking patch of blue disappeared with horrible speed.

The rain hit around Higham Ferrers, Geoff and I ran around the last lock before Irthlingborough with our heads down and our collars up. It seemed to take for ever. *Minerva* bounced around in the lock like a puppy with a flea problem and no amount of power or rope seemed capable of making her stand still.

Finally, after some nervous moments we were on our way again. Three bridges to wander beneath then round the corner and we would be at the football ground where we could hide from the weather for a couple of days.

Geoff, needing the loo, left me at the tiller with many assurances he would be back before I needed him. Watching him edge his way along the slippery windswept gunwales I pulled my hat down over my ears and wished I had needed the loo first.

Noticing that we seemed to have picked up speed I knocked off the throttle as we slid under the iron bridge. This was the first of the bridges, I also noticed that the red light was blinking again, that was odd, it only did that when we were just ticking over.

Wincing as a bucketful of windswept, freezing cold rain hit me in the face I looked over the gunwales at the river and frowned as I noted how fast it seemed to be running. I knocked the throttle off a little further and found that I was at full stop and it was just the river that was carrying us along.

This really was not good. Without power to the prop I had no way of controlling the steering, as we passed at a good lick under the iron bridge I hit the horn hoping to tell Geoff that I needed him up here right NOW!

He's pretty good as husbands go and five or six short bursts on the horn brought him back up on deck. "What's up?" he frowned, I noticed he had rushed out without doing his trousers up.

I indicated the fleeing banks and shouted, "We're going a bit fast."

"Well slow her down." He shrugged like it was no problem.

"I can't, we're already on tickover."

"WHAT?" he peered at the throttle then at the banks which seemed to be gathering speed. Looking over the roof I noticed that the second bridge, the one carrying the A6, was rapidly approaching.

"WELL STICK HER IN REVERSE!" Geoff screamed over the howling wind.

261

I nodded, there was really no point in trying to talk. Slamming poor Min into reverse did slow her down but left me with absolutely no steering at all, so attempting to get around the right-hand bend before the bridge was a bit tricky as I had to keep putting her in forward, turning her a little then putting her into reverse to slow her down. Every time I gained a little headway the wind would slam us back into the side and the rising waters wafted us wherever they pleased, consequently we scraped through the bridge taking a little paint off our sides and some concrete dust from the bridge walls.

As we shot out from under the road bridge I could see the next and final bridge about two hundred yards away and true to form *Minerva* picked up speed and headed towards it like a horse with the bit between her teeth.

I couldn't slow down, there was no time. This bridge had sections beneath it through which I had to steer my runaway boat. A heroic bound onto the back deck he stuck his head down into his collar, closed his eyes and hung on for grim death.

I so nearly made it. As we came through one of the arches the bubbling and heaving water joined forces with the high winds and pushing our backside round, slamming our midsection very hard into the bridge. There was a horrible crunching grinding noise as Min heaved violently over to one side then a huge splash as she slapped back down into the water. Her backside rebounded out and then back again to hit the bridge just by the tiller. With the force of the bump my hand slipped from the tiller and I felt myself falling

262

backward. As the boat slid out from under me Geoff, moving far faster than I've ever seen before, grabbed my arm and dragged me back toward him.

As our nose shot out from beneath the bridge the surging water caught her and spun the front end around to the right. Hanging on to the tiller with some sort of death grip, I slammed her into full reverse trying desperately to ignore the screaming engine that was sending huge clouds of black soot into the air, covering two people that were leaning over the edge of the bridge staring in astonished silence as *Minerva* came to an extremely sudden halt in the weeds at the far side of the river; a sudden stop that threw both of us chest-first into the edge of the roof, knocking the breath out of both of us and leaving us bruised and disoriented.

There is something about an adrenaline rush that really makes you want to check that all your limbs are intact, so for a moment or two we stood there, trying to breathe normally again, moving bits of ourselves to make sure we were still in one piece. I had to smile as Geoff obviously had some difficulties disengaging his white-knuckled fingers from the handrail on the roof, then remembering that it was only that grip that had kept us both on the boat, sighed and thanked anyone who cared to listen that he'd managed to hold on at all. We could have both, so easily, ended up in the river and that would have been disastrous.

The engine was still screaming and with a sigh I killed it with the simple act of pressing the off button. Blessed silence descended broken only by the sound of wind and rain. "You all right?" I spluttered at Geoff.

Not waiting for an answer, I remembered the kids and rushed off down the gunwales to stick my head through the hatch. "Everybody alive?" I called.

"No we're bloody well not," Charlie called back.

"We're fine," Sam giggled.

"What the hell did we hit?" Charlie appeared in the kitchen with a blood-stained tissue in her hand, noting the horrified look on my face she looked down at it and shook her head. "Don't worry, it's just one of Sam's nosebleeds, he didn't bounce off anything, his nose just started bleeding, like it always does."

I sighed with relief, Sam's nose would bleed at the drop of a hat, he had already had one side cauterised and we were expecting to have to do the other side very soon.

"A bridge," I finally answered Charlie's question.

"You managed to hit a bridge," Charlie sneered at me, "big brick thing standing in the middle of the river, did you not notice it?"

I really didn't have time for sarcasm as I could feel the boat moving and we still had no engine.

"Gotta go, just checking you were both fine."

Charlie muttered something at me but I didn't hang about to find out what it was. I headed back to the tiller, Geoff was nowhere to be seen.

For a moment I had the strong urge to check over the side, but then I decided it was a silly idea and stuck my head into the engine room instead.

Sure enough, there he was fiddling with our erstwhile engine. "Will that thing start again?"

264

Geoff nodded. "I think so, give her some boot and see what happens."

At the turn of the key, Min's engine groaned and coughed but finally gasped and spluttered into life. Now came the difficult bit.

Turning her round in a fast-running river with strong winds and still pouring rain wasn't going to be easy and sure enough half an hour later we were still squished against the far bank, held there by the wind, the water flow, an underpowered engine and probably our own incompetence.

"I honestly don't know what to do." Geoff scratched his head and looked glum. "Every time we get six inches off the bank we just get pushed back on again, it's getting ridiculous and more worrying and the waters are getting higher by the second."

I stared down into the muddy green/brown water. It seemed to be getting faster as well. But even more worrying we had gathered quite a crowd. About ten people stood in the rain on the bridge above the river and stared down at our antics (for goodness' sake didn't they have homes to go to?).

I surreptitiously pointed them out to Geoff, "Hey, according to our crowd to problem ratio we have found ourselves with quite an issue."

Geoff grinned. "Come on, one last push," he said, handing me a pole, "you push one way and I'll push the other and we'll see if we can swivel her.

I shrugged, why not? We'd tried everything else.

It worked!! Sort of. With Geoff using his pole as a long leg, he sort of walked the back around, I slammed

265

the pole into the river and basically used it to keep Min's nose in one place. Eventually after a lot of pushing and shoving, swearing and sweating, we were the right way round.

I was soaked through. The rain ran off my hat ran straight down the collar of my wax jacket. I was so cold I really couldn't feel a flaming thing from my knees down. I grinned over at Geoff as we finally managed to start the hundred-yard cruise down river to the Moorings. Poor thing, he looked awful, his hair hung in wet rat-tails over his eyes and two small rivulets of water ran constantly from his beard. Having lost his hat, his ears were bright red and sore-looking. He really looked like a man in dire need of a cup of tea.

By five o'clock he had one, at least he had one under the sofa, he was so tired he had dropped off to sleep on my lap. I only found this out because Charlie told me later, evidently I was asleep with my head thrown back and huge snores rolling sonorously from my open mouth which I had pointed toward the ceiling. She said she didn't have the heart to wake us so had made Sam and herself tea. (I'm fairly sure they had beans and cheese on toast by the look of the three saucepans, three plates, a grill pan, a chopping board and various other items that were in dire need of washing up.) But the desire to help was there and we very much appreciated her thoughtfulness.

CHAPTER
TEN

Amelia's Turn to Cause Chaos

At about ten o'clock Geoff and I woke up enough to send the kids to bed and have a quick chat about his interview the next day.

"Are you looking forward to it?" I asked as I handed him yet another cup of tea.

Geoff gave a huge yawn and then grinned. "Not really, I don't think it will be half as exciting as today."

"I'll be happy if I never have another day as exciting as today. What time do you have to leave tomorrow?"

Geoff yawned again and said, "Well, I want to go into town and pick up some plumbing parts so I thought I'd head off about eleven, if that's all right with you."

I nodded. "Yup, Amelia is due here about midday which is about three in Amelia time, so she might be still here by the time you get back."

"Well, if I miss her, give her a kiss from me."

"I will." I joined him in another long yawning session. "Oh I give up on today. Let's go to bed."

It seemed like only ten minutes later when a gentle knocking on one of the front windows woke us back up. Shouting, "Hold on a mo!" I fumbled for Geoff's watch, ten o'clock! I stared up at the sky, what ten o'clock? Morning? Night? What had happened to the intervening hours? The soft knocking sounded again and I finally managed to throw myself out of bed and grab a big baggy sweatshirt which I threw on over my jammies.

"Hello?" Conscious of my state of déshabille, I peered cautiously around the front doors.

"Hi there!" A cheerful voice sang out.

I winced, coming out of the sun the figure in front of me was merely a black shape with a spectacular aura. The cheerful voice grated on my sleepy senses and I struggled to wake up enough to realise I wasn't experiencing an angelic visitation.

"Erm . . . hi?" I shook my head and tried to get my eyes to stay open without the aid of a couple of cartoon-like matches.

"Environment Agency." The figure blocked out the sun as he crouched down to talk to me.

"Hi." It was such a relief to identify a face. "What can we do for you?"

"Oh, nothing." He pointed down toward the lock. "We just needed to tell everybody that the river's closed for at least another two days. The locks are dangerous and the river's running way too fast so I'm afraid you're all going to be stuck here for a bit, and if it rains again it could be longer."

I stared down the moorings, there were another three boats parked on either side of us. Two smaller narrow boats, one unnamed, one called *Fairy Girl* and a large cabin cruiser.

As we stood there the occupants of these boats joined us and I made a silent vow that I would never, ever come out without getting properly dressed again, it was becoming very embarrassing. The man from the Environment Agency repeated himself for the benefit of the whole group then with a cheery wave and a promise to update us as soon as they had some news sauntered off toward his van, leaving us to introduce ourselves and talk about our various stalled journeys.

Audrey from *Fairy Girl* and her dog Bertie, a big black Labrador, didn't seem too bothered, they lived aboard and generally mooched about pleasing themselves throughout the summer and then when the weather turned inclement, the pair of them would winter in the south of France where they had a small villa. Nice life. John with Sally, a small elderly black and white collie, from the un-named boat in front of us were also unconcerned. They had no place to be and we were in a fairly good mooring spot, a village within walking distance, showers, a skip and good parking. Everything you could wish for actually.

The couple from the motor cruiser weren't so sanguine about the enforced break. They both had jobs and needed to be back at their mooring as soon as possible. So after a brief chat they disappeared with mobile phones to try and organise their hectic schedules. I remembered doing that, I didn't miss it a bit, trying desperately to get a few moments of peace but then life would catch up with you and kick you in the butt again.

With their disappearance, John and Audrey turned toward me. I became even more aware of my sartorial style statement and ran a suddenly sweaty palm down my reindeer-covered jammy bottoms.

"Well," I said, aiming for a breezy tone, "if we're stuck, we're stuck, I'd better go and tell the husband, I'll catch up with you all later." And with a cheery wave I moved nonchalantly back into the boat.

A pair of eyes peered at me, owl-like from beneath the covers, "Wass going on?" Geoff yawned.

I put the kettle on. "We appear to be rendered motionless for a couple of days."

"Wha?" Geoff struggled to focus on me.

"That was the Environment Agency, they've banned all travel on the river until it goes back down to a manageable level."

Geoff frowned, obviously trying to sort out all the connotations of this statement. "Well that should be all right, shouldn't it?" He leaned up on one elbow and peered myopically at me. "I've got the interview today and we can stay here tomorrow and I'll move the car about a day's ride down river, then we can move on the next day." He yawned hugely then yelped as a wide-awake son landed squarely in his midriff.

At eleven o'clock I waved him off into another bout of rainy weather. He was not a happy bunny, after years and years of high-end interviews he felt underdressed if he wasn't wearing a suit and tie but this certainly wasn't that sort of job, an in-house electrician to a large printing works wasn't going to wear a suit very often.

So clean and pressed but suit-less, he had wandered off into the rain in a bit of a grump, obviously feeling that something important was missing. Watching him go I felt an odd frisson of worry, what if he didn't like the job but got offered it. With our finances glaring us in the face I knew he would agree to anything just to keep us afloat.

Laughing at my horrible pun, I wandered about feeding children and generally tidying things away. The kids amused themselves by swearing at the weather and playing some sort of complicated card game. Knowing that I had a million little jobs to do on the boat, I settled down with a good book.

By twelve o'clock the dripping sounds in the boat had taken on the intensity of Chinese water torture. Every time I started a new paragraph the dripping sounds would take on a new tone, then stop for a moment then continue at an increased rate before settling down to a monotonous drip again.

I couldn't stand it any more and I certainly couldn't concentrate on *Hard Boiled Wonderland and the End of the World* by Murakami, this is not a book you can flick through at the best of times, the dripping water made it impossible to even hold the thing without wanting to jump up and down and fling it down the boat.

Sighing, I dumped the book on the sofa and started hunting for the sealant. Damn Amelia, why couldn't she be on time for once, then I'd have a good excuse not to do anything.

271

"She's here!" About half an hour later Charlie's voice dragged me away from desperately trying to poke silicone into the sides of the window with a cotton bud, I was surrounded by little plastic sticks and the silicon was taking on a decidedly lumpy, fluffy sheen.

I huffed, this was ridiculous, the windows were beginning to look so much like badly iced cakes that I was tempted to stick little snowmen and plastic figures of children on sledges along the sills. I ran a finger around the window in an attempt to remove the excess silicone, epic fail: I just managed to get a snow drift at one end.

"MUM!" Charlie bellowed again, "Amelia's here."

"OK, OK." I sniffed and ran my soiled finger down my work jeans, the jeans were getting to the point where they were so stiff with silicon they stood up by themselves. I had tried washing them on several occasions but they, unlike the flaming windows, were completely waterproof, and on top of that I'd had to crack them to bend them into the machine.

"MUM!!" Charlie stamped down the boat. "I've been calling you, didn't you hear me?"

I pretended surprise; it was easier than trying to explain why I was ignoring her. "Sorry, sweetheart, these windows are driving me crazy," I paused and scowled at the offending glass, "do you think there could be a hole in the steel where the water's coming in and it's not the windows at all?"

Charlie shook her head in exasperation, completely ignoring my leaking window woes. "Come on, Mills is here and she's got a big box."

I frowned. "Wow I hope she hasn't brought her washing with her. She's going to be really irritated when I throw it in the river and poke it with a stick."

Charlie theatrically rolled her eyes and physically turning me round, pushed me down the boat.

"Hey, Mum." Amelia stepped into the boat with a huge grin.

Now there are certain psychic tendencies that come with kids, they're like free gifts. I looked at her wide eyes behind her glasses, I noted the way she wouldn't actually look at me, I also noted the way that she talked almost incessantly to Chaos and Disorder which usually meant that if I couldn't get a word in I couldn't ask awkward questions.

Luckily Sam came to my rescue.

"What's in the box, Mills?" He bounced up to the door and stared out at the box slowly collapsing as the rain saturated the cardboard.

"Yes," I asked slowly, "what *is* in the box, Mills?"

Amelia sighed. "Look, I know you're probably not going to be happy, but as I said earlier, it's an early Christmas present for these two, I've bought it now before I become completely broke by being a student barmaid." She shuffled again.

"What's in the box, Mills?" I stared down the gangplank and gasped as the box took a little leap sideways. "Oh God, there's something alive in there!"

Well, honestly I couldn't have said a more stupid thing, on hearing the word "alive" Sam and Charlie lit out of the boat like they were tied to a rocket, leaving me to glare at my oldest who just stared at the ceiling and grinned maniacally. "What have you done?"

Amelia took a deep breath and finally met my eye. "Look, you said they could have one, I got him cheap, and the kids need cheering up because they're living on this heap." She gave me an evil smile. "And do you know the best thing?"

I folded my arms across my chest and glared harder. "What?"

"This present makes me 'The best sister in the world' and that's what I'm aiming for." She patted me on the arm. "You're going to love him, just give him time to grow on you."

I closed my eyes. "Please tell me it's anything but a flaming cat, I really hate cats."

"Mum, Mum! Look." Charlie rushed up the gangplank with a little black lump in her arms, closely followed by her brother shouting, "Let me see, let me see him."

"Amelia's bought us a puppy!"

"Oh God. No!"

Charlie, knowing me all too well, rushed over and dumped the squirming thing into my arms.

Amelia winced. "He might smell, he was a bit sick in the car, and he's twelve weeks old, pedigree but he hasn't any papers."

"Oh great."

I looked down at the sad-looking little thing that was trying desperately to hide its head in my armpit. I wrestled him out and held him out at arm's length and gave him a good looking-over. He was an odd-looking

274

article; all black except for a white chest and one white leg, he looked like he was wearing a plaster cast, a white shirt and a dicky bow due to the little butterfly-shaped black spot under his chin. He also had the oddest eyes, stuck rather far back on either side of his head, he gave the impression of being a black furry fish, with legs.

Dangling in my hands he wagged his long tail, yawned and blinked at me. I cuddled him back into my arms. "What's the matter with his eyes, why are they stuck on the side of his head like that?"

Amelia shrugged and looked shifty. "I assume as his head grows they'll move to the front, all the others looked the same."

The puppy twisted on to his back and lay with all four paws in the air, he started to hiccup, then looking a little surprised, twisted quickly over to his front and vomited down my chest. Amelia winced as I howled.

By the time I had got changed, he had woken up a little bit and, obviously feeling better, was happily jumping on Sam's head, Charlie was fussing around making a list of all the things we would need for him, bed, collar, food and Amelia had made coffee.

As I sank down on the sofa he came waddling over and tried to climb on to my lap. I sighed, Geoff was going to have blue conniptions. "All right, all right." I gently pushed him and his overexcited tongue away from my face. "So," I looked around at the three hopeful faces. "What are we going to call him?"

Leaving Charlie to watch both Sam and Mortimer (the name suited him, with his black suit and dickey bow he looked like someone's elderly uncle), Amelia

275

and I wandered into Irthlingborough to pick up all the dog stuff. Tiny collar, lead, bowls, food, bed, squeaky toys the bill came to around seventy quid. Geoff was really going to have a fit.

Walking back it began to rain again, Amelia was fine, she was carrying the dog bed and found the easiest way to keep dry was to turn it upside down and wear it as a large hat.

"Just a little question." I tucked the food under my coat in a vain effort to keep it dry. "With the boat in disarray, lots more travelling in front of us, all sleeping in one place and trying to avoid the leaks with all this rain, did it, at any point, occur to you that this might not be the best time to throw a twelve-week-old puppy into the mix?"

The one thing I can say about my daughter is that she is completely unable to deal with sarcasm; she gave me a sunny smile from under the dog bed and shook her head. "No, not really, I knew you'd love him."

"Actually, that's another thing," I said, frowning at her, "why is he so old, you usually get puppies at about eight weeks, don't you?"

She nodded. "Well, at least he's had all his injections already, it would have been a real pain if you'd had to keep him in the boat for four weeks until he was safe to go out."

"Yes, but why is he so old?" I stopped and turned to look at her. "Come on, what's wrong with him, we've never managed to get a fully intact animal yet, they're always either broken or insane."

Amelia had the grace to look a little sheepish. "That's the reason I got him cheap, he's the runt of the litter and he's only got one . . . erm . . ." she paused and then took a deep breath and muttered, "testicle."

"Oh great, so half a dog then," I laughed.

"Oh, Mum, I had to take him, I've been watching the pups since they were born and with all the others gone, he was all on his own and they were talking about giving him away, he could have gone to anyone. I knew you'd look after him and the kids would love him." She gave me another big smile from under the dog bed.

I nodded and gave up, I never could resist a charity case, it looked as though Mortimer was here to stay. As we hurried toward the boat I could hear Sam and Charlie laughing as the dog entertained them. Amelia looked at me and grinned. "See, couldn't have brought anything better to cheer them up, could I?"

Leaving Chaos, Disorder and Fuzzy fish to amuse themselves, Amelia and I sat over drinks. "What is he exactly?" I laughed as Mortimer came hurtling past with one of Sam's socks in his mouth, the kids chased him giggling and shouting which just spurred him on to ever more ridiculous antics, they were all having a fine old time.

Amelia stuck her nose into her tea and muttered "Stffforthpshire pthll terrior."

"What?" I tapped my finger on the table. "Is that thing a staffy?

Amelia winced and nodded.

"What were you thinking?" I stood up and grabbed Mort as he shot past and put him on my lap. "Calm

277

down," I called, putting a hand up to Charlie and Sam, "give him a break or he'll be sick again." Mortimer yawned hugely and burped, I held my breath wondering if I was about to have to change into yet another set of clean clothes.

Sitting on my lap with his tail moving at a blur the wide gold eyes stared into mine then slowly began to close, his big head sagged onto my arm and with another yawn he was unconscious. I frowned then sighed, he really was very cute.

Gently holding Mort in one arm I waved the other at Amelia. "You know what I think of these dogs, they're vicious and stupid and shouldn't be around children, you're going to have to take him back." I paused and looked down at Mort who had opened his mouth slightly, I could see his little pink tongue in the darkness behind the white, needle sharp teeth. He snorted in his sleep and turned his head so it was resting on my chest then heaved a huge happy puppy sigh.

Amelia just looked at me. "They're not vicious, they just get bad press, honestly, Mum, this is one of the best dogs with kids, they call them 'nanny dogs'."

I smiled as Mort started a series of little snores, his big paws twitching and flapping slightly, he really, really was terribly cute. "I'll give him a month's trial." I pointed a finger at her. "And that's only if he lasts ten minutes after Geoff gets home."

"Oh yeah." Amelia looked around the boat. "He's gone off to his interview hasn't he . . ." she paused for a moment, "what time's he due back? I wouldn't want to miss him."

"About sixish." I smiled as Mortimer made little grunting noises and tried to bury further into my arms.

At five to six, Amelia made her excuses and scarpered, she cut it really fine as it only seemed seconds after she left that Geoff walked through the door. Mortimer, refreshed and refuelled by his long sleep and a big bowl of food, bounced over to welcome this newcomer.

Geoff stared down at the cavorting pup and nudged him gently with his boot. "What . . . is . . . that?" he enunciated slowly. The boat went silent.

Sam, once again decided to break the tension with a nervous laugh. "It's a dog, Dad, what did you think it was?"

Geoff gently disengaged Mort from his sock. "And where did it come from?"

"It was a surprise present from Amelia," Sam said, then wandered over and picked Mort up, "it's our Christmas present."

Geoff nodded and looked over to me. "Was it a surprise to you as well?"

I nodded and shrugged.

"And where is Amelia?" Geoff raised his eyebrows, I noticed he was still talking very slowly, this really wasn't a good sign.

Charlie piped up, "Ran away when you phoned mum and told her you'd be home in five minutes." she tickled Mortimer under the chin and laughed when he fell over trying to grab her hand in his mouth. "You probably passed her on the way in."

Geoff stared at the pup with extreme distaste. "We can't keep him," he said, ignoring the howls of protest from the kids. "This is ridiculous, having a puppy in amongst all this lot." He waved a hand around at the devastation. Mortimer, his eye caught by the waving hand, leapt up and sank his teeth into one of Geoff's fingers, Geoff yelped, I winced that sort of behaviour really wasn't doing his case much good.

That evening, with Chaos, Disorder and Mort finally fast asleep having worn themselves out chasing each other about all afternoon, Geoff turned to me with that "serious" look on his face, he sighed and picking Mort from my lap where I was happily cuddling him, he put him gently in his bed.

"He has to go back, this is ridiculous." He pointed down at the untidy piles of sleeping children. "Look at us, we're crammed in here like sardines in a tin and you really think that adding a boisterous dog to this mix is a good idea?"

I decided to nip this in the bud now. "I said to Amelia he could have a month's grace." I held up a hand as Geoff frowned. "Look at it this way, if he chews anything in here at the moment it's really not going to make the slightest bit of difference, we promised them a puppy months ago, better he learns to deal with his new family now while we are all up in the air than later when the boat's all beautiful and he decides to cut his teeth on the new woodwork."

Geoff sighed and said, "Well, I suppose . . ."

"And another thing, the kids have been really happy today, it will give them something to concentrate on, I know I'll end up looking after him but that's OK, I like dogs and I like something that will drag me out for a walk."

Geoff waved his punctured hand at me. "Yes, but aren't they dangerous, isn't there a lot of talk about putting them on the dangerous dogs register?"

He had a point, I stared over at the snoring, twitching fuzz ball and shook my head. "I don't know, I checked them out on the net earlier and evidently not, they're good with kids, and love to play and will take a fair amount of abuse from little ones. Let's just see how he goes, shall we? I promise I won't keep a dangerous dog, any signs that he's vicious and he's gone in a flash, all right?"

Geoff nodded reluctantly then snorted as Mort rolled over on to his back exposing his tummy to the warmth from the fire, his little jowls vibrated as he snored and his paws twitched continuously. Geoff shook his head. "He's not very elegant."

I laughed and got up to take the tea cups out. "He matches the rest of the family then, doesn't he?"

The next morning dawned bright and sunny. It actually looked as though the rain had finally stopped. Giving in to a huge yawn I struggled to sit up in bed then froze as a strange noise halted me in my tracks.

Rolling over I came face to face with Mortimer who was happily slapping his tail against the bed, giving my nose a quick lick he shuffled backwards, back under the covers and giving a huge happy sigh closed his eyes again. Geoff opened his.

"What is the puppy doing in the bed?" I lifted the covers and stared into the warm darkness, a pair of shining eyes opened minutely and I swear he gave me a sleepy smile.

"Ah." Geoff sat up and rubbed a hand over his mad morning hair.

"Well?" I frowned down at the floor. "There's no way he'd be able to jump up here yet."

"Um . . ." Geoff gave me a contrite look. "He woke me up at three o'clock this morning, with his crying and when I went to pick him up to put him back in his bed, he was shaking and his ears were cold, so I put him between us and he settled down immediately."

I laughed. "Yeah I bet he did." I poked Mort in the tummy and the tail wagged gently, making a swishing noise as it performed a perfect pendulum across the sheet, then I poked Geoff. "You are a complete fraud, you do know that, don't you?"

Geoff assumed a lofty expression. "I'm sure I have no idea what you're talking about." He began dressing. Mortimer, sensing movement and obviously needing to go out staggered to his feet, Geoff grabbed him and made for the door while I rushed around trying to find his lead.

When all the necessary bodily functions had been taken care of and the kids had shot off with the dog to see if he would play ball, Geoff and I sat over a quiet cup of tea.

"So how do you feel about Mortimer this morning?" I pushed.

Geoff shrugged and said, "He'll probably be OK, he seems fairly open-minded about how and where he lives." Then startling me, he leapt to his feet. "Oh, I forgot to tell you, while you were outside I had a phone call, I've got that job!"

Oh, that was a huge relief, it meant that we could travel down to Cambridge and he'd have a job waiting for him when he got there. I grinned at him, I could feel the grin failing as he looked troubled.

"What's the matter, didn't you want it?"

"Oh yeah, that's not the problem." Geoff ran a hand through his hair again and sighed. "They want me to start on Monday."

"What! No!" I gaped at him. "We've got at least another week of travelling yet, and we can't even start out until they tell us that the river's safe to travel, it might stay up for another two or three days."

As I normally did in a moment of crisis, I leapt up and put the kettle on. "We can't only travel at weekends because they're closing Denver sluice for repairs, so if we don't get there before they close it we won't be able to get through for weeks."

Geoff leaned forward and grabbed my arm. "What! When did you find out about this?"

"Yesterday," I replied, shaking my head and wiping a hand down my face, "I was talking to the EA guy that came to look at the moorings and he told me, so I checked on the net and he's right we have less than two weeks to get to Denver or we'll be stuck for two months."

Geoff slumped back onto the sofa with a look of absolute agony. "That's it, I can't take the job, there's no way we can get there in time if I do." He put his head in his hands.

We stood in silence for a couple of moments, the only sound was the kettle whistle winding itself up to a full hysterical scream. I turned the gas off then, glancing out of the window, waved to Audrey as she came past with Bertie. Watching them meander toward *Fairy Girl*, a germ of an idea planted itself in my mind; it really was the only solution.

Handing Geoff a cup of tea I tapped him on the head. "I'll take her." I gulped as I said it, not something I wanted to do, I have to admit, but it really was the only way.

Geoff looked up at me. "What, on your own?" He shook his head. "Marie, she's huge, and with the river running this fast . . ." he tailed off and stared into his tea, looking worried.

I flapped a hand at him. "Ah, don't worry it'll be fine, Charlie's a lot of use these days, at least there's two of us that can drive and she knows how the locks work, we'll be OK." I kicked him gently then gave him an airy grin as he looked up at me. "We'll be fine." I pointed out of the window. "Audrey travels by herself all the time, if she can do it, so can I."

"Audrey runs a 45 foot boat,. It's tiny compared to this thing." Geoff frowned.

"Geoff," I replied, handing him a biscuit, "tell me what choice we have? The first payment on the boat is due in less than four weeks."

He groaned again and dunked the biscuit into his tea. "None."

Finishing his tea, he stood up and put his coat on. "If you lot are going to be travelling on your own I'd better make sure that engine isn't going to let you down." He wandered toward the door then turned and looked at me. "I'm not really happy about this, you know."

I forced a laugh. "Ah, go on, it'll be fine." I grinned at him as he shook his head again and climbed out of the boat. When I was sure he was out of the way I sank down onto the sofa with my coffee. He wasn't happy about it! Well I wasn't happy about it either, I wasn't happy about it at all.

We spent Sunday trying to keep dry. The sky, dark from horizon to horizon, just continued to pour its contents upon the earth. The windows leaked, the kids were bored cooped up in a long narrow tube, Mortimer got into everything and Geoff wandered around trying to make sure that everything was "ship shape" before he headed off to a new job.

On his third pass through the boat, carrying tools and more bits of unidentifiable equipment I finally grabbed him and made him sit down.

"Look, working yourself up about this isn't going to help." I handed him a cup of tea and launched a packet of ginger nuts towards him. He narrowly missed catching them and only managed to smack the packet with the side of his hand. The packet split and

Mortimer who had happily been investigating the contents of Geoff's tool bag suddenly found he was standing amidst a rain of falling biscuits. This was a good game. He ate two before we could grab him and managed to snag another and took off to his favourite hiding place beneath the new fire.

The first time he had done this I'd been horribly worried, but he loved the warmth and it had the secondary effect of keeping all the dust bunnies at bay beneath the fire. Every time he emerged he was covered in dust and ash and to keep the place clean we just had to throw him outside and let the wind waft it all away. It worked rather well.

Geoff dunked a biscuit into his tea. "The river's not going down at all." He stared out of the window at the falling rain. "You could be stuck here for days."

I shrugged and grinned, Mortimer had finished his biscuit and was now staring at me from beneath the fire, his big paws sticking out on to the tiles and his shiny eyes peering from out of the gloom.

"Marie!" Geoff poked me. "Could you possibly focus for just a moment."

"Hmm hmm?" I grinned and turned resolutely away from watching the fire (Mort had turned around and there was now just a long black tail sticking out and waving at me).

"Look." I picked up a biscuit and dunked it in my tea, there was a sudden scrabbling from beneath the fire. "The river's up, we aren't going anywhere until the EA tell us we can, so what's the problem, we're stuck." A cold wet nose poked me in the hand and I surreptitiously handed Mort my half-eaten biscuit. "There's nothing we can do about it so we do nothing, no point in moaning, I'm stuck here and you have to go to work." I picked up another biscuit and dunked it in my tea. Mort climbed up on the sofa and grinned at me, I sighed and handed him the biscuit.

Geoff heaved himself to his feet and wandered over to put his cup in the sink. "I suppose so," he leaned on the kitchen unit and stared out into the rain. "I don't want to go to work yet. I want to see us back to Cambridge, I don't like leaving you and the kids on your own." He sighed again and frowned up at the sky. "What are we going to do if this doesn't stop and we can't get through Denver?"

"Geoff," I said, heaving myself to my feet, I joined him in staring out of the window, "let's not borrow trouble eh?"

Geoff nodded then, staring over at the sofa, he gave me a kiss. "I'll put the kettle on, you find some more biscuits."

"OK." I gave him a hug then asked, "Don't you like ginger nuts?"

"Love them." Geoff handed me a roll of kitchen towel. "But the dog ate them all while we were talking and he's just thrown up.

I whipped around, Mortimer had indeed been rather ill, and was now sitting on the floor staring at the mess he'd made with a very guilty look, getting to his feet he looked up at me and gave a slow wag of his tail, then bending down he heaved again and added to the mess on the rug. I sighed. "Great, just great."

Seven thirty the next morning and Mortimer and I were in the car park waving Geoff off to his new job.

"Don't do anything daft will you." Geoff leaned out of the car window, wincing as the wind drove the rain into his face.

"Like what?" I untangled Mort for the third time from his lead (he really wasn't getting the hang of it very well) "My whole plan for the day is do some shopping, tidy up, probably read a book and empty buckets of water from under the windows."

"OK." Geoff leaned further out of the car for a kiss goodbye. "See you later." And with that he was off.

I waited until the car had disappeared out of the car park then wandered back toward the river. Mortimer, finally deciding that rain was something he really didn't like, bounding ahead of me.

As I headed toward *Minerva*, I was hailed by Brian the man from the unnamed boat.

"Hello, hello and good morning," he grinned up at the grey and purple sky, "great day, great day." He paused and sauntered over, seemingly oblivious that his shirt was rapidly becoming sodden. "So who's this little chap then," he bent over to give Mortimer a rub and was promptly knocked sideways by twenty pounds of loving and over-enthusiastic puppy. "Wow, he's strong isn't he." He laughed trying to keep Mort's flapping tongue away from his bare knees. (Who wears shorts in the rain?) "Have you been abandoned for the day?" he indicated the car park with a wave of his hand, "I saw hubby heading off into the outer wilds," he dropped his voice to a sonorous whisper, "where the normal folk live." He gave a theatrical shudder and laughed. "I'm glad I'm retired."

Finally managing to untangle the wretched pup from his long lead I laughed. "Yes he's gone off to earn money, and I'm left tending the livestock." Mortimer made a leap for the boat, came up short at the end of his lead and began to cry. I sighed. "Hang on a minute, Brian, let me just get Pestilence into the warm."

By the time I got back to him, Brian's shirt was now so wet it was turning transparent: I could see the string vest beneath. I huddled deeper into my coat and prepared for at least ten minutes of small talk about the weather.

Through the window of *Minerva* I could see Mortimer staring out at the rain he seemed to be smiling, you can go off your pets.

"I don't suppose you're feeling strong, are you?" Brian shuffled a bit in embarrassment. "I was hoping to ask Geoff but he scooted before I could catch up with him."

"Well," I hesitated, "It depends how strong you want me to be, I'm pretty strong for a *girly*." I put as much sarcastic emphasis as I could on the last word but it didn't really have much of an effect.

"I need to get something into that skip." Brian pointed to the rubbish skip. "It's not that heavy, it's just unwieldy and I can't do it by myself." He shuffled again. "I'll understand if you say no."

"What is it?" I put my hood up and winced as the water that had collected there rolled in a short wave down my neck.

"A fridge." Brian gave a sort of hopeful grin. "It really is quite small I just can't get it out of the boat over the side and then up into the skip."

"A fridge?" I raised an eyebrow at him. "I suppose it's broken, is it?"

"What?" Brian frowned. "Oh no, it works, it's just old and needs a really good clean. I bought a bigger one, but I shouldn't have really. It's 12v and 240v and everything, but there's a hole in the plastic moulding of the door and really it has seen better days."

"How would you feel about throwing it into my boat rather than the skip?" I gave him a hopeful look. "We haven't got a fridge and I'm having a lot of trouble keeping milk and other stuff fresh."

Brian hopped up and down a bit with a huge smile, his big feet in their open-toed sandals making a flapping, slapping sound as he leapt about in the puddles. "That's a brilliant idea, fantastic!"

I looked at him, worried that he might be being a little sarcastic, but he was honestly ecstatic about the idea. "Come on," he said and turned toward his boat, "let's get it into yours now, oh I love this idea, I love things being reused and passed on, that's how I got it, you know."

Half an hour later and I was the proud owner of a small, slightly dingy fridge. It had a wooden-effect door and one of its feet had fallen off so it rocked if you nudged it, but it had a small freezer compartment and all its bits were there so it was great. I have to admit I had opened the door with a certain sense of trepidation, but it really wasn't that bad at all. There were some odd blackened "things" lurking in the corners, a couple of rings where milk bottles had stood and the seal around the door was a complete e-coli breeding pen but on the whole it was OK, certainly nothing that some strong bleach solution wouldn't solve.

After about half an hour I had finished and was carefully pouring the used chemicals into an old coke bottle so that I could throw it into the skip. Wedged up on folded cardboard, polished and scrubbed the little fridge hummed away and was wonderful. I placed Lu's empty cage on top of it and was just standing and admiring my handiwork, when screams of laughter made me jump.

"Mum, MUM!" Charlie screamed at me from the sofa, "You have to come and see this."

Taking a last glance at my handiwork I wandered off down the boat, I'd only taken my eyes off them for half an hour, what was going on this time?

"What's up?" I enquired.

"Look, look," Charlie pointed at the dog, she could barely speak for laughing, tears rolled down her bright red cheeks.

"What?" I stared at the dog, "What's the matter with him?"

Mortimer was in the corner, eyes wide and ears flat he looked the very picture of terror. He shook and made little gruffling sounds, he had backed up so hard against the television cabinet that his front legs were on his little round hairless stomach and his back legs stuck out in front of him.

I took a step toward him, both kids screamed at the same time. "Mum stand still!" Charlie bellowed.

"Argh, Mum, watch out for Lu!" Sam screamed at the same time.

"Lu?" I looked down into Mort's bed and there was the hamster. She had her teeth locked into the very end of one of Mort's bone-shaped biscuits. The Bonio was longer than she was and obviously heavy as she seemed only capable of going round and round in circles with one end of the biscuit acting as an anchor, she seemed to be getting quite cross about the whole thing. Mortimer had his eyes fixed on the angry little rodent. Every time she put it down, taking a moment to shout and swear at her recalcitrant snack, his eyes would widen again and he would once again attempt to levitate himself up the wall.

"Oh, for goodness' sake." Leaning over I grabbed Lu and, making sure that she had her teeth firmly embedded in the biscuit and wasn't in danger of attaching herself to my fingers, I manoeuvred her to the kitchen table. Grabbing a handful of muesli I laid out a trail for her and as she pottered off, happily filling her cheeks with the cereal, I stole back the biscuit and put it in Mort's bed.

Mortimer wasn't so easy to appease. It took nearly twenty minutes to coax him on to the sofa, where he shook and whimpered for another half an hour, before finally calming down and flopping out into a terror-filled sleep.

"What happened?" I frowned at the kids who were still grinning cheerfully. "No, Sam, take that maniac rodent away and put her in her cage, she needs to do something with all that food she has stashed in her face." Lu blinked at me from Sam's fist, her fat cheeks pushing up her eye sockets and giving her a slightly smiley look.

Sam wandered off with a huff, leaving Charlie to explain. "Mort and Lu were on the sofa, and Mort was holding his biscuit between his paws and just licking it." She looked over at the dog and sniggered again. "Sam decided that they should meet and we were just waiting for Mort to have a go at her then we'd snatch her up and she'd be fine." She shrugged and said, "But it didn't work like that, Sam put Lu down and she marched up to the dog, bit him on the lip then nicked his biscuit. He screamed and leapt off the sofa and into his bed, Lu and the biscuit got bounced into the air and went over the edge and landed in Mort's bed as well." Charlie grinned obviously remembering the furore that had gone on. "Well, Mort panicked as she landed at his feet and took off over the other side of his bed and into the cupboard."

Charlie stopped for a moment and looked up at me, her smile faded slightly as obviously the look on my face didn't quite meet with her memories of the incident. "We did try to catch her but she kept growling at us and wouldn't let go of the biscuit so we were scared to pick her up and then the dog had a hissy fit and we just couldn't stop laughing." Her voice tailed off as she looked at me and she frowned, "Erm . . . poor dog?" she hazarded a sentiment.

"Hmm, did you, even for a moment, think what would have happened if Mort had actually managed to bite her?" I sighed. Obviously entertainment was needed or else I was going to have two psychotic animals. Actually scrap that, I was going to have another psychotic animal. Lu was already wearing that badge and holding an axe. "Come on get your coat." I shouted the instruction again down the boat for Sam to hear. "We're going out."

Charlie looked aghast out of the window, the rain was now so hard that it was impossible to see anything through the glass — it was just a smeared grey impressionist scene. "But it's raining and Geoff's got the car."

"That's right." I got to my feet and making a quick trip down the boat came back with wellies and coats and umbrellas. "You obviously have time on your hands and if it takes torturing a puppy and a gnarly hamster to fulfil your need for amusement then we need to go and run off some of that energy, don't you think?"

Charlie frowned. "This is a punishment, isn't it."

I handed her a coat. "Give the lady a cigar." I smiled.

That evening I relayed the story to Geoff in an attempt to cheer him up. His first day at the new job had been an unmitigated disaster.

"There's nothing for me to do," he moaned, "we all just sit about drinking tea, the day's so long."

I felt awful, he had really enjoyed his job in Durham. I tried to make light of it. "Look, it's your first day, maybe they thought they were giving you an easy time and it'll get busier."

Taking a sad sip of tea he put his head in his hands, muffling his voice. "Nope, the other lads said it's been like this for months, they were really surprised when I walked in, they hadn't even been told I was coming."

I sighed. This had not been in my plan when I had physically moved my family to suit my whims back on to the boat and into a lifestyle that I loved. The kids weren't talking to me after having a very wet walk this afternoon, and now it seemed that Geoff was blaming me as well because of his job. I felt rather sick. "I'm really sorry," I muttered.

Geoff looked up at me from under his hair and gave me a tired grin. "It's not your fault, what are you sorry for?"

"I moved us here, I made you give up your nice job, I made you take this one." I could feel my throat tightening "I'm really sorry. Maybe we should have just stayed where we were, I'd have got over it, eventually."

Geoff frowned. "Well, thanks a lot."

I could feel my lip begin to quiver. "What for?"

He shuffled over the sofa and put his arm around me. "Thanks for thinking me such a pushover."

"What?"

"Do you really think I am so weak-willed that I would be pushed into something I didn't want to do or thought it was a really stupid idea?" He gave me a nudge. "Do you remember that time, you wanted to move to Canada?" he asked, raising his eyebrows at me, "and the alpaca farm?"

I laughed and nodded. "Yes, yes OK, I get your point."

Geoff gave me a hug and got to his feet heading for the kettle. "Oh no!"

"What?" His pained tone raised me from my reverie; I still think the alpaca farm would have been a good idea.

"Haven't we got any milk?" He looked around the little kitchen, searching for the cool box.

"Oh yes, I forgot to tell you, it's in the fridge."

"Fridge?"

"Yep, I intercepted it as it was heading for the skip." I gave him a grin, "Not quite my first skip-diving escapade because it never reached the skip but I'm getting there."

Geoff wandered off down the boat to look at the fridge and then wandered back with a bottle of milk. "That's a really good find." He laughed. "Have another go and if you get really good at it maybe I won't need a job at all."

I pulled a face at him.

"Look." He handed me a cup of tea and sat down again. "This was just one job, if it doesn't get any better I'll just keep applying and something will come up, I can stand it for a couple of weeks," he stopped and took a sip of tea, "I think I'm just grumpy because I want to see this trip out, get us all back to Cambridge safely."

I nodded and gave him a hug. That night I lay in bed and stared out of the rain-washed window into the unbroken blackness, this journey seemed much harder than the last one, the kids were older, Geoff was unhappy, we were far more broke and now I was really happy that I'd managed to get something out of a skip.

Had I been wrong? For a moment I hankered after the ice-skating cows and our big fire, then firmly made myself remember the bills, the costs, the women at school and all the other ridiculous little annoyances that living in a house brought with it. Geoff snored softly then mumbled and rolled over, I held myself very still until he settled again. When I said I wanted to get back on to a boat, had I just deluded myself? Had I wanted *Happy Go Lucky* back, with her white walls and fitted kitchen, the bath and shower and all the mod cons we had installed?

There were no answers and that night I couldn't have said what was worse, being on a boat with an unhappy family or back in a house with an unhappy me, the last thing I remember before falling asleep was bird song and a brightening sky; it had been a very long night.

The next morning, the clouds hung heavy, grey and threatening but there was no actual rain. I was woken by a short scream from Geoff as he stepped off the boat and had a rather taller step down to terra firma than he usually had. I waved him off then stood staring at *Minerva*'s bow, I could see far more of it than usual, the river had risen so much it was now lapping just an inch below the moorings. As I stood there in contemplative silence, I was aware of a figure behind me and turned around to grin up at the man from the Environment Agency.

He smiled back and stepped forward to stand beside me. "Going to be another two days at least." He nodded downstream. "There's no way anybody's going to get under some of the bridges that-a-way."

"We have to get through Denver before it closes down for repairs," I said, "what do you think our chances are?"

He rubbed his chin and staring at the swirling water, thought for a moment. "Not too bad, actually," he replied, "you should get away from here in a couple of days and then as long as you don't hang about, you should make it to Denver in plenty of time." He refocused on me and grinned. "Let's just hope the weather report is right and there's no more rain, eh?" Giving me a wave and ignoring my rather sickly smile he sauntered off, back to his van.

The kids and I spent that day sorting out clothes and generally tidying, Geoff came home in, if possible, an even more morose mood than the day before. Now it seemed as though his workmates were shunning him. He'd also had a row with his new boss.

"He asked me where all my tools were," Geoff muttered into his fourth cup of tea of the evening, "I told him they were in the car," putting his tea down he leant back on the sofa and ran his hand over Mort's tummy, smiling distractedly as Mort wriggled ecstatically and waved his paws in the air. "He asked me what was the point of having tools in the car and not in the workshop, I said they were more use in the car as there was more work to do at home than there was at work." He sighed and gently disengaged Mort's teeth from around his wrist. "It didn't go down well."

"No," I murmured, "I can see that it wouldn't."

Charlie looked up from the book she was reading. "Don't you like this new job, Geoff?" she asked.

"No love, not really." Geoff bent down to look for his tea.

"Maybe we should have stayed in Durham," she muttered, glaring at me, "you liked that job, didn't you?"

Geoff completely missed the look and wasn't really listening anyway. "Yeah, maybe," he agreed.

She gave me a triumphant smile and picking her book up stamped off up the boat to turn on the computer.

"Thank you, dear," I muttered.

"What?" Geoff looked at Charlie. "Oh, sorry, but she does have a point."

Oh great, now I felt really bad, another sleepless night.

By the end of the next day the kids were merely seconds away from a mutiny, they had argued and fought all day. Sam was reduced to tears when Charlie hit him for tripping over her feet. His argument that they were stuck right out across the boat did little to sway her from feeling that she was aggrieved and trodden on. She ranted that there was no space, there was no privacy and that she was cold and bored and there was nothing to do. Sam joined in and agreed with all that she said. Finally they both found something they could blame for their woes, me.

By the time Geoff staggered through the doors with his now customary sad face and had battled his way through Mort's enthusiastic greeting, both kids had sent me to Coventry and were only too pleased to list their litany of grievances to Geoff.

It was an unpleasant and silent evening, by bedtime, Sam had forgiven me and was happily talking up a storm and beating me at Connect 4 but Charlie held on to her stony silence. Geoff was being introspective, pretending to be asleep on the sofa and the puppy was hiding under the fire again. This wasn't what I'd hoped for, this wasn't what I'd imagined or remembered. Suddenly deciding that I couldn't stand it any longer, I opted to take the dog for a walk. No one said anything as I walked out.

It was actually a pleasant evening. Mortimer bounced along sniffing at every bush, marking each new scent with one of his own. I had brought along a glow-in-the-dark ball and we had great fun rolling it around the car park. We then walked up into Irthlingborough and spent a good hour wandering around the little group of shops before slowly making our way back to the boat. I didn't realise it but we'd been gone well over two hours.

As I walked into the boat, three worried faces looked up at me. "Where have you been? You left your phone behind," Charlie demanded, "we were just going out in search of you."

Sam rushed over and gave me a hug. "I didn't think you were coming back," he muttered into my stomach.

"Why not?" I frowned at them then grinned as poor, over-exercised, Mortimer staggered to his bed and passed out with a heavy sigh, all four tortured paws in the air.

"I don't know," Sam moaned, "you were gone so long, so I told Charlie that you'd run away and it was all her fault for being such a cow."

"OK, OK, look." I pushed Sam down onto the sofa between Charlie and Geoff. "I know it's been hard stuck here in this floating junk yard, but we should be gone soon, the river has dropped a huge amount. I checked tonight, so we can get on again." I looked around at them. "Geoff hates his new job but it's only a job and he can get another one. Sam, you need to stop winding Charlie up and Charlie I could do with a little less anarchy." I fixed both kids with a firm gaze. "When we do pull out, either tomorrow or the next day, it's just going to be you two and me."

Both kids looked horrified.

"Yep, that's right, no Dad, he's going to be at work. Charlie I need your help, I need help with the locks, I need someone to take over the driving of the boat so we can take it in turns. Sam, you can help with the locks and it will be your job to keep pestilence there under control." I waved a hand a Mortimer who snored at me. "We're going to have enough trouble without Geoff being there, but I'm fairly sure we can do it, but we can only do it if we all pitch in, all right?" Both kids nodded so hard they looked as though they had springs for necks.

"I need a cup of tea." I flopped down onto the sofa.

"I'll get it." Charlie jumped up and headed for the stove. "Does this mean I can drive the boat on my own?" She stood with her back to us obviously hoping for one answer and expecting another.

"Yes." I leant back and closed my eyes. "I'm going to need to take breaks and we've got to get to Denver within a week.

There was silence from the direction of the cooker, worried that I'd given the wrong answer I cracked open an eyelid and watched Charlie pump her fist twice and give a silent "YES!!"

I slept surprisingly well that night. Obviously all it took to get life back on track was a bit of direction.

CHAPTER
ELEVEN

Girl Power

Another thirty-six hour boredom break and we were finally given the go-ahead to move, we were so relieved to be actually going that even going on our own didn't seem that daunting any more, or at least it didn't while we were still moored up.

As Geoff left for his fourth miserable day at work we arranged to meet at Thrapston that evening, there was parking and I could walk into town from the mooring, give the kids some exercise and for a first day's trip it should be uneventful and fairly short.

By midday we still hadn't left. I had waved off Audrey and Bertie, they had left as soon as the environment agency man had given the go-ahead. Brian had gone, as had the couple in the cruiser, so now there was just us, a single boat still attached to the wharf and I kept finding jobs to do, each one designed to delay us just that little more.

"Oh for goodness' sake." Charlie stuck her head out of the window and watched me puttering up and down the gunwales sorting out ropes and putting the chimney on. "Are we actually going or not?"

"Erm, yes," I said as I rearranged the same rope for the fifth time. "I won't be long."

"Chicken," she said, grinning at me, "come on, admit it, you're scared."

"No I'm not, I'm fine." I pushed at the rope again. "I just want to make sure everything's right."

Charlie ducked her head back into the boat again making squawking chicken noises.

I sighed and looked down at the water, it was still running fairly fast. Looking ahead I could see the first lock of the day just past the football field. I knew I was petrified of doing this on my own. I had visions of getting the boat hung up on the sill, or having the fast-running water cascade over the back deck, every time I thought about it I broke out in a cold sweat.

For the first time it occurred to me just how important the team work that Geoff and I had built up had become to me, I had taken a big boat through hundreds of locks over the past three years and I'd never had any problems, or nothing that I couldn't handle. But now without him there, the whole thing seemed insurmountable. What I really wanted to do was just bury my head in a book and stay in one place.

"MUM!" Charlie screeched at me, "What are you doing?"

I shook myself out of my worried reverie and took a deep breath. There were no choices, we had to move, we had a deadline to meet and we really couldn't miss it. I was out of opportunities to be pathetic.

"What do you want to do?" I stared at Charlie "Do you want to take her through the lock or do you want to operate the gates?"

Charlie stared back at me. "What?"

"I can't do both, sweetie, remember what I told you last night, not with a boat this big, I need you to do one or the other." I held her gaze and watched as the reality settled on to her, her look became worried and the colour drained from her face. She stepped out on to the mooring and stared down river to the lock.

"I think I'll operate the lock," she said quietly, then chewing on her lip she muttered, "I wish Geoff was here."

I gave her a hug. "So do I, oh God, so do I." We stood there for a moment both breathing deeply, it's true then misery does love company. "So," I gave her a nudge with my hip. "Shall we go?"

She nodded slowly. "We have to, don't we?"

"Yes," I said firmly, "we do."

"OK then." She gave me a shaky grin. "You start her up and I'll push her off."

I nodded then turned and started walking toward the stern. "Hey, Mum!" I turned again at her call.

"Yes?"

She grinned again, stronger this time. "Girl power, eh?"

"Absolutely." I gave her the thumbs up and, trying not to shake, headed for the tiller.

Minerva came to life with her normal belch of black smoke. Charlie untied her mooring lines and pushed her away from the bank, this was it, we were off and without my normal lifeline of a reassuringly calm and organised husband I felt as though the whole operation was far more dangerous than it actually was.

The lock gates were open and I headed in, as we pulled up it all seemed so familiar, Charlie jumped off and closed the gates then, with a final thumbs-up, she began to open the gates on the other side. It was all textbook really and as we pulled away from the lock with Charlie sitting happily on the roof I wondered what all the fuss was about, hadn't we done it all before? I scoffed at my ridiculous fears then smiled as the first rays of sun for what seemed like weeks broke through the clouds, the water ahead of me glinted and twinkled. This was going to be easy.

Sure enough, a couple of hours later after a gentle float past Stanwick lakes we pulled up, still in full sunshine at our designated stopping space just outside Thrapston. The mooring was huge, it wasn't underwater and the kids and the dog were happy to get out and rush around (in a sort of relieved frenzy) on the grass with a ball. I sat on top of the boat with a book and a huge mug of coffee enjoying the warm sunshine and feeling very, very pleased with myself.

Panting hard from all her exertions, Charlie headed inside for a drink. When she re-emerged she jumped up on to the roof with a very serious look. "Mum, we have a problem."

I grinned at her over the top of my book. "What's up, Houston, run out of lemonade?"

Charlie shook her head rapidly and winced. "Lu's dead."

"What!" I put my book down on the roof and lowered my voice as Charlie made shushing sounds casting furtive glances at Sam who was still playing with Mortimer.

"How?" I whispered, "What happened?"

"I don't know." Charlie's forced whisper carried over to Sam and he looked up, curious as to why there was a sudden furious and quiet conversation.

"What are you talking about, Mum?" he shouted.

"Christmas," I shouted back.

"Ooo, great, I've got a list." He happily started to list all the things he needed to Mortimer who completely unperturbed carried on trying to bury his ball in the grass.

"She was fine yesterday," I hissed at Charlie while keeping a wary eye on Sam.

"Well, she has been looking a little moth-eaten lately, and she certainly sleeps a lot more." Charlie shrugged. "She might have just died from old age, she was fully grown when we got her and we have no idea how long she'd been in that pet shop." She shrugged again and winced as she watched Sam kicking Mortimer's ball, missed completely and fell over laughing as the puppy jumped on his stomach. "Let's face it with that attitude she could have been ancient, no one but us would have taken her."

"What are we going to tell Sam?"

Charlie shrugged her shoulders again.

"What are we going to do with the body?"

She shrugged again and shook her head.

"Oh God, he's going to be really upset." I thought for a minute. "Tell you what, let's replace her; all hamsters look alike."

"Don't be daft." Charlie shook her head. "You'd have to take a normal nice hamster and inject it with angry juice for it to behave like Lu, and what about all those weird sounds she used to make?"

"I don't want him upset, we'll just tell him that she's mellowing in her old age." I watched Sam as he tried to swing a stick at some stinging nettles only to find that Mort had grabbed the other end they both fell over the stick, Sam lay face down, Mortimer lay belly up. "We'll just keep him away from the cage tonight, you get rid of the body and I'll call Geoff and tell him to pick up another hamster in Cambridge." I felt as though I was organising the results of a murder.

Charlie crinkled her nose at me. "Why do I have to get rid of the corpse?" She drew out the word "corpse", evidently one of her favourites.

"Because I'm going to distract him with a game and you can give her a burial by water."

Charlie stared into the river for a moment. "OK, but only if I can use the washing-up gloves, I'm not touching her." She shuddered. "I really hate touching dead things." She shuddered again. "Dead rodents are always stiff, cold and lighter than they should be."

Ten minutes later Sam and I were playing a game of Connect 4, Charlie making a huge display of being surreptitious, put the pink marigolds on and wandered, whistling loudly, down the boat toward the ex-Lu's cage.

She smiled serenely at us as she came past, her hands held behind her back, then humming she transferred her hands to the front of her body and stepped out of the boat.

Sam had just won another game, when he looked out of the window. "Hey, Mum, what's that?" we both stared out at the river, then leaving his seat he wandered down to the cage while I sat with my head in my hands waiting for that awful question: "Why is my hamster in the river?"

As she explained later, Charlie had indeed cast Lu with a final farewell into the river, and had stood thinking good thoughts about Lu's short life while she waited for her to sink into the murky depths. Obviously continuing her lifelong goal of doing things she shouldn't, Lu hadn't sunk at all, the current carried her out into mid stream where she had turned over onto her back so that her little pink nose and tiny paws were pointing straight at the sky. Down the length of the boat she slowly floated. To make matters worse the low sun transformed her fur to shining gold and as she meandered gently past, glowing brightly and bobbing like a fat tourist in the sea, the ripples turned her body this way and that causing her little paws to waggle, I was convinced she was waving goodbye as she drifted toward the sunset.

Sam and I watched her exit stage left in utter silence, when she was finally out of sight he looked at me, his expression one of slight confusion. Well, there was no way out of this one, I had to tell the truth.

"I'm really, really sorry Sam, Lu died and we thought we'd replace her with another one before you noticed." I waited with certain trepidation for the hysterics to start.

Sam studied me for a moment then looked down at the Connect 4 board. "I worked out that she's dead, Mum," he said checking which move to make, "I didn't think she'd taken up swimming." He sniffed and clamped his lips shut, obviously upset.

"Right." I waited for a moment to let him get himself sorted out. "So do you want another hamster?"

"No thanks," Sam answered and placed a counter carefully into the grid, "can I have another pet?"

I picked up a blue counter to avoid looking at him. "Erm, it really depends on what you want, I mean, we have the dog now and he belongs to everybody."

Sam nodded. "But I've thought of a pet that would be useful."

This wasn't sounding good, but I had to give the boy the benefit of the doubt. "Oh yes?" I raised my eyebrows to look at him. "What would you like?"

"Chickens." Sam gave me a huge grin. "We could get eggs." With a certain flair he slid a counter into the grid. "Connect 4, I win."

I just groaned.

Geoff found us that night with no problem at all. He really didn't want to hear about dead hamsters or our successful trip, he just wanted to sleep, or at least lie on his back with his eyes closed.

"Have you actually had a busy day?" I handed him a cup of tea.

"No, I bloody well haven't." He opened one eye and glared at me with it, then took the tea with a sigh. "I

310

haven't done anything all day, we just sit there, some of the lads play cards, some of them read the paper. They all sigh with relief when it's lunch time, they get out their lunches, and sit in the same positions, eat their lunch, then the afternoon is much of the same."

He put his tea down on the floor. "I'm so bored I think I'm going to cry."

I decided that being sympathetic wasn't what was required at this time. "Well, if you're so pigged off, why aren't you on the 'net' looking for another job?"

Another sigh. "You're right." Picking up his mug he headed for the laptop.

By the time he had applied for four or five jobs he was in a much better mood and he wandered off with Sam at bed time. I could hear them discussing the swimming abilities of dead hamsters (pretty good according to Sam).

Geoff went off to work with good heart the next day, it was Friday and we had arranged to meet him at Fotheringay, so we didn't have very far to go. With this short run in mind we decided that a short walk into Thrapston would do us all good.

As we walked along, with Sam circling and tripping over, chattering, falling down holes and generally doing his best to get in Charlie's way: if she went to the left he was already ahead of her, she would turn to the right and he would immediately see something that needed studying over that side of the path as well, he didn't do it on purpose, he's never been able to walk in a straight line since he was born. Charlie, desperately trying to keep a bouncing puppy under control finally snapped and tied Mortimer to the back of Sam's trousers, they bounced off together, getting in each other's way and often ending up in a pile on the floor, leaving Charlie and I to wander sedately (and in a straight line) toward the small town.

There isn't a huge amount to see in Thrapston but as we only needed essentials and a mirror we felt that really we were probably going to be OK.

Sam had broken the mirror the previous week and Charlie had taken great delight in telling him that he now would have to endure seven years bad luck. So every time that she pushed him or tripped him she would look innocent and would blame it on his "bad luck". Sam was almost incapacitated with fear and I'd had to put a stop to her torturing him.

Standing in the queue at the Co-op it all started again. Sam tripped over his own feet and only just managed to stop himself from falling by grabbing Charlie's arm. She had waited until he had a good hold then had stepped back and twisted her arm away allowing him to fall to the floor.

As he stood up, red-faced and embarrassed she had started to poke him both verbally and physically. The pokes turned to pinches and Sam's face became a deeper and deeper shade of red. Obviously enjoying herself, Charlie quietly pushed him and pushed him until I couldn't take it any more.

"Charlie, for goodness' sake," I hissed at her, "will you leave him alone?"

Sam couldn't resist piping up, "Yeah Charlie," he sneered, "leave me alone."

I found out later that after I had turned around Charlie had reached out and, grabbing Sam's soft underarm, had given it a huge pinch. But of course, at the time all I heard was Sam's scream.

Turning around amidst the tutting and sour looks of the other women in the queue I prepared a withering speech which should have ended in Charlie being sent outside to look after the dog, unfortunately Sam got there first.

Bright red in the face, and obviously torn between tears and anger my smiling little pacifist finally lost it. Hauling back his left arm he let loose a punch which connected squarely with Charlie's grinning jaw and knocked her off her feet and onto the floor.

Complete silence fell in the shop. Charlie got to her feet and stamped out of the shop, Sam burst into tears and I was horribly torn between telling him off for punching his sister and patting him on the back for finally taking a stand, albeit a rather extreme one.

With him wrapped around my waist I decided that silence was probably the best way to go, so in this state I paid for the items, packed them into bags and left the shop, still with Sam attached to me like some sort of psychologically scarred remora. As we headed toward the door an elderly gentleman stepped in front of us and regarded Sam.

"That's a good left hook you have there young man." He grinned.

Sam tried to smile through his tears but only managed a sort of grimace. I waited for the lecture to start but all he did was smile again and wander off. Sam looked up at me. "Mum?"

"Yes, love?" I looked down at him as he prised himself upright.

"She's going to kill me, isn't she?" He looked fearfully out of the window where Charlie was waiting with the dog, her expression completely blank.

I laughed. "No she isn't, I won't let her."

He stared at his sister for a moment, and then took a deep breath, squaring his shoulders he headed out of the door to meet his fate.

As he walked toward her, she studied him, head on one side, the red patch on the side of her jaw stood out like a neon light.

Sam swallowed and kept walking; I could hear the music from those old westerns playing in my head. As he reached her, they stood and stared at each other.

Finally Charlie grinned. "That really hurt," she said and clapped him hard on the back causing him to stagger slightly. "Well done."

Sam finally smiled and sighed, there was nothing better than getting congratulations from his big sister.

"If, however," Charlie snarled, "you ever do that again, I will kill you where you stand."

Charlie picked up Mort's lead and handed it to him and without even a glance at me they headed out of the car park together. Honestly, kids! I had to grin.

Back on the boat we finally set off again. The river was still flowing quite fast, in the right direction, and we made good time as we headed on toward Peterborough. It wasn't long before we had Titchmarsh lock in our sights. Confident and happy with the sunshine on my face, I pulled into the moorings and yelled for Charlie to come and sort out the lock.

As we pulled into the pound, I noticed that *Minerva* was being a little bouncy, the water was flowing very fast, coming over the top of the open gates. Feeling the start of a nervous moment, I dismissed my fears and concentrated on getting Min over to one side of the pound and making sure that she was roped securely to the concrete bollards on the top of the lock.

Charlie closed the gates behind us and began to lift the guillotine gate at the front of the lock. As the water level in the pound dropped, the river behind began to cascade with ever increasing fury over the rear gates causing a frothing white maelstrom just behind my feet. The force of the water coming in pushed *Minerva* hard up against the front gate and, despite having the engine on full in reverse and two separate ropes around bollards, there was nothing I could do to get her to back away.

We were stuck and I signalled Charlie to hit the emergency stop switch. With the water pushing so hard behind her, if Charlie opened the gates I would be swept through with absolutely no control whatsoever. All my confidence seeped away and I dithered horribly, hopping from one wet foot to the other as water washed over the back deck and down into the back cabin.

Charlie leaned over the edge. "What are we going to do?" she yelled down to me.

"I don't know," I yelled back, "we can't stay here. Just try opening the gate slowly."

Charlie gave me "the look". "I can't, Mum, I press a button and it opens, I don't have any control."

I sighed, I knew she was right, we had two choices either we fill the pound back up again and wait for the river to drop further or we attempt to go through. I dithered again, my feet getting wetter with every passing second.

"OK," I shouted up, "let me get another rope on and I'll try to hold her." I wrapped a rope around a bollard and wrapped it around one of the T studs on the boat. "OK, fire away."

Charlie gave me a doubtful look and hit the button again. The big metal door commenced its inexorable upward swing and with just as much determination *Minerva* pushed her nose hard against the door. It didn't matter how hard I pulled she would not back off. Finally the bottom of the gate reached the point of our bow and with a soft thud edged up and away from the boat.

Like a greyhound from a trap *Minerva* surged forward. The rope I was stupidly holding sped through my hand taking a fair amount of skin with it, I screamed and let go. One of the older ropes snapped and I watched the flailing line fall back toward the boat like a loosely cracked whip. The boat shot forward, sliding the bow and the front deck beneath the metal gate. *Minerva* was pulled up short as the front doors smashed into the gate. There was the sound of breaking glass and a horrible screech of rending metal as our poor television aerial was first crushed and then flattened against the roof as the door passed within inches of the roof.

Luckily we still had one rope attached and as we moved forward, about thirty feet beneath the gates, the push from the water behind slowed and I managed to bring her to a stop just as the gates were about to take off Geoff's new chimney from the top of the boat. He would have been devastated.

"Mum! MUM!!" Charlie screamed down at me, "Are you OK?"

I took stock before I answered, one bleeding hand, one completely obliterated TV aerial, at least one window smashed, I just hoped Sam and Mortimer were both still in one piece.

"Yeah, I'm fine." I gave her a cheery wave, unfortunately I hadn't been careful which hand to wave and at the sight of all the blood Charlie turned a little green.

"You're bleeding," she pointed out.

"I know, it looks worse than it is." I pointed downstream. "Meet me at the moorings I think we need to do a bit of cleaning up."

An hour later, bandaged, and in possession of a hot cup of coffee (with a fair tot of scotch in it, for the pain obviously) and a dustpan full of broken glass I was on the phone to Geoff.

"Can you bring home some wood?"

"Yes, why?"

"We've had a bit of a knock."

"What broke?"

"Both windows in the front doors."

"WHAT! How?"

"Slight altercation with a lock gate."

"Are you all OK?"

"Yeah, we're fine, bit shaky and . . ." I was going to say bloody, but sensibly stopped, it would only worry him. ". . . It's a bit breezy in here, but we're fine, I'll use some duck tape to put up a couple of bin bags and some cardboard for now but we're going to need some wood."

There was a short silence at the end of the phone then. "I'll pick up the wood, shall I still meet you at Fotheringay?"

I hesitated, if I said no, meet us here, he would worry but, if I said yes, I would have to be brave enough to take the boat through another five locks and under numerous bridges, I hoped the rest of the day would be easier as there was no way I could afford to be off-schedule, I sighed. "Meet us at Fotheringay as planned."

"You sure?" Geoff sounded more worried than I was.

"Yes, I'm sure. We'll be fine, now go away and we'll see you later." I blew him a kiss down the phone and hung up.

Charlie looked at me. "You're not serious are you?"

I waved my half-bandaged hand at her, I'd washed it and applied a good glollop of Aloe Vera pulp then bandaged it up, the light green goo and the blood were beginning to seep through the bandage, making a horrible grey stain. "I think we ought to do this again, don't you?"

She nodded and taking a knife cut another leaf from my poor denuded cactus. This time we spread the pulp onto a pad rather than straight onto the skin. I had the feeling that I really ought to take this to A&E but that wasn't going to happen, no car and no town nearby with public transport. I really should be thankful that it hadn't been more serious.

There are certain things that you just can't allow yourself to think about, potential for accidents or severe illness is one of them because most of my life is spent wallowing around in places there aren't even names for, let alone be able to give an ambulance directions to. I studied my hand, it had stopped bleeding but there seemed to be a pinkish water dripping from it. I sighed: this was going to take weeks to heal, slapping the gunk-covered melolin pad onto the wound, I held it out for Charlie to start bandaging. She was uncharacteristically silent throughout the process.

When she had finished and had pinned the bandage in place, she stared at her handiwork for a moment then looked up at me. "Don't do that again, please," she said with a straight face, "I honestly thought the boat was going to sink with you and Sam on it, I'm going to be having nightmares for weeks." She shuddered and biting her lip blinked rapidly.

I gave her a hug. "I can't promise nothing else will happen but I will try very hard not to worry you again."

She nodded, "When the boat hit the gate I felt the thump right through my feet and with the sound of smashing glass and then you screamed and that awful sound as the aerial went down . . ." she sighed and gave me a hug. "I honestly thought you were going to die."

"Oh dear." I hugged her back. "I'm really sorry, I'll try not to do it again."

She nodded and gave me a tremulous smile. "I wish Geoff was here."

I shrugged and replied, "I honestly don't think he could have done anything differently." I stood up and flexed my hand and winced. "I think we did very well and should be proud of ourselves."

She smiled then with a deep breath she nodded and climbed off the sofa. "Shall we get on?"

I heaved myself to my feet and downed the last of my cold coffee. "Yeauch! Yes I think we should."

We took it very slowly and having had one major disaster it seemed as though we would be finally allowed to enjoy the sunshine.

As we were meandering slowly through Oundle the wind, which up to this point had been present but not really that invasive, picked up and began to make its presence felt, by the time we reached the Cotterstock lock it was blowing strongly and steadily in from the south-east. Coming up on the lock I noticed with a sigh that the pound was empty, our gates closed and the bottom gates open, no chance of just pulling her into the pound then.

I gave a double blast of the horn which brought Charlie, moaning and complaining, out on to the roof.

"I'm fed up with this," she announced, "I just get settled doing something and we find another bloody lock." She frowned as I wrestled with *Minerva* and the wind and completely failed to get her anywhere close to the moorings. "Erm . . . Mum, didn't we want to park up there?"

"Yes, Charlie," I snapped through gritted teeth. "I am desperately trying to get her over there, but as you might notice she doesn't want to go."

Putting *Minerva* into reverse we paddled in vain against the wind trying desperately to get back far enough that I could take another run in at the moorings.

"What are you doing?" Charlie shouted over the wind.

"I can't get her to go backwards," I shouted back, "the wind's pushing us away from the moorings and the water is flowing fairly fast straight down that channel." I pointed ahead. "I can't do anything, I'm going to try and turn her nose into the lock gates so that you can jump off, I'll throw you a rope and we'll try and pull her in."

Charlie looked dubiously at the sharp right turn that led into the lock. "Are you sure that'll work?" she shouted.

"No, but it's the only idea I've got." I put *Minerva* into full reverse and, wincing at the huge cloud of black smoke that billowed up from the exhaust chimney, I ignored the screaming protests of the engine and did my utmost to pull her back.

Finally with a lot of swearing and wearing of engine parts, I managed to get her nose buried in the lock gates. Charlie skipped down the gunwales and jumped easily onto the far bank where she ran across the lock gates and stood waiting for me to throw her a rope.

Being only about six stone and built like an elf is great for climbing, running and leaping. It is an incredibly bad body shape for pulling twenty tons of steel against wind and current.

Seeing that she was being pulled closer and closer to the edge of the mooring I had to scream at her, "Just let go of the rope, you moose."

She did and *Minerva*'s rear end swung free to bury itself in the far bank.

I had another moment of déjà vu, here we were stuck across a river again. Our nose wedged firmly into the gap between lock gate and wall and our backside stuck in the reeds. I sighed and killed the engine.

Charlie ran back over the lock gates and stared in consternation at the drop into the pound. "What are we going to do?" She nervously rubbed her hands together. "What if the lock gates give way and we fall into the water, over the drop?"

I wasn't really listening; I was trying to work out how the hell I was going to get out of this mess.

We stood there for about fifteen minutes, trying desperately to move and failing every time. Finally Sam appeared.

"What's going on?" He stuck his head out of the side doors. "Can I have a sandwich? I'm hungry."

Irritated that he had interrupted my chain of thoughts (admittedly they were thoughts that were going round and round in circles), I snapped at him.

"Not now, Sam, can't you see we have a little problem here?"

Sam climbed out of the boat and following Charlie's route leapt on to the concrete. He stood for a moment working out all that was going on. Then he shrugged and sitting on a bollard began to play on his DS.

"So what are we going to do?" Charlie asked for the fifth time. "Those gates keep creaking, the boat's going to fall in, I know it is."

Sam looked up at her and frowned. "What's the matter, Charlie?"

"Oh for goodness' sake, Sam, just stay out of the way." Charlie, worried beyond coherence, snapped at him, "You can see what's going on, what if those gates give way and we fall into the lock, it's a long way down, we'll sink the boat."

Worry, and especially nonsensical worry, is obviously catching. Finally she convinced me that the gates were going to give way and I decided that as *Minerva* was locked solid across the river it was safe to get off and have a look at those gates, just to make sure they weren't going to give way. We had been at a complete stop for nearly an hour at this point.

Charlie and I leaned cautiously over the lock and peered into the water. Sam shrugged again and sat back on his bollard. "So can I have that sandwich?" he repeated.

I grabbed Charlie as she headed toward him, furious beyond words.

"Not yet, Sam, let's see if we can get out of this mess, then I'll get you something to eat." I stared back at the boat wishing that Geoff were there, not that he'd be able to do anything, it's just that misery loves company.

Sam sighed and stood up. "It's cold." He wandered over toward the lock; I put a hand out to stop him falling over the edge. He looked at the lock, then back at the boat. "Is the lock broken then?"

"No, love. We're just stuck, what about if we get that rope back and all three of us pull the back end round?"

Sam looked at me and frowned. "Wouldn't it be easier to fill the lock up, open these gates and then pull the boat in?"

Silence, broken only by the sounds of wind and water fell over our little group. Charlie and I looked at each other then down at the lock.

Without a word spoken I climbed on the back of the boat, Charlie took her key and began to lower the bottom gate.

We'd had to back *Minerva* off a little to open the top gates, but after that she'd gone in easily enough, we'd dropped gently down to the next level and were soon on our way again.

At the bottom moorings I pulled her in with no difficulty at all.

Putting the kettle on, Charlie and I refused to look at each other and Sam was confused by the silence.

I put a tuna and cucumber sandwich in front of him and gave him a kiss. "Well done you."

"Eh?" he queried around a big mouthful, "Wha' for?"

"For keeping your head when all about you are losing theirs." I gave him a hug. "When you're around it's like having a little one of your father in the boat."

Sam really had no idea what he'd done that had been so right, but he was happy with the praise so he beamed at me.

Charlie sniffed. "I hate it when he does that." She took a mouthful of sandwich. "You know he's going to grow up to be a lawyer or something that needs lateral thinking and maths, don't you?"

"No I'm not." Sam frowned. "I'm going to be an accountant."

Charlie and I grinned. "Good for you, Sam." I gave him another hug. "That will be lovely."

Boat, containing tired, slightly frazzled family, and car, containing a worried Geoff, arrived at Fotheringay within a very short time of each other. He surveyed the damage and in his usual organised and quietly efficient style he set to, straightening the aerial and putting wood up at the doors.

As we were sitting down to a rather wonderful meal of fish and chips, Amelia phoned.

I spent a happy hour talking to her about the wonderful Chris and how college was due to start in a week's time. She had slipped back into her old ways of talking at a hundred miles an hour, changing subjects at the speed of light so that when she asked how we were doing, it took me somewhat by surprise.

"Well, we've had a bit of a time of it really, Lu died, Charlie tried to put the body in the river but it wouldn't sink and she waved at us as she went past the windows, that was yesterday. Today Sam punched Charlie in the face, and we smashed the windows in the boat and totalled the aerial by running it into a lock gate and I lost most of the skin on my palm to rope burn, then we got stuck across the river and Charlie and I became stupid and thought the boat was going to fall into the pound but Sam sorted it out." I blurted out.

There was silence on the end of the phone. "Hello? Amelia are you still there?"

"I don't really know what to say to all that," she said, "Lu's dead . . ." she paused obviously trying to get all the information into a straight line, "hang on, Sam punched Charlie . . . really?"

I laughed, trust Amelia to go straight to the unexpected, obviously pets dying was just sad and us running into things was now commonplace in her view.

"Yep, she wound him up so much he gave her a good smack right in the kisser." I waited for the inevitable.

"Sam?" Amelia sounded confused. "Our Sam?

"Yes, he actually does have a breaking point," I said, laughing, "I was beginning to think he didn't have one at all."

"Hmm." Amelia was silent for another moment while she obviously, like me, adjusted her mental image of her youngest sibling. "Anyway, I'd better go, I'm working tonight, then after work, Chris and I are going out with friends so I'm glad you're all still alive."

"Sounds great, so when are we going to meet Chris?" I laughed as there was a sort of glurkling sound down the phone.

"I don't know," Amelia said, coughing, "but he keeps asking to meet you lot as well, so I think I've said too much to both of you."

"Good, well the sooner you bring him over the better, then you'll get both of us off your back." I waited for the usual excuses.

"Right, I will." She laughed. "This will be make or break for this relationship. As soon as you get to Cambridge we'll be down, when are you likely to be home?"

"As long as we manage to get through Denver, we should be home in three days, four at the most, maybe five." I winced, well that didn't sound vague at all.

"Good, we'll see you then." Amelia completely ignored the range of numbers I had given her and there was silence for a moment. "Mum?"

"Yes?"

"I really like this one." Another short pause. "Could you please TRY and be a little normal."

I laughed. "Nope, if you've told him all about us, then it would just confuse him if we suddenly become two-up two-down suburbans, don't you think?

There was a huff. "I suppose so," she sighed, obviously this was really worrying her. "See you soon . . . and Mum?"

"Yes?"

"Erm could you please stop trying to kill yourself and the kids, if you actually managed it I'd be sad." There was a click and she was gone.

I slipped my phone back into my pocket as Geoff wandered up the boat.

"Two things." He poked me gently in the shoulder.

"Yes?" I put the kettle on.

"One, all you have to do is drive the boat, please stop breaking it." He poked me gently with each word then he gently lifted my bandaged hand. "And stop breaking yourself, this could have been really nasty, you should see the dent across the front, you must have hit that gate really hard."

I grinned at him. "I didn't really have any choice. She was going and we were going with her whether we liked it or not."

"And two," he continued, "I have an interview for a proper job with a maintenance company in Cambridge, same sort of thing as my job in Durham, comes with a van and all those sort of benefits." He gave me a big grin. "Fingers crossed, eh?"

"Hello in there," an unknown voice called in through the bow doors, interrupting us before I could start asking questions.

"Hello?" Geoff and I turned as one.

A bearded grinning man stuck his head in our doors. "I don't suppose I could borrow you for a moment, could I?" He indicated with a thumb over his shoulder. "We've just parked up next door and our collie pup has run off with your staffy. They're having a great time, but I think it's going to take more than me and your son to round them up again."

Two hours later there was blessed silence, both kids and dogs had collapsed after an hour of chasing each other about the large field below Fotheringay castle. After the first half an hour, as the dogs didn't seem inclined to actually run away, they just wanted to chase each other about, occasionally buzzing their owners as they hurtled past us, the adults had given up, Geoff had made tea and we had all sat down to watch kids and dogs miss each other by inches. Sarah, Lawrence's wife, had made scones and, pausing only to call the kids over for one, we had sat, drinking tea, and eating scones and watching the game (I think the score ended up dogs 3 kids 1) and moaning about Titchmarsh lock.

Their boat, *Butterfly*, was only fifty foot so hadn't had the traumas in the lock that we'd experienced, but even so Sarah said she wouldn't want to attempt it again, she had also phoned the Environment Agency, a course of action I hadn't even considered, to tell them that it was dangerous.

After kids and dogs were asleep I came out with tea for Geoff and Sarah and, accepting a glass of wine from Mike, settled myself down we prepared to watch the sun go down and the lights in the church come on. It was a very peaceful scene, the wind had dropped with the setting sun and sitting huddled inside a big coat I was warm and happy.

"I can't believe you'd do this on your own." Sarah shook her head. "I wouldn't dare, we've had this boat four months now and I'm still running into things and panicking. You must be really brave."

I sighed. "Not really, we just don't have a choice, with Geoff working now we absolutely have to be in Cambridge as soon as possible, just to get the kids to school." I shook my head with a grin. "Believe me, I wouldn't do it if I could possibly avoid it."

Sarah shook her head firmly. "No, I just wouldn't do it; we'd have to find some other way, just travel at weekends or something." She looked worriedly at her husband. "This is Lawrence's boat, and if he wasn't there to drive it, I don't know what I'd do."

Obviously this wasn't an argument I was going to win so I just nodded and gently changed the subject on to her cooking skills and what sort of equipment they had on their boat.

Later, lying in bed I went over the comments again. How on earth could you live this life if you weren't both committed to it? "This is Lawrence's boat." It echoed around and around in my head. I couldn't imagine being able to get away with being fragile or girly in this environment, today had proved that. You have to have a slight amount of insanity and a certain ability to turn a blind eye to the possible dangers, my throbbing hand reminded me that those dangers can be very real and a situation can go from being safe to downright dangerous in the blink of an eye.

Four years, on and off, we've been puttering up and down this same stretch of canal and river. The three trips have all been very different. My hand throbbed again and I could feel the itching where the liquid that was still seeping out of the wound trickled into my palm. I stared out of the window, I was forty-five years old, was that too old to be taking on another great big project?

I rolled over on to my stomach, careful not to wake Geoff, and stared down the length of the boat. For another single moment I missed our house then, even

more strongly and for the first time in four years I
longed for our old life, a life that was easy, a big house,
with enough money to live on, my lovely warm Aga, the
huge bath, the big garden.

I sat up and climbed out of bed, moving quietly to
put the kettle on. Why did I want this life? My hand
throbbed and I winced as I quickly put the kettle down
so that I could pick it up again with my uninjured one.
What the hell was I doing? I turned the gas on and
moved quietly down the boat to look at the kids, they
both lay in their usual tumbled positions, what I was
doing to them and how would all this effect them later?
I swallowed against a sudden lump in my throat. It
wasn't worth it, I was only doing this because I hated
the bills and the postman! Suddenly all my reasons
for wanting this life back seemed banal and stupid,
unreasonable and selfish, Sarah was wrong, I was
wrong, I wasn't brave at all and quite frankly I didn't
want to play any more.

Geoff's hand on my shoulder almost gave me a heart
attack. "What's up?" he whispered loudly.

I sniffed as the tears began and he got the whole
sorry tale in one big blurt.

Depositing me with a pile of tissues on the bed he
went to make tea.

Ignoring all my sniffling and snorting he sat down
beside me and started moaning that he didn't have any
clean socks.

I stared at him incredulously, bloody socks? I think
he was missing the point.

"Tell you what." He dunked a biscuit in his tea and still staring at the wall he deliberately ignored my outrage at being taken to task over the laundry. "Why don't I take the boat to Peterborough, tomorrow, you take the car and my dirty socks, find a launderette, sort the washing out and then you can have a wander round the town, buy a book, sit in Starbucks with one of those disgusting coffees you like so much. Take some time for you, you've been dealing with boat and rain and scary locks and psychotic children all week while I've been sitting around drinking tea and learning flaming suduko, it's no wonder you're having a meltdown." He gave me a hopeful grin, "It's like the worst-case scenario of single parenting."

I leant on his shoulder for a moment. "Thanks sweetie, I think I'd like that a lot."

"Good!" He leapt up and took my cup away. "Now can we please get some sleep?"

CHAPTER
TWELVE

I Need Some "Me Time"

Even Peterborough is gorgeous when the sun's out. Shooting off early, I'd got all the washing done (five loads of it, I knew I was falling down on some jobs but really, I didn't realise we'd got so short of everything), by ten o'clock and as Geoff wasn't due into Peterborough until late afternoon I was free to wander the town.

Sitting in Starbucks I revisited my feelings from last night, it didn't make any difference and it didn't matter which way I studied the problems, I just couldn't work out whether I had pushed my family to do the right thing. There was no doubt that the next two to three years was going to be hard work but the question kept coming up, "is it worth it?"

There was one big difference on this trip and it was undoubtedly Charlie shaped. She'd arrived on the old boat looking for a family and happy to try a new way of life. Now, however, she was a hulking teenager with all the little idiosyncrasies that teenagers have, wild mood swings, a need to be by herself and an intense desire to consider us all ridiculous and downright damaging to her self-image.

As so often happens in times of crisis, the phone rang, I checked the screen and smiled. "Hi, Mum." I grinned down the phone. "Just the person I need to talk to."

There was a small silence. "Oh dear, not more trouble?" Mum sounded quite subdued.

I pushed aside my worries for Charlie's wellbeing and focused on the phone. "Are you OK? You sound a little frazzled."

"Your father's having some real problems with his ankle." She sniffed. "And I'm having some trouble with my knee so between us we've only got two good legs and they seem to want to go in different directions."

"Well, let's start with Dad's ankle." I wandered over to the counter and ordered another Mocha — this sounded like it was going to be a long conversation. "I thought that was all healed up, he broke it nearly three years ago." I stopped and thought for a moment. "Didn't they put all sorts of plates and screws into it to hold it all together?"

My father had broken his ankle while falling from the roof, he'd been walking with a stick ever since, his swollen ankle and leg had never really healed properly. I have to admit I'd felt that due to his age he was as mobile as he was likely to be and hadn't really given the whole thing a lot of thought.

"That's the problem." Mum sighed again. "Some of the screws have worked themselves out and are now pushing out of the bones. He's in quite a lot of pain and I'm no use, my knee is getting worse and worse so we've only got two good legs between us and just lean on each other whenever we go out. I feel about one hundred and five."

Mum had damaged her knee playing badminton about twenty years ago, at the time the treatment had been to remove the cartilage but I was beginning to suspect that now it would be a different story. I kept quiet — there was every possibility she would soon need a new knee.

I realised Mum had been talking while I had been reminiscing and hurriedly concentrated on the conversation again.

". . . So we're going to sell the boat." I only heard the final part of her statement and consequently panicked.

"What, my boat?" I was horribly confused. "Why would selling our boat help your collective legs?"

"Not your boat." My mother huffed as she realised I hadn't been paying attention to what she'd been saying. "We're selling our boat." She paused for a moment. "And the house in France."

"Oh." I couldn't think of anything to say that wouldn't sound condescending. "I can understand selling that great big sailing boat of yours, it takes a lot of work to get it running properly and with you two at the helm both of you with dodgy bits." I stopped talking, at some point I really must install that filter between brain and mouth, I'd been intending to do it for years but never quite got round to it.

But I had a point, the *Emmarie* is very exciting. The wretched thing heeled over in the slightest wind and scared the life out of me every time we went out on it. For Charlie, each trip was just one long sequence of screams, she really hated it. Sam just hung over the side and giggled. "Why sell the house in France? It's beautiful over there."

Mum and Dad also owned a big three-bedroomed country house in La Chapelle de Brain just outside Redon. They'd bought it about five years ago and had done a lot of work to it. Now, it was gorgeous, set in a huge wooded garden and backing on to the river, it was an oasis of country *tranquilité*. We had visited a couple of times and I had always harboured a secret desire to learn French and move over there. The people were lovely and time always seemed to slow when we visited.

Mum sighed and said, "It's just the travelling and now that your Dad's got to have a series of operations to get all this metalwork out of his leg it's just all too much, we really should have done this when we were younger." She paused for a moment. "It's going to take ages to heal up and we just won't be able to go anywhere for a while."

We chatted for a few more minutes and I avoided questions about the boating life. Then after sending my love to Dad I put the phone down and concentrated on my coffee.

Strangely enough, even though the conversation hadn't really been a happy one, I felt much better. Mum was right, if you're going to do something stupid do it while you're young enough to cope with the traumas. I looked down at my still weeping hand, we had enough problems without having health problems as well so waiting another ten years to sort myself out really wasn't an option.

I mulled the question over all day, trying new scenarios for life, one where we go back to working with computers and two where we just get a house and sell this boat, three where we try to make this work. But as I wandered down the waterfront waiting for Geoff to pull in, I still didn't have a definitive answer.

Sitting in the shade of a big tree I had been so deep in thought that I hadn't really noticed the huge fair behind me. I only really re-joined reality when a huge wet nose was stuck into my face, followed rapidly by a warm wet tongue.

"Hello again." A voice drifted over my shoulder. "You look miles away. Oh for goodness' sake, dog, leave her alone."

I struggled against Bertie's enthusiastic greeting to give Audrey a feeble wave. "Hi, Audrey, you made it all right then." I laughed and pushed the big Labrador away. "Give over Bertie, or at least get a breath mint."

Audrey sat down beside me and stretched her legs out in the sun. "Yeah we got here," she paused to drag Bertie away. "Titchmarsh was a bit of a bitch, though, how was it when you came through?"

I shuddered. "Horrible, smashed two windows, dented the front, trashed our Aerial and gave me the heebies which will last for about a month."

"Oh my God." Audrey looked a little stunned. "*Fairy Girl* was just thrown about a bit."

"How do you do it on your own, Audrey?" I stroked Bertie and stared out over the river. "Even with a small boat it must be fairly hairy sometimes."

Audrey looked at me for a long moment. "I suppose so, but I think it's the adrenaline that keeps me going." She smiled and stood up. "I need to move the boat, I'm not staying here tonight — it's going to be bedlam," she said and waved a hand at the rides and lit stalls behind us. "You going to take the kids?"

I turned around and looked at the fair, I hadn't even considered that. "Yes, I think they could do with a bit of fun."

She nodded. "Ah well, better go, catch you again some time."

With that she and Bertie headed off.

I watched her go and thought about my parents, both now well into their seventies, after years of rushing about the world buying tumbledown houses and doing them up they had finally reached the end of their tether.

I honestly never expected them to finally slow down, but now sitting here feeling tired and worn-out, I could understand Mum's sentiments. Was there a time where you just switch over to being old, or middle-aged and everything changes? Do you wake up one morning and say to your reflection, "Today I need a tweed suit, a blue rinse and some sensible shoes?

I sighed and got to my feet as *Minerva* pulled in further down the waterfront. I needed a long hot bath and a week in Spain. Squaring my shoulders I marched toward the boat ready to catch ropes. I wasn't going to get either so I might as well get on with what needed to be done.

None of us were really happy to see the next morning. We'd had a late night, full of coloured lights and loud music, candy floss and fast rides. We'd discovered that Sam was a speed junky with no fear of heights and that Charlie now had a certain sense of her own mortality, something she certainly hadn't possessed a year ago.

Geoff and I had wandered the fair waiting patiently beneath each swooping, screaming monstrosity, neither willing to go on the rides and both thankful that as we had two children we actually didn't need to.

During the long walk back to the boat (we'd taken Audrey's example to heart and had also pulled well out of town), Geoff had asked me how I was feeling.

"Fine, fine." I grinned at him. "A good coffee always does the trick."

"Look, how are we going to do this?" He peered into the darkness trying to keep Chaos and Disorder in sight.

"Do what?" I staggered around in the dark, cursing my ridiculously bad vision.

Geoff grabbed my arm and steered me around a bend in the riverside. "Move the cars and get everybody and the car in the same place at the same time."

I decided to push my luck a little. "Well you could take the boat and the kids through Stanground tomorrow morning early as planned. I'll walk back and pick up the car and the washing, go and do a big shop, meet you at Whittlesea. We can transfer all the washing and shopping on board, then one of us can take the car on to March, check out the moorings and put the car in the car park for the night." Good grief it was like planning a military campaign.

"OK." Geoff grinned, his teeth flashing white in the darkness. "You get another boat- and child-free day and we'll meet you at Whittlesea."

We walked for a moment in silence just enjoying the peace and quiet, I could see the boat ahead of us, the kids were sitting on the roof, their silhouettes showing against the moon.

"Oh no!" Geoff suddenly blurted out, "We can't do that."

My heart sank, I had just planned another hour with coffee and a book before I had to set out for Whittlesea. "Why not?"

"Because you'll miss doing Dracula's lock and the Whittlesea bend." Geoff grinned at me. "And I know you'd want to add those to your 'things I have done on my own' list."

There is a big problem with having no night sight, when the person who is acting as your eyes runs away, giggling, there is no way you can catch him.

Seven o'clock the next morning, I waved the boat off and turned back for the walk towards Peterborough. It was a lovely morning, with more than a hint of autumn in the air, the mist rose in lazy spirals from the river and heavy dew glistened in the morning sun, turning patches of grass, hedges and all the spiders' webs into glittering art pieces.

I certainly didn't rush and it took me about an hour to get back into town. The car was just where I'd left it (never an absolute certainty in Peterborough), and after taking a moment to get my bearings I headed for the nearest Tesco.

I'd been at Whittlesea for an hour or so before Geoff, kids, dog and boat turned up.

Charlie clambered out of the boat and stretched, then showed me her arms. "Look, this is awful, I've got muscles." She bent her arm at right angles and her skinny arm changed from a piece of string to a piece of string with a small knot in it. I wasn't really that impressed.

"Don't worry, I don't think you're going to give Schwarzenegger a run for his money just yet." I laughed and gave her a poke. "You got here all right then."

She pursed her lips at me. "Yeah, but Geoff tried to kill us."

I looked askance at her and she grinned. "We were a bit too close to one of the lock walls and the Gunwales got hung up on one of those big metal rings, the water kept dropping away and finally she fell off and hit the water with a hell of a splash."

"Whoops!" I grimaced. "I bet your dad wasn't happy about that."

She shrugged and started rummaging through the shopping bags as she was joined by her ever-hungry younger brother.

After they had raided the groceries and scampered off, Geoff also started nosing through the bags. Finally finding a bag of doughnuts, he settled down to enjoy the late sunshine. "I'm going to try and get the day off on Tuesday so that we can both get her through Salters Lode and Denver."

"Oh, thank God for that." I had been almost on the verge of panic about getting through the two locks, especially having to pull the tight right-hand turn out of Salters and round toward Denver. "Do you think they'll let you take it?" I crossed both fingers and sent a quick prayer up to whoever might be listening.

"Well, we haven't any work on, so I can't see why not." Geoff shrugged.

"When's your interview for that other job?" I asked, the sooner the better as far as I was concerned.

Geoff heaved a sigh. "The bloke who's interviewing is away on holiday so it isn't until the end of October, I'd have to check the exact day."

"Three weeks at the most then." I laughed. "They can't fail to be impressed by your general attitude and huge willingness to work."

Geoff frowned. "You have a lot more faith in my interview technique than I do." He shook his head and looked worried for a moment. "I don't want to appear too desperate but honestly if I don't get this job I think I'll scream."

A scream, for a moment I thought that one of the kids was just putting sound effects to Geoff's words but as the hubbub from the front of the boat grew I realised that something was seriously wrong.

Geoff and I both bolted for the front and found both kids leaning over the side desperately trying to reach something in the water.

"What's going on," I shouted above the noise.

"Mortimer fell in." Sam turned round to me. "He was screaming at one of the swans, got both sets of feet up on the side and before Charlie could catch him he'd gone in."

"Don't worry." Geoff waded through the kids. "All dogs can swim."

"Ours can't." Charlie looked worried. "He keeps turning tail up in the water."

"What?" I peered over the side and sure enough there was a black bottom and a tail and a lot of splashing, occasionally a pair of panic-stricken eyes and a couple of nostrils would break the surface but then they'd submerge again and the tail would move further down the boat. "Oh my God! Geoff grab him!"

Geoff leaned out as far as he could but couldn't reach. Quickly turning around he grabbed Charlie (for a minute I thought he was going to throw her over the side), then taking a firm hold of her trousers and sweatshirt he hoisted her up onto the gunwales and held her out at arm's length. Realising that he wasn't going to be able to hold that position for long I grabbed the back of his jeans with one hand and the side of the boat with the other and leant backward hoping to give him more stability, even so, the veins at his temples still stood out and he went a lovely shade of puce, passers-by stood and stared, we looked like the family from that children's book *The Magic Turnip* all in a line and all heaving mightily.

Charlie, after a moment's panic, grabbed Mort's tail and dragged him back toward the boat. Geoff dropped Charlie unceremoniously onto the deck then reaching over the side grabbed our poor pup by the scruff and the tail and hauled him out of the water.

"Sam." I gave him a swift nudge. "Go and get a towel."

I wandered over to the dog who stood up, belched water out onto the planks of the deck then wagged his tail feebly at me. "You stupid animal." I gathered him up heedless that he was wet and shivering. "You really are very badly designed." I mentally added a dog lifejacket to our growing list of needs.

Sam rushed back with a towel and we swaddled our rather glazed dog into the folds.

This is probably the incident that led to Mort's love affair with towels and his deep and abiding hatred of swans, to this day he still can't see a swan without going into complete conniptions, so far he has been bitten, beaten and stamped on by the wretched things, not once has he ever managed to cause even the slightest damage to one but he never stops trying. He gets on with cats, ferrets, other dogs, loves people but swans are his nemesis, I have lost count of the times I have been dragged out on deck to break up a screaming match between the two species.

With the dog still wrapped up in a towel and the two children rushing to give him anything they thought he might need, I helped Geoff get *Minerva* through the Whittlesea lock. Watching them pull out I realised that my handbag with the car keys in it was still on the roof with all the shopping, and had to run down the towpath shouting for Geoff to throw it to me.

The onlookers give me a nervous smile and a rather wide berth as I stamped back toward the car muttering imprecations under my breath about drowning dogs, swans and leaky locks.

That evening, happily ensconced at the moorings in March, I went all out and cooked a veggie curry and settled down for the evening. "You could always just not bother going in tomorrow." I know that I'm not helping Geoff's work situation, but I really don't want another day of taking the boat on my own.

"Oh, don't tempt me," he groaned, "I keep dreaming that I've been fired and wake up really happy."

I got up to put the kettle on. "Look on the bright side, at least you'll be able to get Tuesday off, then we can have all the fun of taking her through Denver together."

"I hope so." Geoff muttered.

I pretended not to hear him, because I knew, if he wasn't there, then the boat probably wasn't going through, and if we didn't get through due to tidal problems tomorrow there were no guarantees that he'd be able to take another day off, we HAD to get through tomorrow.

Geoff waved goodbye with a laugh as he watched me struggling to get Mortimer over the edge of the bow to go out for his morning jaunt and empty. After yesterday's debacle there was no way in hell that dog was going anywhere near the side of the boat. He dragged his feet, lay on his back and just cried continuously until, in the end, I had to pick him up and carry him. He rushed about doing his business, then we had the same fight getting back on to the boat. But at least the added friction and exercise woke me up and had me ready to go far quicker than my normal three cups of coffee could have accomplished.

The rain started just as we pulled away and, huddled in my waterproof on the back of the boat, I decided that this was not going to be a good day. We had talked to the lock keeper the night before and he hadn't sounded very positive about our chances, we had a week to get through these locks before they closed for repairs and we'd be stuck on the wrong side of the sluice.

On our previous trip we had been stuck at March for a week so I knew that the tides were a bit iffy around this time of year. All I could do was pull my collar up, put my head down and hope.

To compound all my trouble and woes, Minerva was handling like a pregnant cow. With hardly any power, her steering was like swirling a stick in a bowl of thick porridge. Eventually after about an hour and a half of difficulties, I pulled her in at the side of the river and tried to think of something else that could be wrong: something which wouldn't necessitate me fishing about in the cold water beneath the weed hatch.

One cup of coffee later and I'd worked out I had no choice but to put my hands and arms into that water, I had tried poking beneath the boat with a stick but that hadn't come up with anything useful so there was nothing for it, I was going to have to face the dreaded weed hatch. I shuddered, tried to bribe the kids to do it for me, but even at ridiculous amounts of money being offered they both just grinned and shook their heads at me. (Possibly because they both knew that even if they actually did it I was almost guaranteed to welch on any deal they made.)

They did turn out to watch me do it though so that was nice. I opened the hatch and stared with distaste down into the water, putting one hand in I felt around the skeg (the pointy bit that the propeller is attached to) and from there to the little gap between boat and prop. There wasn't one, the gap was entirely filled with something rough and filled with leaves and tendrils. Ah well, at least I knew what the problem was.

It took about three-quarters of an hour to get all the rubbish from around the prop, two different types of rope, one quite thick and coarse the other a nice blue bailer twine which in turn had gathered up every weed and floating bush for the last ten miles and turned it into a foliate ball which had almost completely obscured the prop. By the time I had finished, both hands were blue to the elbows and I had dropped two knives into the river.

Closing the weed hatch, I gibbered gently at Charlie and amazingly she managed to work out the nonsensical sounds coming from between my chattering teeth meant "Go and put the kettle on".

About an hour later I was almost warm again. "I'll take her on, Mum." Charlie gave me a cheerful grin.

"What?" I didn't manage to get the entire word out but at least I was making more sense than I had been earlier.

347

"There aren't any locks, are there?" She looked at me quizzically. "I'll take it slow and you can warm up for a bit more." She waited for a reply and when I just looked dubious she pressed on. "Honestly it will be fine."

I took a moment to get my ice-locked jaw mobile again. "There is a lock, it's about three-quarters of an hour away. It's a manned lock but the route is pretty straight till then." I looked longingly at the fire and made a decision. "Any problems and you give three short blasts on the horn and I'll be out quicker than you can say Wah!"

Charlie grinned and scurried off in search of coat, hat, gloves and all the other bits and pieces that would make her stand out on the back less boring, (cup of tea, mp3, magazine, etc., etc.).

Sam had been paying close attention while all this had been going on and as Charlie rushed off he grabbed my arm. "You're letting Charlie drive the boat, by herself?" He put on a dramatic and worried expression.

I nodded.

"We're all going to die!" he screamed and threw himself backwards onto the sofa then closing his eyes he extended one hand dramatically toward the ceiling. "Mother! is that you calling me into the light?"

"No." I poked him in the ribs until he screamed with laughter. "This is your mother calling you a twit."

He laughed and rushed off down the boat to sit on Mortimer, who took the whole thing with fairly good grace.

We made the next lock within the hour. Charlie, on the whole, had done exceptionally well. There were only two occasions where I'd had to stick my head out of the doors and tell her to slow down.

The couple at the Upwell lock are lovely, chatty and helpful. I think they were a little surprised at such a young driver and were quite relieved when I appeared out of the boat to take over.

Charlie pulled *Minerva* very slowly and carefully into the lock and apart from a few nudges and instructions I let her get on with it. She seemed perfectly content to stay on the plate so I was quite happy to get off and have a quick chat, not only with the lock keeper but with the owner of another boat who was waiting on the moorings on the other side.

Charlie brought *Minerva* out of the lock and parked her carefully on the moorings at the far side.

"Do you want me to take over now?" I asked as we sat over a cup of tea.

Charlie thought about it for a moment. "No, not really, unless you really want to."

I shrugged and said, "I'm happy in here, and you seem to be doing a good job, but there's a really horrible right hand bend coming up in a little while, and you might need some help with that."

"OK," Charlie grinned and said, "I quite like being in control of this great lump." She put her coat back on and disappeared outside.

The bend at Outwell was, as predicted, pretty hairy but between the two of us we managed it and passed gently into a landscape that can only be described as terminally boring.

The Middle Levels stretches in a flat plain toward the horizon with only little clumps of houses to break up the monotony. The waterway is long and straight, the road which runs alongside is long and straight. The grey sky touched the grey earth and we all plodded along in the gloom.

When it was my turn to drive (we were taking hour-on, hour-off rotations by that point) I tried to put the radio on, but the cheerful voice of the announcer and the bouncy music seemed so at odds with the glum landscape that I had to change it, I felt as though the sound was cutting through the melancholy like a knife. I turned to a classical station hoping that something statelier would be a better accompaniment. Unfortunately they were playing Carmina Burana by Carl Orff and that fitted the landscape so well it gave me the creeps: I turned it off.

As we finally passed through Nordelph, ducking under the last low bridge on the other side I was smitten by completely opposing feelings. On one hand I was ecstatic to be nearly out of the Middle Levels, and I was happy that the journey was nearly over, through the two big locks and home via Ely, only one more day remaining. On the other hand I was worried that we wouldn't get through those locks and also I didn't really want the journey to end because then we would just go back to living on a boat. It was the journey that was the exciting part and I was worried that the living part wouldn't be as much fun as I'd remembered it.

It is always a bit of a surprise to arrive at Salters Lode, one minute you're plodding along a fairly slim passage between high weeds, the next you go under a road bridge and find the river just stops dead and there you are.

The car was parked on the side and I could see a figure sitting slumped inside. Hitting the horn, I smirked a little as the figure jerked up and then stretched and got out of the car.

Geoff had a face like thunder. Whoops! I hadn't realised he was that fast asleep. "I'm sorry," I shouted, "I didn't mean to wake you up, I was just letting you know that we're here." I tailed off: his face hadn't changed, "What's the matter?"

"I got fired," he muttered through gritted teeth.

Well I wasn't expecting that and held up a hand to stop the following explanation. "Hold that thought, let's get her tied up and put away, we can get the kettle on and you can tell me all about it over treacle tart, OK?"

Geoff nodded, his angry face melting into a sort of glum and forlorn look and when I reached over and gave him a big hug he just slumped into my shoulder with a sigh. Obviously it had not been a good day.

Tea made, tart eaten, kids and dog rushing around outside, he finally got around to telling me what had happened.

"First thing this morning," he began, "I asked for tomorrow off and that seemed to be OK, then I went back to sitting around waiting for some work to come in." He paused to take a sip of tea. "About three o'clock

351

I was called into the office and was basically told, thanks very much but don't bother coming back."

"Oh dear, you must have felt horrible." I gave him another hug. "Do you think it's because you asked to take the day off?"

Geoff shook his head. "No, I don't think so, I haven't actually done anything since I've been there and it doesn't look like there's any work coming in." He paused and sighed. "It's been such a waste of time."

"Well you're getting paid for what you've done, aren't you?" I got up to put the kettle on again, this obviously wasn't going to be a one-cup conversation.

"Yeah, but I could have been with you and the kids." He put his head in his hands and stared at his boots. "The aerial, the windows, your hand," he continued, waving at my, now slightly grubby, bandage, "none of that might have happened if I'd been here."

"Humph." I sat down next to him. "I think you flatter yourself a bit." He looked up hurt. "Oh, I didn't mean it like that." I gave him yet another hug. "Unless you've suddenly become King Canute, there was no way you could have slowed down the water in Titchmarsh Lock, so it may well have been your hand, not mine that got hurt, but as we usually run so that you do the locks and I work the pound I can't see that anything would have been different."

Geoff shrugged and nodded.

"Look," the kettle chose that moment to blow its whistle but I continued, "we're here, we have an extra week's money in our pockets, you are definitely going

352

to be here to get us through the lock, you have another interview in a couple of weeks . . ."

"Two actually," Geoff interrupted, "I got another call today, there's a job in Peterborough, they need an electrician with data and UPS experience to work in a banking data centre."

"Oh," I grinned. "Well that's great."

I stood up and reached my good hand out to pull him up as well. "You're being a fraud, this is for the best, if we can't get through here tomorrow then you're going to be around the next day to help out and the next, and the next, so I for one am incredibly relieved."

Geoff gave me the first real grin of the afternoon. I took his cup from him, turned him around and pushed him out of the doors. "Now go and see the lock keeper and see what our chances are of getting home tomorrow."

Geoff grinned again and went.

Shaking my head slightly, I gathered up cups and plates and began to wash up before making some dinner. I had to smile as I looked out of the window, the kids had found sticks and were sword-fighting across the grass outside. Mortimer was almost beside himself and spent his time launching himself indiscriminately at any moving stick, the children had to reclaim their weapons from the dog before he or she could hit the other. He was doing a damn fine job of peace-keeping.

Not much had changed since the last time we were here, except that, unlike last time, Helen and Dave weren't here and I was actually sober, which I most certainly wasn't on our last visit.

The phone rang and drying my hands rapidly I looked at the incoming number and smiled. "Hi, that is so weird: I was literally just thinking about you."

"Oh yeah?" Helen sounded wary

"Yep, we're back at Salters Lode." I laughed down the phone. "I can't remember much about our last visit, can you?"

We chatted for about an hour, finishing only when the kids bounced back in with Mortimer barking behind them.

"Is that a dog I can hear?" Helen, a massive dog lover herself, could almost recognise which breed of dog it was just from its breathing.

"Yes, Amelia bought Chaos and Disorder a pup for Christmas." I retrieved one of my socks from the puppy in question. "He seems to have fitted in quite well."

"What is he?" Helen laughed.

"Staffy," I said shortly, "but so far he hasn't shown any signs of aggression."

Helen seemed surprised. "Why on earth should he? They're lovely and really good with kids."

I sighed, I knew I should have called her to get her view on him when he arrived.

"But Marie . . ."

"Hmm?"

"Actually, that's what I'm calling about," she suddenly sounded hesitant.

"What, Mortimer?"

"Mortimer?" She laughed. "Only you would call a dog Mortimer." She sighed. "No, it's Herbert I'm calling about."

Herbert had been our very, very ancient and incapacitated terrier when we had lived on *Happy Go Lucky*. By the time we had decided to put her up for sale, he'd been quite ill and wasn't dealing with life on board at all well and we'd been told by the vet after one particular scare that he really ought to be put to sleep or at least find him a final home where life wasn't so exciting and active. I had been devastated at the time and Helen had come to our rescue, finding him a place with her friend Linda in Scotland who had a lot of old dogs and was quite happy to have another potter about her bungalow.

"Herbie?" I smiled, he'd had the most horrible smell and unlike our current enthusiast had spent most of his life cuddled up to the fire or wrapped in his blankets, he was ugly and battered, half-blind and had fallen into the river with alarming regularity. "How is he?"

Helen sighed. "He died this morning."

"Oh."

"I'm really sorry," Helen paused, obviously trying to find the right thing to say.

I saved her from the search. "Hels, don't worry, he must have been about a hundred in dog years. What happened?"

"Well, nothing really, he just died in his sleep." Helen laughed. "He spent most of his life asleep so it was sort of expected really, but he wasn't in pain, he just didn't wake up."

355

We spent another ten minutes chatting then, spying Geoff walking back toward the boat, looking a bit concerned, I assured her I'd call as soon as we got home and ended the call.

"What's up?" I called over to Geoff as I pocketed my phone.

Geoff carried on trudging toward me with no sign that he'd even heard the question (he really must get his ears tested sometime soon). When he finally reached me he gave a small shrug. "No answers, I'm afraid."

I must have given him a quizzical look because he continued, "He can't say whether we'll get through or not." He shrugged again and said, "We're just going to have to play it by ear."

Later that evening, Mortimer decided that nine o'clock was the perfect time to want to go for a walk. I took one look at the kids engrossed in some Disney film and decided that even asking one of them to take him out was just going to be met with blank stares, Geoff was asleep and snoring on the sofa, so, avoiding the gambolling, leaping puppy, I wandered around the boat, putting on walking boots and coat, I then filled the pockets with phone, torch, and secondary torch and filled my travel mug with coffee.

After losing Mortimer in the dark the previous week, Geoff had brought home a brightly coloured and reflective collar with tiny LED's set into it at odd spaces, I hadn't had the chance to use it on him yet and tonight seemed the perfect opportunity. I told the kids that I was going out (I'm not sure they even heard me) and, turning on the torch that was attached by straps to my hat I headed out into the night with Captain Enthusiast.

There was a definite scent of autumn in the air so with Mortimer flashing like a small Christmas tree and me taking a sip of coffee every other step we headed away from the water and down a small lane. It was a very still night, thick clouds obscured any moon and I was glad of my two torches.

As we wandered along I watched Mortimer and thought of Herbert. The final loss of the little dog gave me a small ache; it was another part of another life that had now vanished. He had never really got his head around living on a boat and fell off with alarming regularity, I grinned as I remembered some of the troubles he got himself into. "Seeya Herb," I whispered, then jumped as the light on my head went out.

Stopping for a moment, I placed the other torch carefully onto the ground and took my hat off. It was obvious that the battery had gone on the head torch but I bashed it a couple of times just to make sure (this percussive maintenance had never worked for me before, but there was always going to be a first time).

Obviously wondering why I wasn't immediately behind him, Mortimer came bouncing back towards me. Jumping up at me with his ball in his mouth he misjudged the whole thing horribly and landed directly on the big torch that I had placed so carefully on the ground, trampled to death, it too went out and plunged me into darkness.

357

I think I may have mentioned before that I have no night vision. I've heard other people say this but they always have a little, I have none, none at all. Plunged into an inky blackness, I immediately panicked. There were no houses around, certainly no street lights and with thick clouds covering the whole sky there wasn't even a glimmer of starlight, let alone moonlight. All I could see was an alternating flash of bright blue and white lights that emanated about a foot from the ground and appeared to be moving in circles (Mortimer was apparently chasing his tail).

Feeling a little like Thelma from *Scooby Doo* I knelt down and felt around for the other torch, I must have taken a couple of steps away from where I was before and I couldn't feel it anywhere around. Taking a few deep breaths in an effort to calm the real panic that was building, I decided that Mort's LED's were so bright that they were probably blinding me every time they flashed, I could see where the dog was but they certainly weren't lighting up anything around him so, reaching down, put him on his lead and turned off his collar. It made absolutely no difference at all, I could feel Mort tugging on his lead and there were other sounds, a wind seemed to have sprung up and there was a rustling and sighing among the trees so, just to have something to look at, I turned it back on.

I waved a hand in front of my face but obviously there was no point in waiting for my eyes to adjust to the darkness. They just weren't going to. My big problem was that I wasn't sure if I had turned around or not so I couldn't just do an about face and walk slowly and carefully back to the boat.

I stood for a moment in an absolute rictus of indecision, the sounds around me grew in intensity, the wind became stronger and I was positive I could hear something rustling around in the bushes by the side of the lane

There was nothing for it, I pulled out my phone and dialled Geoff. (Oh, I was not going to live this down for a long, long time.)

"Hi," I squeaked as his bleary voice asked me where the hell I was, "I've got a bit of a problem, my head light has gone out and Mort trampled the other torch to death, so I'm in the dark."

There was silence for a moment at the other end of the phone as Geoff assimilated this information then he laughed. "You can't see a thing can you?" he deduced.

"Nope." I relaxed a little at the sound of his calm and steady voice. "Can you come and find me? I think there's something in the bushes just waiting for me to make a move." I could hear Sam in the background asking what was wrong.

"Did you go up that lane?" Geoff asked then without waiting for me to answer he went on, "It's all right Sam, your mum's torch has broken so I've got to go and get her."

"Yes, I haven't turned off or anything, I just walked in a straight line." I frowned; I could hear the kids laughing and making comments about "blind as a bat" and "maybe Mortimer should be trained as a guide dog".

"Can't you just turn round and come back?" Geoff asked, "Surely you can't have got that far, as soon as you get around the corner you should be able to see the boat, we've got all the lights on."

"Well I would," I snipped at him, "but I can't remember if I've turned around, well, I know I've turned around but I'm not sure how many times and what direction I'm facing in."

Geoff laughed again. "Hang on, let me get my boots on and another torch and I'll come and find you."

"Thank you," I muttered; the snuffling began again in the bushes. "If you feel like jogging I would really appreciate it."

"I'll be there as soon as I can." Geoff turned his phone off.

Even the light from my phone was comforting so I kept pressing buttons to keep it on but soon the battery started to beep so I desisted and stood in the dark. Mortimer, who could obviously see perfectly well, ran around on the end of his long extending lead for a while, then, bored and wondering why we were standing still, came back and jumped up at my legs. I knelt down to stroke him but as I did he turned away from me and began to growl.

"Oh please don't do that," I whispered, desperately trying to see what he was growling at. No good, still completely black. For a moment I wondered how the blind cope and my admiration for anyone with a sight problem increased one hundred fold, to be forever in this darkness, with sounds and smells growing out of proportion was just something I couldn't contemplate.

They must be incredibly brave, every small trip for them must be an exercise in heroism, I resolved there and then to put a very large amount of money in the next Guide Dogs for the Blind box I came across.

Mortimer's growling took on a new intensity and he pressed himself back on to my lap, his little body shaking with the force of each rumbling snarl. I could feel my heart trying to beat itself out of my body, I was actually quite irritated with it, the sound of the flustered beating was actually blocking out my ability to listen to whatever it was that had upset the dog so much.

I wiped my sweaty palms down my jeans and looked this way and that down the lane hoping for a glimmer of light that would herald the arrival of my knight in shining armour, there was no sign of illumination but the rustling in the bushes got louder.

Mortimer leapt forward toward the sound, barking and snarling, stopping only when he reached the end of his lead and as I was already on my knees this pulled me completely off balance and face down on to the ground. Finally getting my feet sorted out I pulled him back toward me and stood up trembling, trying not to make any noise I kept myself completely motionless while I desperately tried to listen to what was going on around me.

The soft and warm breath on the back of my neck finally dissolved any bravado I may have been hanging on to and turned me into a big fat girly. I screamed, then when I ran out of breath I stopped, refuelled and screamed again.

At the end of the second scream, Geoff had arrived, out of breath and eyes wide, he obviously thought I was being murdered or at the very least eaten alive by one of the elusive big cats you see on the news.

"Huff . . . what's the . . . puff . . . matter?" He shone the light around.

Now that there was light I stared around looking for the source of all my fears, straight into the eyes of a rather puzzled-looking Friesian that had broken away from the herd and come over to investigate the barking dog. The track I had been walking along was sunken between two fields so the cow was a lot taller than she had any right to be and hence the breath on the back of my neck.

Mortimer hadn't even noticed the cow, he was busy in the bushes still growling and scouting around.

"So what's the matter?" Geoff stood with his hands on his knees breathing heavily; he had obviously run at the sound of the screams.

I could feel myself blushing. "Mortimer was growling and then I got breathed on by a cow and I couldn't see so I thought there was something really big behind me, and I couldn't see and all I could hear was this rustling and Mort was growling and snarling and I was really scared," I gabbled at him.

"You got breathed on by a 'cow'," Geoff enunciated. He shook his head and taking a deep breath stood up and shone the torch on the dog. "Mort!" he snapped, "come here."

Mortimer backed away from the grasses and bushes and trotted over with his tail waving.

"I know it sounds stupid now." I grabbed his arm and began dragging him back toward the boat. "But it was really frightening and you know I can't see in the dark." Well that sounded pathetic even to me.

Geoff just snorted.

Back at home, I made tea and had to endure an hour of the kids creeping up behind me, blowing on my neck and shouting "Moo!!" at me before running away and giggling.

When all was finally quiet later on that evening, the kids were in bed and Geoff and I were having a last cup of tea, it occurred to me that as a species we haven't really come all that far. I had never actually seen anything on any dark night to be frightened of, so why should my imagination run riot? Why would I not think "cow" or "horse"? Maybe it's just inbuilt in all of us, a way of keeping safe, from back when our species was young. It also occurred to me that while it may be darker and scarier in the country, these days the dark is more dangerous in cities. I didn't really come up with any answers but I did manage to make a promise to myself that I would never again go out without at least two torches and a backup, and a backup for the backup.

Standing in the sunshine, looking down into the lock the next morning, I finally realised how the lock worked. Never actually having been through Salters Lode in this direction, I had always been slightly confused by descriptions of the two sets of lock gates, but taking a long look I could now see why only smaller boats could go through when the water was high.

At first glance it seemed like any other lock but, as the tidal waters receded, there slowly appeared another set of gates, these are set further back and are only half height, when the tide is high they are completely submerged so there we were waiting for the waters to drop enough so that those half-height gates could be used to get us through the lock and out into the tidal waters of the Great Ouse.

We spent much of the morning wandering about doing little jobs and occasionally peering over the lock gates. Slowly, very slowly, the waters began to drop. First the top of the gates could be seen, then a little more.

Eventually the lock keeper decided that it was as good as it was going to get and said we could give it a go.

I have to admit I didn't like the sound of that very much, I wanted more assurance than just "give it a go". Out on the Great Ouse the wide river looked to be running very fast, far too fast for my liking.

But there really wasn't any way to turn back now. So we all piled aboard and Geoff brought her steadily in through both sets of rear gates.

"The best thing you can do," the keeper shouted over the sound of running water, "is to get her to turn as quickly as possible." He pointed out toward the other lock. "How powerful is that engine of yours?"

"It's OK," Geoff shouted back at him.

OK! OK!! I was horrified, there was nothing about our engine that was remotely OK. It was lolly sticks, string and Blu-tack and that was on a good day.

The waters began to drop beneath us and within no time at all the big gates ahead of us opened up. There was no doubt, we were in for a bumpy ride.

The difference in water speed was horribly apparent as we pulled out of the lock and into the tiny channel that led out on to the river.

"Pile on the power and turn," the keeper shouted again.

Geoff did just that, with a huge belch of smoke that drifted out of the chimney and covered the lock keeper who was standing above us, we moved forward with a fairly rapid acceleration. Geoff kept the tiller far over, intending to get her nose around to the right as soon as he could.

Utter and complete failure. The rushing waters caught her nose as she emerged from the channel, dragged her out to mid stream and without a by your leave carried us away toward Kings Lynn. It was shocking how fast we were travelling, Geoff pushed the tiller over as far as he could and desperately attempted to get her nose round.

By the time we managed to get the situation under control, we were at least half a mile from the lock. We'd travelled that distance in about five minutes. Getting back past the lock and up to Denver Sluice against the tide took us much longer.

The lock keeper waved as we chugged slowly past and made exaggerated relief movements, then grinned and waved again. We weren't dead, we were heading in the right direction he was happy.

365

Once inside the huge pound of Denver Sluice I could finally take a breath and peel my rigid fingers one by one from the top of the boat.

Geoff turned to me with a big grin. "That was exciting!"

It was no good, I really had no other choice, I had to slap him. (But only gently.) This was the second time in twelve hours where my heart had speeded up to at least twice its normal rate, one of these days it was all going to be too much for the poor thing and I was going to be looking at an extended stay in Addenbrooke's Hospital.

CHAPTER
THIRTEEN

Nearly Home

Three hours travelling and we finally had Ely in our sights, another boat had been following us for a while, it obviously was going faster than us because slowly, very slowly, it had been catching us up.

Deciding that this would be a good time to fill with water and pump out before sorting out the final leg of the journey to the moorings, we pulled into the pump point and busied ourselves with water and the huge pipes of the pump-out machine.

Minerva is a little odd because she actually has two pump-out points. The waste tank forms a "U" shape across the boat and down both sides. It is actually two "L"-shaped tanks joined together with a huge pipe across the centre. Consequently it's quite hard to get a completely empty tank. We decided that just to make sure we had done everything properly we would pump out on both sides.

The boat following us drew closer. Finally we finished and noticed that they were holding position behind, obviously waiting for us to move on so that they too could use the pumping facilities.

We returned everything to its rightful place and closed the gates on the pump out and climbed back onto *Minerva*.

"Oy!" A voice hailed us over the water. "Are you going to get your lazy bloody arses out of there or do we have to come over and give you a wee bit of a shove?"

Geoff and I looked at each other, the last major altercation I'd had with anybody had been almost on this very spot. We'd pulled *Happy Go Lucky* in for a pump-out and had managed to mortally offend a particularly grumpy angler. Things had gone downhill pretty rapidly that time. This time I was older and wiser and not in the mood to take any crap from anyone.

Turning around to deliver a withering mouthful I was arrested by the sight of two grinning faces. It's an odd feeling and I am positive that everybody has experienced it at one time or another. It's when you see someone that you know, so very well, but they're not where they should be, so for a split second you don't recognise them at all.

The other boat drew alongside, both occupants laughing uproariously at our stunned faces. "Oh you should have seen your face," the woman said, her incredibly long hair floating out behind her in the wind. "If looks could kill, I'd be face down in the river by now."

Her husband, sitting on the roof laughed. "Hello," he said, "fancy seeing you here."

All I could manage was a strangled, "Wha the hell?"

At that moment Sam stuck his head out of the double doors. "Uncle Scum!!" he shrieked.

"Hello Sam," both of them said in unison, "so how do you feel about having us as neighbours?" Drew laughed at Sam's stunned face.

Bill (Sarah) and Drew (Andrew) have known Sam since he was a bump. They were one of the reasons we originally thought of buying a boat, we'd been to their wedding, and had generally eaten, drunk and had a good time with them for what seemed like for ever.

They bought their boat *The Blue Boar* a couple of years before we even considered taking to the water and had spent most of the last six years swanning about around Oxford and Reading. They certainly never came as far as Cambridge.

"What the hell are you doing here?" I finally managed to gasp.

"We're heading for our new mooring." Bill grinned at me as she leant on the tiller. I think we're two boats down from you.

"Seriously?"

Drew nodded. "Yep, got fed up with wandering around Reading and decided to come back to Cambridge." Bill had worked in Cambridge for some years before she met Drew.

"Weather's closing in." Bill pulled her collar up around her ears. "Was going to suggest a barby tonight but how about we just come round with a bottle of something and some food?"

I nodded, still unable to really speak.

"OK." They gave us twin evil grins. "We'll see you later." Drew put a foot on *Minerva's* roof and pushed off.

We followed their progress in silence.

"Are we going to be living next door to Uncle Scum?" Sam shouted up to us.

Geoff nodded. "Evidently so."

"Yay." Sam disappeared inside, we could hear him shouting the news at Charlie.

The last leg of the trip, took us down such a well-known route. Out through Ely, along the river to the pub, a quick right turn into Mill Creek and once again, we were home.

For the last twenty minutes of the trip I'd felt physically sick. Here we were again, when we left to deliver *Happy Go Lucky* to her new owner I had never, for one minute dared to hope that I'd be back, we'd intended to buy a sea-going barge. But here we were. Shocked faces that we knew so well looked out at us from boat windows as we meandered past. Jude, in particular did a wonderful double-take then almost flattened herself against the window she was waving so hard.

A couple of people that we didn't know, then Lewis the grumpy electrician, Disco Steve and a wonderful gap where our new boat would just fit in like a foot in Cinderella's shoe.

Minerva stuck her nose into the space as though she'd done it a hundred times before, then pulled her backside in snug and tight to the bank.

It was as though time had stood still, our little patch was overgrown and untended but the mooring posts that Geoff had sweated and sworn over were still there. The tyres that we'd pinched out of a skip were still dangling on heavy rope over the side of the mooring and even our steps were still where we'd left them.

Charlie leapt out of the boat, followed closely by her brother. "We're home, we're home," she chanted and leapt from the gunwale onto the grass. It was beautifully choreographed, the overgrown grass covered a multitude of sins and when her feet touched ground level she found that it was merely long grass and disappeared up to the waist in the river.

Geoff leaned over the side as Charlie, scowling and dripping, soaked to the skin climbed out on to the bank. "I take it you forgot about that hole, it's the same one you fell into at least twice when we were last here."

Charlie, muttering and shedding clothes as she went, stamped around to the front of the boat. Obviously intending to dry off and get changed just as she'd done the last time.

Geoff reeled out the electric cable and plugging ourselves back into the old electricity post, Geoff switched her over to land power. *Minerva*, suddenly given a blood transfusion, lit up like a fairground ride and as the clouds rolled in making it much darker than it had any right to be at four thirty in the afternoon, she looked very much like home.

I couldn't get the grin off my face. As neighbours and old friends emerged from boats to say hello, I tried to let go of any doubts or worries that I had been holding for the trip down. The next two years would be hard work but it was definitely going to be worth it.

CHAPTER
FOURTEEN

Home at Last and
Everything's Perfect?

We'd managed to turn up only two weeks before half term so the kids were quite happy to go back to their old schools, each knowing that they only had to suffer a short while before they'd be off on holiday again. Geoff was also happy, he began making long lists of things he had to do before winter set in and I waited for instructions.

The very first thing on our list was to put up temporary fencing so that Mortimer would have an enclosed space to rush about in. We spent the first week doing just that, it was only a set of metal posts and green heavy duty netting but Mort was daft enough that if it looked like a fence, it was obviously something he couldn't get through so he didn't even try, it worked quite well.

Knowing that we really wouldn't have long before the cold weather settled in for good, we purchased a wood shed and set about filling it as much as we could. We emptied the boat of all the bits and bobs that we had thought we might need for travelling and filled her up with stuff for just general living. However, our first real building job was to make Charlie a proper bedroom and get her some space of her own. It took Geoff about a weekend.

The back cabin was exceptionally classical, with a bed and a set of cupboards and drawers that miraculously turned into a table and another small bed, it was really ingenious. There was a tiny stove in one corner and the whole was painted in the ubiquitous roses and castles designs. It was like standing in a dolls house — it was unbelievable that whole families used to live in these conditions.

Charlie, although she appreciated the history, hated the whole thing on sight so Geoff took to removing large amounts of re-created history and using what was left to make a bedroom fit for a teenage girl.

As each piece of decorated wood clattered onto the bank I winced knowing that the purists among the boating crowd would surely be shaking their fists and howling with rage at such vandalism. But it couldn't be helped; no fourteen-year-old wanted to live in something that looked like Granny's cupboard.

By the end of the weekend he had created a bed, a wardrobe and a table, we had painted over all the (slightly faded) roses and castles and the whole thing was pristine white and smelt of paint rather than damp wood and oil.

Although originally very happy about the whole thing, when the time came to actually go to bed Charlie was more than a little reticent.

"What if something gets me?" she asked in a slightly quivery voice. "I have to walk round the boat to get to you, will you hear me if I shout?"

Geoff gave her a hug, "I've thought of that," he said, "just above your bed is a button." He wheeled her toward the door of the boat. "Come on I'll show you, all you have to do is press it and a door bell will ring in here and one of us will be out like a shot." He grabbed a torch and opened the front door, gesturing for Charlie to accompany him. "OK?"

Charlie looked at him dubiously. "Will you actually come if I press it, though?" She looked worried.

"Absolutely," I confirmed. "Ring the bell and we'll be there before you take your finger away."

Frowning she gave a small nod and went out with Geoff. "Night, Mum," she said as she left.

An hour later there was the sudden sharp buzz of a doorbell ringing.

Sighing, Geoff got to his feet. "I'll go," he said.

Ten minutes later he was back. "She can't sleep and keeps hearing funny noises."

I nodded vaguely, unwilling to take my eyes off the television programme I was watching. "Well, it's only to be expected, she must feel a little isolated down there." I paused for a moment, remembering the conversations that we had had about the rear cabin. "She definitely wanted to sleep in there, didn't she?"

Geoff took a sip of tea and nodded. "Yep, said she needed some space for herself."

"Hmm," I replied, draining my mug just as the buzzer sounded a second time, "I think this might actually take some getting used to for her."

That evening Charlie rang the doorbell a total of seventeen times and it was well past two o'clock in the morning before she finally fell asleep. By that time Geoff was so tired he had finally given in and agreed to put in an intercom system.

Getting Charlie up for school the next morning was more than a little difficult, she had locked her door (just to stop "something" getting at her) and there was no way I could get into the back cabin to give her the shaking she so often required. At every threat there was a mumbled affirmation that she really was getting up and every time I shouted she just promised to come out then went back to sleep.

I couldn't get through the metal doors and there was no access cut between the main body of the boat and the back cabin as yet so there she stayed, safe and out of parental control. Finally I gave up and took Sam to school (he felt this was entirely unfair) leaving Geoff with strict instructions to find a way to get her out by the time I got back.

On my return I could see Geoff standing on the bank staring at the cabin with a cup of tea in his hand. "How's it going?" I enquired.

"Badly," he replied, "I've shouted and banged and even taken a hammer to the side of the boat, but there's been no reply."

"Really?" I frowned at the rear cabin. "Do you think she's OK?"

"Yes." Geoff scowled. "I think she's fine, I think she wanted a day off school, I think she's warm and comfortable and I think she's just ignoring us."

I studied the back of the boat for a moment then, moving closer to my fuming husband, I whispered. "Do you think you could take out that porthole window?"

He opened his mouth to speak but I stopped him by putting a finger to my lips. At his frown I lifted the carrier bag I had brought with me from the car and opened it, allowing him to peer inside. "I made a little stop on the way home," I whispered.

The grin that slid across Geoff's face was almost pure evil and he took a long look at the porthole that was one of the two windows to Charlie's bedroom. "Do you know," he paused for another grin, "I think I probably can."

"Just loosen it off, quietly," I whispered, "Then come in for a cup of tea, I want her nice and relaxed, I want her to think we've given up."

Geoff nodded and tiptoed toward the boat taking a screwdriver out of his pocket as he went.

An hour later and we had finished our tea, washed up the breakfast things and had clattered around in the main body of the boat enough that Charlie should have been well asleep.

Geoff checked his watch. "Now?" he said.

Reaching into the Halford's bag, I took out the can and air-horn attachment I had picked up on the way home. "Yep, I don't think we'll wake anybody else up now, most normal people are up and about."

Trying not to giggle, we tiptoed down the length of the boat, Mortimer gambolling at our heels obviously wondering what the hell was going on. Geoff gently pulled out the glass and gestured me forward.

I peered into the back cabin and sure enough, as I had expected, Charlie was fast asleep, one arm hanging off the side of the bed, the other thrown above her head.

Giving Geoff one last smile I tucked one ear into my shoulder and stuck a finger in the other then, sticking the horn through the open gap, I depressed the button on the can of compressed air it was attached to. The sound was even louder than I could have expected and Charlie's reaction so much more than anyone could have hoped for.

At the startling screeching sound she sat straight up in bed with a scream, then arms flailing she hit the floor with a thump, bed clothes and various books slid off the bed and landed on top of her, suddenly plunged into darkness, she panicked further and kicked her way out of the obstructions to stand all wide eyes and chaotic hair in her tiny cabin, she stared around, obviously wondering where the sound had come from.

Staggering over to the door, she flicked the bolt off and stared out into the morning sun. I slid along the side of the boat brought one hand around the back of the boat and hit the horn again. Charlie fell back into her cabin with yet another scream.

Convinced that she was now wide awake I stuck my head through her doorway. "Rise and shine, sweetie," I said and gave her a smile, "it's time you were up and about."

As I wandered back toward the front doors I realised it was quite depressing the amount of swear words that child knew and even more depressing that she was willing to use them, honestly where's the respect? But it was difficult to be cross while giggling with your husband.

About half an hour later Charlie emerged, red-eyed and angry in the living room, but before she could get her sense of injustice revved up and her list of excuses going she was read the riot act.

One, thou wilst not lock your parents out of your bedroom; two, thou wilst not ignore said parents and pretend to be getting up; three, thou wilst not grab a sneaky day off school by performing number two. It went on and on there were about ten points in total. Charlie ended up grounded and spluttering in fury.

She was told that if this happened again Geoff would take the lock off her door and she would be left to worry that anyone could get in at night, also the next time I had to wake her up it would be the horn attached to a hosepipe spitting freezing water.

Charlie stamped back to her cabin and although she didn't lock the door she refused to come out and we didn't see her again till tea time when hunger finally drove her, still sulking and petulant, back into the living room to be fed. The next morning she was up and dressed on time but still acidly silent.

The next day, as Geoff and I were sitting over a pile of paperwork trying to work out what the first job would be in the peace and quiet of a child-free boat, my mother rang.

"Would you like to get rid of the kids for a week so you can get on?" she asked.

I think we may have caused permanent damage to her ears; we were so exuberant with our agreement. The plan was that Charlie and Sam would go with Mum and Dad over to France for the half-term holiday. Dad wanted to mow the lawn and get the house on the market and it seemed like a good time to have a last break before winter set in.

With this much time offered to us and with Geoff's interview for a new job on the Wednesday of half term, we decided to tackle the biggest job we had, a new kitchen.

The children were very much in favour of a half-term trip, so, loaded up with clothes, passports and other bits and pieces, we waved them all off early on Saturday morning and looked forward to a week of heavy building.

Geoff had already got all the wood and bits necessary for building a new kitchen but was unhappy with my plans. I wanted a "walk through" kitchen with the work surface on the river side coming out at 45 degrees which would match a decline of 45 degrees on the land side. This would give us as much work surface as possible and put the sink in a nice little unit of its own.

We had a nice round sink that would go in and we planned to move the cooker from the kitchen that was already on the boat (it couldn't really be called a kitchen it was a box with a cooker in it), so we had one week to re-line the walls, put in a new gas line, move the cooker and get the whole thing up and running.

I have to admit it would have been nice to relax a little and enjoy each other's company but with only a limited amount of time, we were up at six in the morning and worked through till midnight each night.

Geoff found the kitchen units particularly trying and by the end of the week could only actually mutter, "45 degrees" to any question he was asked. However he did a wonderful job and by the time the kids came back, we had a proper kitchen complete with herb rack and tea towel holder, it was lovely.

Geoff had taken one day off and had attended an interview for a maintenance electrician for a company in Cambridge. As we were waiting for the kids to return on the Friday, he got the long-awaited call, he was, thankfully, once again gainfully employed.

On the day the children were due back we had a call from my mother. "Hi there," she chirped down the phone, "just making sure you were home, we'll be there in about half an hour."

"Oh OK. Did you all have a good time?" I mentally ran through all the things I could do in half an hour.

"Well, most of us did," Mum said and laughed, "but don't worry I'll tell you all about it when we get there."

"Right." I wondered what had gone wrong, with my kids it really could have been anything. "We'll see you in a bit then."

"Make sure you have a very soft chair handy." Mum laughed, then there was a click as she cut the call.

In less time than it took to drink a cup of coffee, I could hear Sam's voice wafting toward me on the wind. Remembering that both parents were slightly mobility-challenged at the moment, I grabbed a rather affronted dog and locked him down the other end of the boat. I had just put the kettle on when my youngest leapt into the boat.

"Mum, MUM! Hi." He leapt toward me and almost knocked me down with a huge hug. "I missed you but I had a great time."

"I missed you too, what do you think of the new kitchen?" Sam never noticed anything unless it was pointed out to him.

Sam ignored me and laughed. "Nanny and Granddad will be here in a minute, they're waiting for Charlie." With that he rushed off with his bag to go and unpack and bury himself in a computer game. "The kitchen's nice," his words diminished as he left.

"Hi, Mum." Charlie limped into the boat and giving me a quick hug made a great show of sitting, very carefully, on the sofa.

"What happened to you?" I noticed the look of pain that spread across her face as she settled onto a cushion.

"She's the only person in the world that has managed to break their bottom." Mum stepped into the boat with a laugh, followed closely by my father.

"What?" I wondered if I'd heard right. "Her bottom, how do you break a bottom?"

Mum reached over and turned the kettle off. "We can't stay, we have to get home." She turned to regard

381

a rather red-faced Charlie. "She decided that she was going to climb a tree and set up a swing." My mother shook her head and looked disapproving. "Then she fell out of the tree and landed on the woodpile, they think she's cracked her coccyx, and there's nothing to do but wait for it to heal. Well they can't bandage it or put it in plaster, can they?"

"Really?" I winced "Ouch, you're going to be standing up for a little while then."

"Thanks, Mum." Charlie pouted at me. "Your sympathy is really welcome."

"Sorry, love." I tried not to laugh. "It must be really painful, we'll have to dig out one of Sam's old swimming rings for you to sit on."

Charlie stuck her nose in the air. "I'm going to unpack," she stated and wafted out of the boat.

We were very good, we almost made it to a whole minute before we all fell about laughing.

Even with the kitchen and the fire in, the winter was, without doubt, one of the hardest we have ever had to face. The run-up to Christmas was particularly gruelling. The river froze and the snow came down during the day then froze at night. We had no water as the pumps had all frozen and the road to the marina became a mile and a half of skating rink. I gave up going out for a week and braved the school's ire by refusing to use the car.

Cars, bikes and delivery vans crashed and as we lived on the main corner of the road Drew, Dion and Geoff spent a lot of time digging them out of the snow, anybody with left over carpet became very popular and huge gangs of people gathered together to dig marina dwellers out of ruts. With the weather so cold and still, it was extremely difficult to get the fire going with any enthusiasm. It just wouldn't "go" and one particularly cold day Geoff caught me just as I was about to soak the logs in petrol and see if that would give them some oomph. He explained long and hard and in words of one syllable just exactly what was wrong with my idea then after removing the petrol can he went out and bought a couple of oil-filled radiators, they were horribly expensive to run but at least we could feel our extremities once more. Even so, we still spent most of the run up to Christmas wearing at least five layers, even the dog had a jumper.

With all the water in the marina frozen there were no showers, no washing machine and we spent a fortune on bottled water which we would buy in bulk whenever one of us was brave enough to face the frigid outdoors and the four-mile trip to the local supermarket.

Washing was done in a baby bath and after ten days of being frozen in, the house in Durham, even with the mad neighbours started to look like paradise.

Just to make our lives complete our little Daewoo Matiz finally died a complete death so, without any transport at all, we had to spend the last of our money on a new car, we finally settled on an old but seemingly solid Volvo.

Two days after we brought it home, the radiator froze and sprung a leak. Geoff was furious. "Why didn't you put any antifreeze in it?" he moaned. "How the hell are we supposed to get to your mother's now?"

I actually managed to hold it together until the children were in bed before I finally found the guts to voice my fears. "We're going to have to sell up," I gabbled at Geoff, "we haven't got any money, I'm cold, really cold, we don't have a car so I can't get the kids to school, so we're going to have social services raining down on us, the kids haven't got any presents, it's two days away from Christmas Eve and quite frankly I can't do this any more."

Geoff looked up, surprised, then came over and after giving me a long hug put the kettle on (we were down to our last ten teabags things had never been so grim). "It's not that bad," he said.

"What do you mean it's not that bad?" I shouted at him. Mortimer looked up, startled at the tone of my voice then sliding off the sofa he crept, tail between his legs, beneath the fire (it was getting to be a bit of a struggle, he was almost too big to fit). "How can it not be that bad?" Leaping up, I flung open the door of the fridge, apart from something horrible singing to itself, cuddled in its own little green fur coat at the very back (at least something was enjoying some warmth), there was a small lump of cheese, a half-used can of beans, a pint of milk and some slightly wilted broccoli. "Look at this, what am I supposed to do with this, I can't feed four on this." I slammed the fridge door shut and slumped back on the sofa head in hands. "We should never have bought another boat," I sniffed, "it's all my fault, nobody else wanted to move, just me and now I don't want to be here either and I'm fed up with saying 'hey look on the bright side, it could be worse'. It can't get any worse, it's as worse as it gets."

Geoff made tea and waited for the emotional tide to recede. Then, carrying two steaming mugs, came over and sat on the sofa. He started to hand me a mug then thought better of it and put it on the floor. "Look, I got paid today and bought some radiator welding stuff so that should put the car right and we should be able to get to your mum's, the kids presents have already been bought, or at least the main ones, and we can rely on your mum and dad to get them all sorts of little bits and pieces, she's already told us what's waiting for them there." He handed me a hanky. "We only need to buy food for one more day then we're off up to Worcester."

"You got paid today?" I frowned. "I didn't think you were being paid until after Christmas."

He nodded and gave me another hug. "Yep, and they've paid me in advance for all the time I'm off over the holiday."

"Really?" I felt like a drowning woman who had just been thrown a lifeline.

Geoff shuffled over and snuggled up with his arm around me. "Look, I know it feels cold and miserable at the moment but if we can limp along till spring," he tailed off. "I don't want to sell the boat do you . . . really?"

Shrugging, I stuck my nose back in my tea. "No, I don't but the kids are cold and fed up with being broke." I stroked Mortimer who sensing things had

385

returned to a more even keel had crawled out from beneath the fire and had climbed up into my lap. "The weather's so bad that even when I do manage to get them to school we're always late." I studied Mort's paws. "I haven't managed to buy you a Christmas present either and I feel horrible about it."

Geoff grinned at me. "I don't want a Christmas present." He hugged me harder. "Although I'll tell you what."

"What?" I sniffed.

"I bet you'd love a stocking full of coal right about now, wouldn't you?" He laughed.

Christmas was over way too soon, we managed to limp the car to my mother's and spent a happy week there, sitting in her Jacuzzi, luxuriating in front of her fire and being fed an extraordinary amount of food.

Mum, knowing me all too well, took me to one side on the morning of our departure and pressed a surreptitious envelope into my hand. "This will keep you going for a little while." She grinned. "Don't tell your father."

I opened the envelope and looked inside; two hundred pounds in twenties looked happily back at me. Not really knowing how to thank her I just burst into tears on her shoulder. That seemed grateful enough and it reduced her to tears as well. "I wish you weren't so far away," she said, "I could help more if you were closer."

"Ah, Mum," I sniffled, "I shouldn't need help, I'm too old to need help. I feel like a teenager again who just can't stop getting into debt or can't make her money stretch to the end of the month." I shook my head and took a deep, deep shuddering breath. "I should be way past that by now, in fact I should be making plans to help you as you slip happily into your dotage . . . OW!"

Mum gave me a half-hearted slap. "Dotage indeed," she frowned. "Well you could always just give up, sell up and go back to a normal life again." She looked hopeful.

I thought about it for a moment. "If you'd said that three months ago I would have given you a resounding no!" I shook my head and felt sad. "But now? I really don't know, we're so broke and so cold and every time it rains some of the windows are still leaking and the water's frozen so we can't wash," I tailed off as I caught sight of Mum's look.

"Marie," she gasped, "there are poor people in Nepal that live a better and more luxurious life than you do, this is getting ridiculous, what about the kids," she broke off for a moment to prod a finger into the kitchen worktop emphasising her argument. "This can't be healthy for them."

"We're fine, Nanny." Charlie, who had been listening to the argument from the shadow of the bookcase in the hall, wandered into the kitchen, her stockinged feet making no noise on the parquet flooring. "Honestly my little room is lovely and warm, it's the warmest room on the boat and Sam just wanders around in bare feet and a T-shirt — he doesn't seem to feel the cold at all, it's only these two old worry-worts that sit and gibber."

Mum humphed and shook her head. "It all sounds absolutely terrible."

I wandered across her huge kitchen toward the kettle. "It'll be better when the spring's here." I laughed and pocketed the envelope. "At least things can't get any worse." Even as I said it I regretted the words and desperately tried to think of a way to undo the curse . . . "At least I hope they can't," I amended.

Four weeks later at six-thirty in the morning I was "enjoying" my morning walk around the boat for my normal attempt at raising the dead. "Charlie!" I shouted through her door. "Come on, time to get up, breakfast's ready." There was silence and I sighed. "CHARLIE!!" I kicked the side of the boat. "Come on, don't ignore me."

Very faintly from inside the back cabin came a faint moan and I felt alarm bells begin to ring in my head. Jumping on to the back deck I stuck my head through her door (after the first week she'd decided that there wasn't anything that was likely to "get" her and had left it unlocked). "Charlie, are you awake?"

A white face peered at me from under the covers, she looked awful, red eyes ringed in dark skin stared at me from beneath flat wet hair. "Mum," she whispered, "I feel awful."

I felt my stomach turn over and knew immediately that she had the dreaded "swine flu". The story had been on the news for a fair while and living in such conditions we had really hoped it would pass us by, obviously not.

Jumping down into her cabin I stuck my hand on her forehead; she was burning up, her eyes seemed to stare through me and off into the distance. "Come on." I gently pulled her into a sitting position. "I need to get you into the main boat."

She nodded and tried to swing her legs over the edge of the bed. "I just can't move," she whispered and sank back onto her pillow.

I wondered what I was going to do, I couldn't carry her, she was now way too big for that, well, what I needed was muscle. Sighing I reached up and pressed the doorbell above her bed — five or six quick rings.

A couple of minutes later Geoff stuck his head into the cabin. "What's up?" He looked over at Charlie and paled then without a word jumped down into the cabin and gathering her up, quilt and all, just hoisted her up on his shoulder and left the cabin.

Taking two minutes to feed the rats, I gathered up her pillow and a blanket and followed him. By the time I got back into the boat, he had arranged her on the sofa and had taken her temperature. Charlie, oblivious to everything tossed and turned in her quilt.

"Thirty-nine point two," Geoff frowned down at the digital readout. "She's definitely not pulling an 'I want a day off school' sickie."

Sam wandered up and stared down at his sister, his expression concerned. Reaching forward he gave her a gentle poke on the arm. "She must be sick." He shook his head, frowning. "Normally she'd have hit me for that."

"Go and get ready for school, Sam." Geoff turned Sam toward the other end of the boat and gave him a small push. "I'm taking you in today."

"Oh dear, is that going to make you late?" Geoff had only recently started his new job and was enjoying it a lot. However he was on a three-month trial and the last thing we needed was for him to get into trouble at work.

"No." Geoff wandered toward the kitchen and began making his lunch. "Luckily I'm working near Sam's school so I can drop him off then go on. Are you going to be all right with Charlie?"

I looked up from where I was rummaging through the drawer trying to find the paracetamol. "Yep, I'll give her some of this and set up her old bed for her, if her temperature doesn't come down within half an hour of taking it, I'll just call an ambulance."

For two weeks Charlie coughed and spluttered, moaned, slept, complained and generally did everything that a teenager with a bad case of flu tends to do. By the time she felt ready to go back to school and back to her own room I was a complete wreck. Her coughing kept everyone awake all night and we all felt very frazzled. Being in such close proximity to each other only made things worse, you could almost taste the germs in the air.

On the day Charlie returned to school I came home from dropping them both off, set an alarm for the pick-up run, collapsed on the sofa and slept the day away. I was woken at about two by Geoff staggering through the door.

"Hey." I shook myself awake. "What are you doing here?"

Geoff winced as he stepped carefully and slowly down into the boat. "I've got no work on so I've taken a half day."

390

"Oh, right." still more than half asleep, I yawned and stretched. "Put the kettle on, can you?"

Geoff winced again as he sank down onto the sofa. "Could you do it? I've put my back out."

Well, that woke me up. "What? What do you mean you've put your back out?" I jumped up and put the kettle on. "Do you want some painkillers?"

Geoff nodded and slumped sideways into the warm spot I had just vacated. "Yes please."

Ten minutes later he had a mug of tea and a handful of paracetamol (we were going through the things like travel sweets). I stood up and put my coat on. "I've got to go and get the kids." I pulled on my hat and gloves. "Will you be all right?"

Geoff nodded. "I think I'll just sleep." He shuffled carefully into a more comfortable position. "Ouch!" He sighed. "If I can."

"Hmm, where's the pain?" I looked up from ferreting around under the sofa with a pair of fur-lined boots in my hand.

"Right down the bottom," Geoff gasped, "I can't move it at all."

I checked my watch, I was going to be late. "I'll pick up some stronger painkillers for you."

Geoff nodded then closed his eyes.

In the chemist, I hedged my bets and bought the strongest painkillers they would sell me, more cold and flu tablets, various painkilling creams and some Ibuprofen. (I decided that if all this was going on I was probably going to get a headache as well.) I was just about to pay when a display of boxes caught my eye.

"Is that a TENS machine?" I asked the woman behind the counter. She nodded and taking one from the pile opened it for me to look at.

"They're very good," she said, "they get rid of all sorts of pains."

"I used one when I was in labour, it worked well, are they good for backache too?" I studied the little blue machine nestled in its polystyrene nest.

"Excellent." The assistant smiled, she took out the four little sticky pads and plugged each one into a wire which she then plugged into the machine. "These little pads send out a small current and if you put them around the area of pain, they stimulate the nerves and block out pain." She frowned. "I think that's how it works."

I hesitated, thinking of my ailing bank account. "It looks very expensive."

"Not at all," she said and turned the box around, showing me the ticket, £14.99, "they're very good value." Smiling again she put everything back in the box and stuck her hands into the pockets of her overall. "Would you like one?"

I was torn, we had to get Geoff back to work as quickly as possible and if the pain killers didn't work we were going to be in trouble.

For a moment I felt ashamed, Geoff was obviously in a lot of pain and here was I worrying about the fact that he didn't get sick pay. I shook my head, if he didn't get paid it wasn't only going to be him in pain, it would be all of us.

I dragged my debit card out of my purse and turned to smile at the assistant. "Yes, I'll have one and I'd better have the batteries as well."

I left the chemist with a large bag of goodies and a receipt for well over thirty pounds. Heading for the car I realised that I had just used the last of the week's money, thank goodness it was Thursday and tomorrow was payday so at least we could eat.

Geoff took up the sofa for the entire evening. Charlie, obviously feeling aggrieved that she wasn't the only one sick in the house, took herself off to bed after moaning that her chest hurt. It was a quiet and peaceful evening, with Geoff wired up to his little buzzing machine and drugged into insensibility, he could finally sleep. Mortimer and I watched the telly revelling in the peace and quiet.

I woke Geoff to make him go to bed and had to wrestle his TENS machine off him (he was obviously one of those people it worked really well for). We dosed him again with yet another round of pain killers and went to bed, hoping that in the morning all would be well.

It most certainly wasn't, waking at about six I leapt out of bed and hurried to turn the fire up and get the boat warm. By the time the fire was blazing and the kettle screaming I turned my attention to my determinedly sleeping husband.

"Geoff . . ." I waited for a few moments, nothing. "GEOFF!"

One eyelid cracked open and a red-surrounded amber eye looked at me. "What?"

"Come on, time to get up, kettle's on." The morning was so like a hundred others that I had completely forgotten the pain he had been in yesterday, it was brought back to me when he tried to move.

"Argh!" Geoff yelped as he tried to roll over. "My back."

"Damn," I griped, "I'd forgotten about that."

Fishing around in the drawer again I popped two codeine and paracetamol tablets from a blister pack. "Here, take these." As I turned from the sink with a glass of water in hand I saw that Geoff had crawled out of bed and was attempting to stand up, he wasn't doing very well.

"Hang on," I said and put the drugs and water back down on the kitchen surface. "Here grab my hand and use it to steady yourself."

Geoff shook his head and, still bent double, crabbed his way around the bed toward me until I had a wonderful view of his behind clad in stripy pyjama bottoms. Reaching out his right hand he braced himself against the kitchen work surface and attempted to stand upright.

I watched as he obviously hit a position that was incredibly painful, his face contorted then the blood drained away leaving him white and shaking. As I opened my mouth to say something comforting his eyes rolled up into his head and he fell, very slowly, backward toward me.

I still don't know how I managed, but I caught him under both arms and lowered him to the floor, unfortunately I went with him and we ended up in a pile between the kitchen units with me on the bottom and my normally indestructible husband in a dead faint on top of me.

I was completely stuck, there is only space for one person between the units and Geoff was unconscious, I tried to roll to the left and met the fridge, rolling to the right only got me into a cupboard. Eventually I managed to push Geoff off me and by rolling on top of him finally was able to get myself upright, by this time he was coming around again.

Finding himself on the floor he looked confused then, as he tried to move, his already pasty face paled further and turning his head, he heaved then groaned, luckily nothing came up.

Of course both children chose this moment to appear. Sam seeing the state we were both in beat a hasty retreat back to his bed and Charlie, mid-moan about chest pains, stopped in the middle of her sentence and just stared.

It was pure chaos, there was just no room to manoeuvre. I decided that the first thing I would have to move was Geoff.

"Sam, get out of bed please." Sam's head appeared over the partition.

"Is Dad all right?" he quavered at me.

"He will be, but I need your bed . . . NOW!" I held out a hand for Geoff to grab, he ignored it.

"OK, OK." Sam leapt out of bed and headed for the toilet.

"Charlie, just park on the end of our bed for a couple of minutes and let the dog out, will you?"

Mortimer, wondering what on earth was going on, was preparing to jump on us from the top of the bed.

Geoff, with my help, managed to very slowly roll over onto all fours. I didn't press him to get up and he just crawled down the boat then climbed slowly into Sam's bed. I handed him the tablets and the water then marshalled the kids to help me get the bed put away.

Eventually we were all sorted. Rolling Geoff gently over on to his front I attached his TENS machine and, as soon as he was happily buzzing away, his breathing steadied and became less tortured with every minute that passed.

Making sure he had the controls to hand, I left the kids to make their own breakfast and went down to start the car. Covered in ice, it appreciated fifteen minutes running to get itself ready for the day. (I felt this was completely unfair, I'd have liked fifteen minutes to get ready for my day as well but I didn't have that luxury.) On the way to school Charlie kept coughing until frazzled beyond endurance I finally told her to shut up.

"Oh, thanks very much," she muttered between hacks. "My chest really hurts."

I sighed. "Look, it's Friday, both of you get through today and we've got the whole weekend to relax."

She muttered something beneath her breath and went back to staring out of the window coughing occasionally.

By lunchtime Geoff was feeling much better, he'd had three solid hours of electrical current passing through his back and could actually walk about. He was a little high from painkillers but was coping pretty well.

"How're you doing?" I passed him a cup of tea.

"Pretty good." he gave me a slightly spacey grin. "Quite a lot better actually." He took a sip of tea and stretched slowly and deliberately toward the ceiling, grinning as he did so. "I called work, they were very good about the whole thing. At least I have the weekend to sort this out."

I nodded and looked up from the jobs website I was perusing. "Do you think you will?" I winced at my tone; I didn't want to force him back to work but . . .

Geoff laughed. "I think I'll be fine, I'll take the TENS with me." He laughed again. "Hey, I'll be the only battery-operated electrician for miles around."

I just groaned.

The next morning was Saturday and, not expecting to see Charlie before midday, I was surprised to find her standing over me at seven o'clock in the morning. "You all right love?"

"No," Charlie said clutching her chest, "my chest really hurts and I can't breathe." She puffed her cheeks out at me as she tried to breathe out. "I think I've got the flu again."

I struggled out of bed and throwing on a long padded work shirt I use as a dressing gown, grabbed the thermometer. While I was waiting for it to go "beep" I took a long look at her, she was pale and sweaty, her breathing coming in short gasps and squeaks.

Reading thirty-nine degrees on the thermometer, I reached for my phone and dialled 999. I put one hand under her arm and propelled her toward the bed. "Sit down," I hissed. She nodded and collapsed onto the bed with Geoff, they made a fine pair alternately wincing, groaning, wheezing and coughing, they sounded like a terrible alternative one-man band.

The ambulance took about half an hour to arrive during which time I poured Charlie, between coughs, into leggings, big socks, boots, a baggy sweatshirt and a big coat. Leaving her in the boat I went outside to await the arrival of the paramedics. When it arrived, a man climbed out of the back and stared up the flood defences at me.

"Where's the patient?" he called.

I indicated behind me. "Up here," I called back.

He looked worried and dithered about. "I can't bring the ambulance on to that grass, we might not get off."

I put a hand up to him. "Just wait there."

Unable to bear the messing about, I went back to the boat and half-carried, half-guided Charlie up the steps, over the flood defences, down the other side and over to the ambulance. By this time a small crowd of onlookers had gathered on top of the flood defences, trying to work out what was going on. They didn't really get a chance, after ten minutes of prodding and poking, Charlie, eyes somewhat panicked behind the oxygen mask she was wearing, was on her way to hospital.

A TENS machine is obviously a wonderful thing, five hours later Geoff had managed to pour himself and Sam into the car and picked us both up from A&E. It had been confirmed that Charlie had pneumonia in one lung and was given antibiotics and strict instructions to stay in bed for at least a week.

Three weeks later she finally went back to school. Geoff had gone back to work after the weekend but he was still occasionally attached to his TENS machine and with all the panic and worry of the winter I realised that I'd completely failed to notice that spring had arrived.

I found myself staring at a small group of daffodils while out for a walk with Mortimer. It had been, without a doubt, the worst winter we had ever been through, but I was now so tired that I had hardly noticed the last month and had gone through the motions of my days like a zombie. The long green shoots pushing up through the icy grass almost made me cry, the boat was still a cold wreck, Geoff might still have had occasional back problems and Charlie still had a cough that could be heard through five millimetres of steel, but the very sight of these little plants gave me just enough of a boost: I could see a light at the end of the tunnel.

CHAPTER
FIFTEEN

Finally, Winter's Over

Slowly, so slowly, the world grew warmer, there were more sunny days, the surrounding trees and bushes developed small buds and then seemingly all at once exploded into bright new greenery. Sam took to riding his bike around the flood defences and Charlie, having made two good friends, started spending weekends at either Scarlet's or Jack's house, she seemed to be enjoying life much more.

I wholeheartedly approved of her two friends, Scarlet, tall and statuesque, reminded me of a somewhat gothic burlesque girl, her long red hair matched her name and she had a ready smile and an airy nature, I often imagined that if she hadn't been wearing such huge boots Scarlet would have floated away on some mad flight of fancy or other.

Jack on the other hand was as sarcastic as one human could possibly get, tall and thin to the point of emaciation, his well dressed exterior seemed seriously at odds with our outdoorsy lifestyle but his cold-hearted commentary on life, people and work often had me in genuine fits of giggles. He had superb timing and could cut a conversation with a single

400

comment. He also had a laugh like a constipated donkey, a certain personality trait that Sam mimicked immediately and within minutes there were two of them braying away at some joke or other. Even though they filled up the boat and ate all my bacon and eggs they were always welcome to visit.

We hadn't seen Amelia since Christmas and although we had spoken on a regular basis, she had decided that we were all too ill or infirm to cope with a visit and had used this as an excuse to keep Chris as far away as possible.

Eventually there could be no more excuses and on a sunny weekend in late March she turned up with "Mr Right" in tow.

Leaping into the boat she dragged him, looking rather bewildered and confused, to meet us. He was tall and seemed to be genuinely amused by Amelia, her siblings, the mad dog and her odd family. He had longish mouse-coloured hair which was definitely wayward and gently floppy, actually that described Chris exactly. With his big black duffle coat, slightly baggy jeans and well-loved trainers, he looked the epitome of the eternal student, softly spoken with a quick wit and a ready laugh he grinned at the world that he could only see through fairly strong glasses, I could certainly see why she was so enamoured of him.

After spending the afternoon with him my last worries vanished. It didn't look like we'd put him off at all and he had spent most of the afternoon with Sam and Charlie trying to teach them to spin poi, while laughingly fending off an overenthusiastic staffy who

401

felt that balls on strings with long coloured tails were still balls and therefore belonged to him.

The next day Amelia rang. "So, what did you think of him?"

I laughed. "You are of course completely right, he's lovely."

Amelia squeaked. "Oh he is isn't he." She gave a happy sigh. "He thought the same about you lot as well which was a huge relief, anyway it was lovely to see you, I'll call you during the week I have to go I'm on my break at work."

With that she was gone.

With the kids settled and Geoff happy in his job (his three-month trial had ended without fanfare and he just carried on with the company), I decided that I needed to find a job. The extra money would be great and would just make life that little bit easier.

The only problem was what to do, I needed a job close to both Sam's and Charlie's schools and preferably needed to work between nine-thirty and two-thirty. I knew that trying to find a position with those specific criteria was not going to be easy at all.

Looking through the paper one night Geoff said, "How do you feel about fixing tellys?"

I frowned. "I'm sure it would be a very useful skill." I looked back down at my book. "Unfortunately it's one I don't have."

Geoff handed the paper to me; he had ringed a small ad on the jobs pages. "It says full training given." He tapped the paper with his pen. "It's working for Addenbrooke's."

My interest was piqued. "Really? That'll be those entertainments units they have above each bed, we were using one when Charlie was in A&E." I looked at the advert. "Oh, it's part-time as well, I'll give them a ring tomorrow."

The job wasn't actually working for Addenbrooke's, it was a company that had offices at the hospital site. Hospedia had the contract for maintaining and supplying all the bedside entertainment units in the hospital and after going through a couple of interviews I happily donned my bright pink shirt and joined the ranks of the "telly" staff.

For about two weeks I followed one of the other staff about, learning the ropes. It was an easy job and with my background in IT I had no problems at all dealing with the technical side and it didn't take long to get used to the patients even though some of them could understandably be a little tetchy.

There were five other staff, Debbie the boss was lovely, tiny and blonde, she smiled her way through the day, took all traumas in her stride and generally sorted us out and laughed while she did it. Angela the relief manager was different from Debbie in almost every way, small and stocky with long fair hair, she was much less laid-back but had an equivalent sense of humour; she laughed at different things to Debbie but it didn't really matter, they both laughed a lot.

Rob, the youngest member of the team, sported a vast amount of tattoos and a tall Mohican. Rob's looks belied his nature, he was very good at all the technical bits and pieces with an evil sense of humour. Jolly, so small it was a wonder that she could reach the units that were positioned above the patients' beds, could often be found giggling with one of the patients on the wards.

Beata (known to all as Betty) was the other member of the team. Betty was one person I got on well with immediately, very intense and determined to do the best job she possibly could. A qualified teacher in Poland, she was totally committed to perfecting her English and we went out on the wards together a lot. She had a great sense of humour and her often comic comments on life made me laugh a great deal.

My first day alone on the wards made me realise that this was definitely the job for me. I had noticed that some of the patients with the more gruesome injuries, bike accidents and that sort of thing, thoroughly enjoyed regaling anybody they could with the intimate details of both their accidents and the following treatment. I worked out pretty quickly that showing the least bit of disgust or horror didn't go down well at all, and my twenty years in customer service stood me in good stead when I had to have a poker face.

That day I was out on the wards by about ten o'clock. My first call was to the plastics ward, it was one of my favourites; new and gleaming, the four huge wards stood at the end of the small village-sized institution that Cambridge calls its hospital. I wandered into the ward and approached a bed next to the window.

"Hi there," I announced myself to the man in the bed, he was about thirty, his leg, obviously in a bad way, was supported on some sort of gantry affair outside the covers. It didn't look to be healing at all well. "I'm from Hospedia, I understand you've got some problems with your television?"

He looked up from his book and nodded. "Oh hi, yeah." He reached over and pulled the television down on its long arm and turned it around to face me, there was a double white line across the screen. "It just sort of stopped." He gave me a big smile. "Can you fix it?" He pointed down at his leg. "I think I might be here some time."

I nodded and, taking out a screwdriver, climbed up on the chair beside his bed. "I think so, I just have to reboot it." That procedure completed, I sat down on the chair beside him and waited for the machine to run through its start-up sequence. "So what happened to you?" I pointed down at the leg.

There are some patients you feel you can ask and some you just know that you can't, it's definitely down to instinct. Some are smiley and bored and want to talk, others are just so ill that you get in and out as quickly as you can, doing the least you can to disturb them. This was definitely a smiley chatty type.

"I fell down a manhole." He grinned and winced as he applied pressure to his thigh. "Fell into a load of pipes and one of them pierced my ankle," he went on, sticking his lower lip out and frowning down at his leg, "made a right mess."

I nodded. "Didn't you see the manhole, or didn't it have warning signs?" I figured when he got out of the hospital someone was going to be sued to their last penny.

The man leaned back on his pillow and closed his eyes. "Yes, I knew it was there and yes, the signs warning people about the hole were perfectly positioned." He opened his eyes and gave me a sad grin.

"Ok . . ." I was a little confused "So how . . ." I tailed off, I didn't really want to ask, "Did you jump?" — it seemed a little insensitive.

The man in the bed (James) pushed himself to a more upright position. "It was my manhole, I was working down there."

"You fell down your own manhole." (Poker face, poker face, don't laugh, definitely don't laugh.)

"Yep, stepped backward while talking to my mate and just went straight down the hole." He shook his head. "That was three months ago, and I'm still here."

"Wow, unlucky." I made a show of checking the unit, seeing how far the reboot had progressed, it gave me a moment to get my face under control.

"Do you want to see pictures of my leeches?" James reached over for his iPhone.

"Leeches?" I was confused; had we slipped back into mediaeval times?

"Yeah." James began flicking through pictures on his phone. "They use them for pulling blood through grafted skin, I had loads of them."

"Erm . . . OK."

James had about twenty pictures of his little slimy friends working away on his leg, I was quite horrified to note that although they started out quite small, by the time they had finished, one in particular, had grown so large it was attached to his ankle but its tail was wrapped around his shin. I just couldn't help myself at that picture and let out a small "Ewww".

James sat up and looked over at the picture. "Oh, that one was great, he was my favourite. I named him you know."

I noticed that the reboot had finished and, reaching over, picked up the phone and put in the code that would tell the unit that it could continue working. Replacing the handset I stood up and, gathering my kit together, got ready to leave. "Go on." I turned to James who was grinning at me from the bed. "I'll bite, what did you call it?"

James looked hurt. "Not 'it', it's a 'him'," he paused for effect, "that one was called 'Lawyer'."

I laughed and groaned. "Thanks for that, that's an image that's going to stay with me for the rest of the day."

Laughing, he waved me out of the ward and went back to his book.

My next port of call was the children's ward, then transplants, then the maternity hospital, after that there were a couple of other calls as well, one I couldn't get into, because the patient was very, very poorly, finished off my day.

Back at home that evening Geoff asked me how my day had gone. "Pretty classic, I should say." I looked up from mending Sam's school trousers (small boys seem to treat school trousers like their own personal nemesis). I explained, laughing about the leeches and about the man who had backed into an electric fence with an armed shotgun, the shock from the fence had caused his finger to depress the trigger and he had shot two of his own toes off.

"You sound like you're quite enjoying this job." Geoff raised his eyebrows in question. (I have to admit I'm fairly renowned for starting a job with great gusto only to fall out of love with it after about a week.)

"Well the money certainly makes a big difference." I bit the last thread from Sam's trousers and held them up to examine the repair, it wasn't great but at least it meant he would be less obscene for the next couple of weeks until I could afford to buy him a new pair on payday. "The job itself is the same day after day but the patients all change so you never know who you're going to talk to or the stories you're going to hear." I thought about it for a moment. "It definitely has its ups and downs, some patients, their story is ending and it's really sad, their families are so helpless and hopeless that it's heartbreaking."

I took a long look around our skanky boat. "I know I moan about living like this, but there are at least fifty people with money and big houses in that hospital at the moment that would swap their lives for mine in an instant." I heaved a big sigh remembering a scene of quiet grief I had witnessed that day. "It's all about what's important, really, isn't it?"

Geoff nodded and handed me a cup of tea, there wasn't really much to say to that so instead we took advantage of a moment of peace and quiet to indulge in ten minutes of leaning on each other. Enjoying my tea I indulged in some fairly miserable thoughts of how much worse life could be and counted our blessings.

That summer wasn't great. The weather, after a brief spell of ridiculous high temperatures in June settled down into that sort of grey nothingness for which Britain is famous.

Charlie and her friends had taken to camping with a vengeance, and most weekends she would disappear with Jack, Scarlet and a constantly changing crowd of others to a piece of waste woodland where they would set up camp and spend the weekends getting muddy and exhausted.

I had a call fairly early one Sunday morning: "Could you come and pick me up, Mum?" Charlie sounded fairly subdued and I wondered if she'd fallen out with her friends.

"Sure," I replied, looking around for my keys, "you OK?"

"Not really," she said in between sniffs, "could you hurry please?"

It took me about half an hour to get to her and as I got out of the car I realised almost immediately that it wasn't an argument, she'd hurt herself, again. I had to sigh, what had she done this time?"

Jack and Scarlet were sitting with her, the little group looked forlorn and fairly grubby. They had packed up their campsite and were sitting amongst a pile of tents and sleeping bags.

"You all OK?" I shouted as I got out of the car.

"I think I've broken my finger." Charlie held up the offending swollen digit. "It really hurts."

An hour later, after dropping off her friends and their equipment I was back at work again but this time on the receiving end.

"How did this happen?" asked a young doctor who turned Charlie's hand over and studied it carefully, "We've had the X-ray back and it's not broken, but there's obviously something wrong."

Charlie looked a little embarrassed. "Well I was running and I tripped over and fell into a bush."

The doctor looked up. "What sort of bush?"

Charlie shrugged. "A spiky one, I think it was a blackthorn," she said and looked down at her hand. "I got a thorn in it as well, I had to pull it out, it was in quite deep." She pointed to the middle joint on her swollen finger. "It went right in there."

"Hmmm." He nodded then turned to me. "I think I need one of the plastics team down to look at this. Has she had anything to eat today?"

Alarm bells started ringing, I know full well that eating is only a problem if the hospital intend to put you on the operating table. Charlie put her hand behind her and began telling us how much better it was feeling and if it wasn't broken then surely it would be better to just go home now, wouldn't it?

Doctor Steve just grinned at her. "If you'd broken it, it would be fairly simple to fix, but I think you've pierced the tendon sheath and now it's all filled with pus and bacteria, we have to clean it out."

Charlie gulped and went pale.

Two hours later I helped her into bed on ward L4. She looked very young amongst the older women there. I set the television up for her and made sure she had a lot of time on it. "You're lucky." I checked the phone on the unit. "I only fixed this one yesterday, good job really otherwise I'd have had to fix it now."

Charlie stared at me in silence, then looked down in utter disgust at the backless short cotton robe the hospital had put on her.

"Do you want me to stay with you?" I asked.

"No way!" She looked horrified. "I've got friends coming in to see me later, but if you could leave me some money I could go down to the concourse and get a burger."

"You can't eat." I ferreted around in my handbag looking for my purse.

"I can until six, while you were getting a coffee the nurse said I wouldn't be having my operation until early tomorrow."

I checked with the nurse and gave Charlie some money and a book I'd bought for her then, with a slight frisson of anxiety and a lot of requests for her to call me, I went home.

"I'll be back tomorrow morning," I assured her.

Charlie caught sight of a tall girl wandering down the corridor then turning me around she gave me a push toward the door. "Yes, yes, I'll see you then. Stop fussing, Mother. I'll be fine."

I took the hint and left.

It was quite useful working at the hospital and the next morning I swapped my area with Betty so that I could work in the ATC and be near to Charlie. No one minded.

"Hey you." I wandered into the ward and waved at Charlie.

"Where have you been," she hissed, she looked panicked and upset.

"Why, what's up?" I sat down on the chair next to her bed.

"I'm going now!" She started taking out all her earrings and struggled with her tongue piercing. "I have to take all these out. Will you keep them safe for me?"

I nodded then looked up as a nurse bustled into the room. "You ready?" she asked Charlie.

"One more earring to go," I said.

The nurse looked at me, confused. "Can you fix her telly after we've gone?" She used the imperious tone they always use to move non-essential staff on. "I need to get her changed."

"I think I'll stay." I couldn't resist winding her up just a little.

"No I don't think so." She took a deep breath in and was just about to give me the full force of her ire when I cut across her.

"I'm her mother."

"Oh!" she deflated like a balloon and smiled. "Sorry, didn't know and we see you so often," she pointed to my ridiculously coloured uniform.

On the way to theatre Charlie gave up the tough teenager persona and became young and worried again. "What if I don't wake up?" She tried to sit up on the trolley but the porter glared at her and she sank back into her pillows. "What if I die?"

Another nurse who was walking with me patted her on the hand. "You'll be fine, you'll wake up a bit groggy but you'll be fine."

"Mum?" Charlie obviously needed a lot more confirmation. "Can some people not wake up?"

"Yes, but there is always another reason why they don't, bad hearts, body too frail and a load of other reasons, but you're young and healthy and really you will wake up."

"How would you know?" Charlie snapped, worry making her rude and badly behaved.

"Your mother's right." The nurse patted her hand again. "People don't just die, there's always a reason."

Charlie pulled her hand away and turned her face to the wall; she was obviously very worried.

"Look, if you see a light just don't go toward it, OK?" I waved my fingers at her and whispered in her ear in the spookiest voice I could manage, "Stay away from the light. Stay away from the light."

Charlie giggled and waved as her gurney was pushed through into theatre.

"Strange sense of humour," the nurse commented.

I had to agree with her.

Three days later I took Charlie home, she was very subdued. "Are you OK?" I asked.

She nodded but didn't say anything.

"Does your hand hurt?" I glanced over at the padded brace she had that covered the stitches in her finger and palm, supported by a shoulder strap.

"A little." She stared down at her feet. "Mum, you know that nice lady in the bed opposite?"

"Mmmhmm," I acknowledged, "the one that kept giving you chocolate."

Charlie smiled. "Yeah. She didn't have any hair and wore a headscarf, does that mean she's got cancer?"

"Probably, that is one of the side-effects of some of the treatments." I wondered where this was going.

"The doctors came to see her last night and they pulled the curtains round." Charlie stared out of the window. "When they left, she started crying . . ." Charlie broke off with a sniff, "she cried all night, but really quietly so the nurses wouldn't hear her, but I did." Charlie glanced up at me then back out of the window again. "I feel bad because this morning the curtains were still around her bed and I couldn't go and say goodbye but I was relieved because I didn't know what to say and now I feel guilty because she was so nice."

We drove in silence while I desperately tried to think of something to say to her, some major pearls of wisdom that would make the whole death and dying thing easier for her to deal with. After a couple of minutes I gave up.

"There aren't any answers to that one, new treatments are being developed all the time and it's natural to not want to make things worse for someone by saying something stupid." I paused and wondered how much she really wanted to hear. "I think we're all nervous around terminally ill people because we know they're heading toward something we know nothing about and that lack of 'knowing' scares us silly."

Charlie nodded emphatically.

"And you're so young that the idea scares you more than others."

"I don't want to die," she shuddered.

"Well you've seen what such a little thing as a thorn can do to you." I pointed at her bandaged hand and arm. "Maybe a little foresight in the future about what you're doing and you may just live to become a burden on your children."

Charlie looked up at me with a small smile.

"I certainly intend to become a burden to you," I said.

Charlie grinned "Mother ..." she hesitated for effect, "believe me, you already are."

Our only real problem was that as the family grew, the limited space on the boat became quite an issue.

One morning in early July I found Charlie face down on the sofa. "Mum, I've got loads of homework," she moaned.

"So what's the problem?" I have to admit I wasn't really listening, this conversation had been going on and off for about a month. "Just set the computer up on the dining room table and do it there."

Charlie heaved an aggrieved sigh. "I can't, you know I can't. Sam keeps coming and bothering me and Geoff keeps wandering past with tools and banging things, I just can't concentrate."

"Then take the laptop into your bedroom and do it there." I picked up the bowl of salad and turned to head outside with it, we'd recently become the proud owners of a wooden trestle table and benches and a big sun umbrella. It was lovely to eat outside so we took advantage of it as often as we could. "Look, can we talk about this later, Bill and Drew are coming round and I need to poke your father into starting the barbecue so he can burn stuff."

Charlie huffed. "There's no room in my bedroom," she shouted, "and it's really hot and dark."

"So work outside." I probably wasn't being as sympathetic as I could have been but quite frankly there was very little I could do.

Charlie huffed again and stamped off down the boat, pausing only to grab the laptop as she went by. Slamming through the doors she pushed past a bewildered Geoff and stamped off down the mooring.

"What's the matter with her?" Geoff got his hand slapped for pinching bits of tomato out of the salad.

"Same thing as usual." I covered the bowl with cling film then handed him a box of matches. "Barbecue?"

"She's got a point." Geoff followed me out into the sunshine. "There really isn't any room for her in that ridiculous back cabin."

"Oh don't you start." I took the matches from him and handed him a bag of charcoal. "What are we supposed to do about it? Surely one small teenager can fit in a space that was originally designed to be inhabited by a family of four?"

Geoff placed the bag of charcoal into the barbecue and set fire to it, from his expression I could tell he actually did have an idea what we could do about it but was worried I wouldn't like the solution. "I've just been chatting to the new security guard up in the marina; he's bought a new boat," he said.

"Oh yes?" The management of the marina had changed fairly recently and we now had things like security and a shower block, it was all becoming most civilised. The new security guy was lovely, he was happy and smiley and altogether a nice guy, his dog was far more frightening than he was and I had to assume that he had well-hidden threatening depths.

Geoff nodded. "He asked me if I'd do the electrics on his new boat."

"Hmm mmm." I wasn't really paying much attention, Geoff spent most of his time in other people's boats sorting out their sparks.

"But he asked me if I'd like his old boat in exchange for the work." Geoff shrugged. "Evidently Charlie was talking to him and saying how much she'd like to buy a little boat like that one."

"What?" I put the bowl down and turned to concentrate on what he was saying. "The little tiny one. That one that looks like a floating metal shed?"

Geoff nodded. "What do you think? It's only twenty-seven foot long, if we asked Dion and Charlie if they would consider shuffling up toward Bill and Drew a bit, and if Steve doesn't mind our backside hanging over his garden a little we could probably get it in front of ours."

"Hold on a minute." I held up a hand. "That means we'd have two boats to fix up, that thing's got no running water, no toilet, no heating, it's just a box."

Geoff nodded. "Well she hasn't got any of that now and she has to walk down the length of the boat to get to the front doors, but if we moved her out into a boat of her own we could use the back cabin for storage while we're doing them both up. She'd still have to use the facilities on the big boat but she'd have somewhere to go that was hers."

I ran a hand through my hair, it really was a wonderful opportunity and, with money tight and time even tighter, what did it matter if we had two boats to do up instead of just one? The way we were going neither was going to get finished any time soon.

"Can I tell her?" I grinned at him. "Actually no, that's not fair, you sorted out the deal, you can tell her."

Geoff laughed and shook his head. "What and deprive you of winding her up? I wouldn't dare."

Laughing I shot off and banged on the back of the boat. "Charlie!"

"What?" came the short, snappy and slightly muffled shout.

"Can you come out for a moment please?"

"I'm busy."

"Yes I know, that's what I wanted to talk to you about, come out."

"Later." There was a short thump from inside the boat. "I'm busy."

"Charlotte Alyse!" I very rarely used her full name. "Get out here right now."

There was a certain amount of muttering and grumbling but eventually she stuck her head out of the back doors. "What!" she snapped.

"Come with me." I turned and wandered over toward Geoff.

Obviously realising that this was important, she only heaved a tortured sigh before climbing out of her cabin and trotting after me.

"Geoff's got you a boat of your own." I stared at her. "Will that sort out your space problems?"

There was a long silence, I could actually see the words going round and round in her head, obviously they weren't making any sense. She frowned, then she shook her head, then she looked confused, it was wonderful. Eventually she said, "What?"

"The little boat that belongs to Stuart?" I waited for her to nod. "Well, he's offered to swap it for Geoff doing the electrical work on his new boat, you get one offer, do you want it?"

If Charlie's jaw hadn't actually been attached to her face it would have hit her in the foot. I sat down next to Geoff on the trestle table and we sat and watched her face go through a range of emotions. Eventually I turned to Geoff. "Well, there's no reply so that's obviously a no, then."

Charlie spluttered and grabbed my arm. "Yes, YES! Yes I want it, can I do anything I like to it, and can I paint it and put things in it and make it like a real bedroom and have a lounge space and a sofa for friends and a telly of my own?

Geoff and I nodded in unison.

"Can we go and tell him now?" Charlie was literally hopping up and down on the spot. "Geoff, can we?"

Geoff laughed. "Come on then, you probably can't have it till next weekend, but we'll tell him now."

"GREAT!!" Charlie rushed off up the flood defences leaving Geoff to trot along in her wake. As they left, Sam appeared riding the new bike that Nanny and Granddad had bought for his birthday. He'd been down on Steve and Jude's boat, little Charlie, their oldest was just learning to ride a bike so Sam was "helping". Obviously his stomach clock had alerted him that food should be ready about now.

"What's got Charlie all happy and smiley?" he asked as he wandered down the slope, "Actually I don't care, I've got a puncture, can Dad fix it?"

"He's busy with Charlie for a moment." I stood up. "I can fix it."

Sam looked at me in confusion then shook his head. "No thanks, it's all right Mum, Dad fixes things."

Poor Geoff.

The next week was a week too long for Charlie. As we expected, all the neighbours had been very good about having a small metal box inserted into their midst and had shuffled around to make room for it.

That Saturday there was a definite carnival feeling in the air. As the floating shed (Hedge pig was its name) had no engine Stuart had arranged for a friend to tow it up the river, from one end of the marina to the other. Unfortunately Geoff had been called into work, so I was left to deal with it.

As the little craft approached, I looked around and realised there were quite a few people suddenly milling about, Drew and Dion were standing, chatting up on the flood defences, Steve and Lewis were hanging about in Steve's garden. (Lewis was smiling and this small change to his usual demeanour threw me completely.) As the little boat pulled in there was a sudden flurry of activity. Ropes were thrown, boats were moved, I didn't have to move a muscle. Within ten minutes Hedge pig was parked, moored up and there were already people turning up with things that they thought Charlie might need, chairs, rugs, small tables and cabinets all appeared in a pile beside her boat, there was even a Hoover, an iron and an ironing board (I doubted that the last two would get much use but the thought was nice).

Then they all vanished again. It was like magic, I doubt even a wizard could have managed it so well and Charlie and I were left staring at her little boat.

"See ya, Mum!" Charlie, once she had finished thanking people, grabbed a load of goods and clothes and prepared to move into her new room.

Over the next month Charlie painted and created, turning her little box into a tiny bedsit, we often found Scarlet and Jack sitting in there with her, mostly moaning that they wanted a boat of their own. Geoff put in a tiny log burner and between them they created a raised bed. We were lucky enough to get a futon which just fitted through the door and a television,

421

which didn't. (We had to pass it though the large sliding windows, it was ridiculously huge.)

As summer moved inexorably toward autumn we managed in our own little way to achieve small but significant stages in boat building and live-aboard luxury. There was no way this winter was going to be anywhere near as bad as the last.

On one of the last sunny days, Amelia and Chris turned up unannounced and out of the blue.

"Hello," I shouted up, "what are you doing here?"

Amelia padded down the steps with Chris close behind her. She gave me a hug then, unable to contain herself any more grabbed Chris's hand and screamed. "We're getting married!" She waved a hand in front of my face.

I know I'm getting old because I can't see things at the end of my nose any more. I took a step back the better to see.

On her finger a small but glittering piece of ice. "Isn't it pretty?" She looked worried, obviously concerned that I wouldn't get the implications of the sparkling piece of jewellery.

"Gorgeous." I gave her a hug, then because he was looking a little nervous, wandered over and gave Chris a big hug as well. "You are one mad bloke." I laughed and poked him gently in the stomach. "Who in their right mind would willingly join in matrimony to a family like this?"

Chris just laughed and gave me a hug right back. "Only the very bravest." He raised his head and put on a heroic look. "I do what I have to do . . . ouch!"

What a wuss, I only gave him a little pinch.

"And the other big news . . ." Amelia hopped from foot to foot trying to contain her excitement, irritated that I was ignoring her while attempting to put Chris at ease.

"Yes?" I prompted.

"I got into Cardiff University." She reached back to Chris who wandered up and peering at me over her shoulder gave me a big smile. "We're moving to Wales."

That evening, with Sam snoring away in his recently finished bedroom, Charlie, alternately banging and singing in hers (I'd told her three times to turn the music down), and the dog, now fully grown and very muscular taking up most of the sofa, I finally managed to talk to Geoff.

"I think next year is going to be a bit of a strain." I snuggled up to my husband.

Geoff, watching "NCIS", was completely immersed in the story line. "Oh yeah," he murmured "why's that then?"

"Well, Amelia's finally off to University then later on she's getting married so there's a wedding to sort out. It's Charlie's GCSE year, then she'll be off to college and Sam will be going up to High School." I shook my head. "It's like the Mad Hatter's tea party, you know . . . all move round one."

Geoff finally focused on what I was saying. "I think you had these children either too far apart or not far enough apart."

I laughed. "It's nice that they do things together."

423

"Hmm." Geoff stared down the boat and winced. He was obviously looking at all the half finished bits and pieces that we had lying about. "And what about us, do we move on as well?"

I frowned. "Move on to what?" I thought for a moment, "We're going to have our hands full just dealing with them for the next twelve months, think of all the changes they've got to go through."

"They should be used to change by now," Geoff said, chuckling.

"I suppose, but all the changes that we've dragged them through, have been instigated by us, these are changes they have to do for themselves and we really can't get involved. All we can do is sit back and catch them if they fall."

"So what about us?" Geoff persisted. "We've got loads to do as well."

"I can't see us changing any time soon, can you?" I replied.

Geoff shook his head. "No, too much to do." He began ticking lists off on his fingers. "We need to finish this boat, we need to put a new bathroom in and cut that passage through the back wall and into the boatman's cabin, we still have to work and the kids still need to be dealt with."

I nodded. "I think this is going to be another slow year for boat restoration."

Geoff answered, sighing, "As long as you're not going to tell me you want it all done in the next six months we should be fine."

I took a long look down the boat and for the first time in months wondered whether I could now live a normal life in a house, making cakes and meeting other mums for coffee.

Snuggling further under my husband's armpit I pushed the thought quite viciously aside. No, there was absolutely no way I could go back to that now. I wouldn't want to and even if I could I knew it would only last until the spring when the warmer weather would drag me out in search of change.

"I don't think I want it done in six months," I assured my now rather worried-looking husband, "in fact I think it's time to slow down and just enjoy doing what we do. Six months, six years I really don't care, it'll get done when it's done and we'll take it from there."

Geoff looked a little surprised. "What, no plans to sell it and get another one?"

"Nope."

"Move it to another location?" He frowned. "Another town, somewhere different?" Obviously a wife without a "plan" wasn't something he was used to.

"Nope."

"Really?" His voice showed how much he believed this new laid-back attitude. "There's nothing you wouldn't change about this situation right here and now?"

"Nope, nothing major anyway, although it might be nice to win the lottery." I tried to put what I felt into words. "This is home, it may be half-finished and it may be a pain and it may be small and we may be a bit

425

broke, but, eventually, we'll get it how we want it but that's only half the story, the boat's not really that important in the grand scheme of things. It's the people, the life, the whole enchilada really.

"The kids are going to take off, Amelia's already planning her next stage and Charlie's flapping around getting ready for hers. Sam's will come in time and then it will be us and the boat." I shrugged. "I'm not going to look forward to that time, because, quite frankly, it'll happen whether I worry about it or not, the days pass so quickly. If I look forward to tomorrow, before I know it I've already missed most of today."

Geoff nodded then sat up with a worried look. "Well, before you settle into some weird philosophic and euphoric haze, we do have one major problem at the moment."

"What's that?" I asked grinning at Mortimer who was waving his feet in the air in an effort to get someone to rub his stomach.

Geoff stared into his empty mug. "I'm out of tea and it's your turn to put the kettle on."

As I filled the kettle and set the gas alight it occurred to me that happiness has to come at a price and I wondered, if we hadn't suffered through last winter and all the illness and problems that we'd had this year, whether I would even be able to recognise those moments of true contentment when they finally arrived. I thought of the proverb that was etched into a big plaque above the main desk of the hospital, I read it every day as I walked through the main doors: "This too shall pass". How true, there would no doubt be other dark days, things would go wrong and there would be times that just needed to be endured and sighed over.

But for now, this fleeting moment, with Charlie singing in her bedroom, Sam snoring in his and Amelia almost giddy with anticipation for the future we really had nothing to worry about and if being out of tea was our only gripe then I could say, hand on heart, that life was good.

Other titles published by Ulverscroft:

NARROW MARGINS

Marie Browne

Faced with the loss of everything following the collapse of the Rover car company, Marie Browne moves her long-suffering husband Geoff, chaotic children and smelly, narcoleptic dog onto a houseboat in search of a less stressful, healthier, alternative way of life. Strapped for cash, the family buys a decrepit seventy-foot barge called *Happy Go Lucky*, which had been run as a floating hotel. Outdated and in need of a complete refurbishment, Happy becomes their floating home as they negotiate the trials and tribulations of life in the slow lane.

THE STY'S THE LIMIT

Simon Dawson

Years ago, after a drunken misunderstanding, Simon Dawson gave up his job in the city, moved to the wilds of Exmoor and became an accidental self-sufficient smallholder surrounded by animals. But now his life is changing all over again: horror of horrors, he's getting older. Enlisting a cast of best friends — including Ziggy, a panicked soon-to-be father; Garth, an annoying teenager; and the General, a rather handsome pig — to work through their age-related angsts, a plan is hatched to help each other mature (or immature). Hilarity and heartfelt discoveries ensue — all with a fair dose of pigs, chickens, goats and animal madness along the way.